Anna T.
Opacity – Minority – Improvisation

Queer Studies | Volume 27

Anna T. (PhD), born in 1984, has worked as an artist, theorist, and educator in Greece, England, Germany, and Austria. Since 2003 she has exhibited and participated in numerous group and solo exhibitions and new media festivals in Europe, the Americas, and Australia. Between 2014 and 2017 she was a board member and curator at Mz* Baltazar's Lab, a feminist hackerspace for creatives in Vienna, and since 2017 she has taught at the Academy of Fine Arts and the University of Art and Design Linz.

Anna T.
Opacity – Minority – Improvisation
An Exploration of the Closet Through Queer Slangs and Postcolonial Theory

[transcript]

Bibliographic information published by the Deutsche Nationalbibliothek
The Deutsche Nationalbibliothek lists this publication in the Deutsche Nationalbibliografie; detailed bibliographic data are available in the Internet at http://dnb.d-nb.de

© 2020 transcript Verlag, Bielefeld

All rights reserved. No part of this book may be reprinted or reproduced or utilized in any form or by any electronic, mechanical, or other means, now known or hereafter invented, including photocopying and recording, or in any information storage or retrieval system, without permission in writing from the publisher.

Cover layout: Frederik Marroquín
Printed by Majuskel Medienproduktion GmbH, Wetzlar
Print-ISBN 978-3-8376-5133-1
PDF-ISBN 978-3-8394-5133-5
https://doi.org/10.14361/9783839451335

Contents

Acknowledgements 9

Introduction 13
Methodology, Methods, Aesthetics 22

The Chronicles of the Closet 31
Μια φορά κι έναν καιρό … 31
Περί Νισεστόκουτου 38
Άει μωρή καλιαρντή! 44
Εσύ μωρή, που κάθεσαι; - Situating the Denizens 55
Queer / Lavender Linguistics 56
Performance 63
A Little Outing 68

Opacity 75
Opacity and the Closet 75
Tensions 78
ΛΕΞΙΚΟ 80
Social Queetique - χαχα. χα. 81
Opacity, Detour, Silence 87
Opacity and Postcolonial Critique 90
ʹ   ʹ 98
Detour 105
The Opacity of the Rainbow 110
Opacity and I 112
Disenfranchised 113

Minority 119
Orality - Literature 123
Minor Art Practice 128

Mom's the Word or Take Sertraline with Me (if you want to) 139
queen 139
Affective Staying Ins 140
Looking back 141
Backwardness 142
'Yaaass queen' *snaps fingers* 147
Εσύ μωρή ποιανού είσαι; 150
Phenomenology of the _____ 155
Μαριναρίσματα 155
Nextness 162

Tô passada! 169

Endnotes 181

Bibliography 219

To my thirteen-year-old self, που το χρειαζόταν πολύ.

Acknowledgements

I would like to first and foremost thank my publishers Roswitha Gost and Karin Werner, as well as Mirjam Galley and Jenso Scheer for trusting me, supporting me, and believing in my work.

Thank you Renate Lorenz, Anette Baldauf, and Moira Hille for supportingme through the PhD this book is the result of. I would also like to thank Andi Ferus, the Academy of Fine Arts Vienna and its Center for Doctoral Studies, the Austrian Students' Union (ÖH), and the WIASN for their support, material and emotional. Thank you Frederik Marroquín for pushing me to chase this, thank you Giorghis Despotakis and Rafał Morusiewicz, Janine Jembere, Ruthie Jenrbekova, Patrícia J. Reis for your feedback, corrections and suggestions, and Sandra Monterroso, Nastja Goloskokova, Giulia Cilla, Maria U. Hera, and Müco, for your help. Ευχαριστώ τους γονείς μου, και τους τρεις. A big thanks to Dervla for her wise words of comfort, and all her help with this project. A big thanks to Piran and Acacia for their genuine hygge. Thank you m and Lari for your hospitality-turned-friendship and all the cookies you have baked for me over the years. A big hug and a warm thank you goes to Zori for her love and gentle reminders of what is actually important.

I want to thank everyone who taught and helped me to take care of myself during this strenuous process, and were by me when I got ill. I would also like to thank Pêdra Costa, Diego Wiltshire, Fer Nogueirra, Ju Correia, Nicholas Kontovas, Paul Baker, Ya'ar Hever, Liat Granierer, George Tsitiridis, and Paola Revenioti for helping me better situate myself within the beauty of Pajubá, Lubunca, Polari, Ókhchit, and Kaliarnta. I couldn't have done this without the support of all those who helped me find djobs. Finally I would like to thank all of Dorothy's friends, all those who play for the team, those who ride the other bus, όσες το κανελλώνουν το γαλακτομπούρεκο, τα σπάνε τα μπετά, all the Donald Ducks, those who are a bit funny, those drinking from the furry cup, όσους την κουνάνε την αχλαδιά, those wearing sensible shoes, και όσες το γυαλίζουν το πόμολο.

sits down and is given a tiny pillow that remained after everyone else sat on theirs

'...so I began this project with an intention to explore the proverbial closet and work mainly on interactive installations. Over the course of the project, a lot changed, and I created a body of work that includes videos, performances, a six-channel video installation, performative writing, and unsolicited public art.

I start with a negation. A willfulness to show the works. I decided against an exhibition or screening format for several reasons. The artistic practise component of my project has been one of the research methods used to approach my topic, as well as a dissemination tool of the current state of the research. To re-screen or re-install the works would have stripped them from the context in and for which they were created. A replication of the circumstances would be a failed one. It would be a perfunctory re-setup of something that is no longer current as much as it might still be relevant. Έπρεπε να έχω και λίγο μπλα μπλα για να σπασει η ακαδημαϊκή ορολογία και να στραφούμε λίγο σε πιο periférica καταστάσεις, να αβέλει και η φαεινοπαρτουζα εδω πέρα. My work is about opacity, performative silence, and passivity, with a focus on oral tradition. For all those reasons, I decided to share my artistic practice via narration, focusing on the kinds of knowledge that orality carries: the emotive, the memory-based, the embodied. I want to share my work and working process with you in the way a voice can do, being always already a commentary.

So I'm going to lay the groundwork for narrating my artworks to you in a way that will hopefully make sense for everyone. Είναι κάπως ζόρικο και καλιαρντό τώρα αυτό, αλλά tô passada!
But let's get back in track, starting from the beginning-ish. Initially, my focus was on how the closet was constituted by language, but soon after my interest shifted to the phenomenology of the closet. Something that acted as a dominant theme was the relationship between the notional closet and its physical counterpart with its capitalist implications. What are the objects related to both the proverbial and the physical closet, and how are they gendered and politicised? What happens if a deconstruction is attempted? Would that destabilise the closet or the performances surrounding it?'

Introduction

This book was mainly produced in the framework of my doctoral studies in the Academy of Fine Arts Vienna in tandem with other aspects of my artistic practice. My time in the PhD course was one of intense work habits, existential crises, and life-changing events. What I very naively began as a delving deeper into the ways concealment and queerness inform my work turned out to be a thorough exploration of neoliberalism, unpaid labour, the academia in several lingual and cultural contexts, and an embracing of failure as the most productive and positive thing I could have done. My arms failed me, my mind failed me, I failed my expectations, and most of all, an open and transparent dealing with queerness failed my need for opacity. The PhD in Practice being a group programme offered many opportunities to think about belonging, collective work, antagonism, ambitions, and sharing, as did the fact that for most of my time in the programme I lived with several other people in homes shaped by politics of sharing. It has also been a tough time in terms of finances, employability, and maintaining this work pace for several years while trying to make ends meet, heal the repetitive strain syndrome on both arms, and thinking on the politics of the country that allowed me to work on something I am passionate about without having to pay tuition fees in the neoliberal times since the socioeconomic crisis of '08. Re-working this book for a publication that would allow it to reach more people has allowed me to rethink parts of it and re-examine certain positions, incorporate thoughts derived from conversations with friends and colleagues I have had the honour to be part of, as well as include reflections on events that have happened more recently and which added to the emotional tension of some of the content. Over the past years, I have been teaching on an academic level, an experience which has been inspiring and fruitful and which has helped me re-frame certain things as well. Over the time it took to put together this book, other aspects of my 'artistic practice' begun to fade. I mean the aspects that are readily accepted as such: photography, video, installations, street art, which are usually exhibited in relevant spaces. Instead, what became more and more important to me was group settings of sharing such as seminars, workshops, the *production* of exhibitions or publications. Teaching, I learnt, is quite creative and includes the elements of care work, collective working and thinking, and sharing that are so valuable for me. Thus, I have now started seeing these aspects of teaching (ones that are collective, participatory, processual and don't necessarily lead to a gallery or museum) as part of my practice, or a practice which I am a part of.

Situated in the intersection of queer, postcolonial and decolonial studies, (lavender) linguistics, and artistic research, this project employed the artistic methods of video, video installation, performance, the familial method of storytelling, and the scholarly formats of the lecture and (performative) writing to investigate the proverbial closet and its creations. To do so, I rely on opacity, a postcolonial concept, in order to open up queer to periférica knowledge (Γνώσεις της Περιφέρειας / των Περιφερειακών) and non-Western methodological paradigms. Opacity is a concept borrowed from Édouard Glissant to refer to the tactic employed by native and enslaved peoples in the Caribbean to escape the demand for transparency and understandability by the colonisers. Those indigenous populations would manipulate language so that meaning would escape oppressors, and thusly both communicate more safely and flip the exclusionary paradigm.[1] 'Creole', writes Britton with regards to Glissant's work, was 'a subversive language whose purpose from the start was not simply to communicate but also to conceal its meanings, thereby turning the master's language against him. In this sense, it is a typical form of opacity'.[2]

Within the field of lavender linguistics—a field that examines the language LGBTQ+ people use—there have been similar creations. Lexicography has been slow to document these slangs, and most linguistics' journal articles explore one or two at a time. In my research, I focus on eleven such slangs namely Kaliarnta (Greece), Polari (UK), Pajubá (Brazil), Swardspeak (Philippines), Bahasa Binan (Indonesia), IsiNgqumo and Gayl (South Africa), Hijra Farsi (India), Ókhchit (אוחצ׳ית) (Israel), Gayspeak (English-speaking world), and Lubunca (Turkey). I use Kaliarnta and Polari and further look into the neologisms and semantic alterations that form them (which indicate not only strong counter-cultural elements but the construction of parallel worlds in which deviance is celebrated, and normative mores are questioned) to create my own words and use them in my lectures and performances. In this project, I synthesise lavender linguistics, queer theory, postcoloniality/decoloniality and artistic research to investigate how 'queer' can be practised as a methodology through a non-Western epistemological framework and how my subjectivities are both shaping it and being shaped by it. Throughout this book, both lavender linguistics—introduced and researched by William Leap—and queer linguistics are discussed. The former is the field that examines the language LGBTQ+ people use (ranging from dialects to mannerisms, pronunciation, and coded language). The latter is a subfield of the former where people try to create inclusive and respectful language and mores and which has become more and more visible lately. This field includes discussions on gender-neutral pronouns, establishing (preferred) pronouns in group settings (and the pros and cons of that), as well as terminology that more accurately describes identification subjectivities, orientations (or lack thereof), and affinities. While both provide a framework through which cisheteronormativity is often mocked, they do so from distinct positions. Their differences have to do with how the users position themselves within the social, their status, education, and intentions. Of course temporalities here are an essential factor too; while the slangs have been mostly in use in centuries and decades past, having lost their life-line attributes with the dawn of the internet, queer linguistics seems to have taken off precisely in the internet era, though in several cases the two have overlapped and to some extent still do.

This is a project created as artistic practice, as a research method, as a dissemination method, as a 'scientific' elaboration on the 'artistic' methods and tools employed parallel to it. Doing academic research and obtaining a doctorate is something I have wanted for several years, and had I known earlier it was available to me, I believe I would have pursued it earlier. It was really crucial for me to continue my artistic work while supporting it theoretically and eventually working on theory as much as practice in an academic institution. It has also been a way for me to legitimise my work as an artist, work that is often overlooked, snubbed, and is, of course, majorly underpaid. It has been a way for me to try to prove that I am not many of the things that are projected/interpellated on me due to my background. Given the field I work in (queer theory), I think it has also been my way of legitimising myself. I have often found myself struggling with what I call precarity syndrome; the need to continually prove oneself and find odd jobs, create connections, leave no stone unturned in the search for making ends meet, be recognised, and be heard, always be working, always be productive / producing.[3] Working in the intersection of artistic practice and theory and trying to introduce myself through my work in various social occasions familiarised me with the scorn many have towards the arts and their suspiciousness towards any attempt to bridge it with anything academic. These comments and behaviours often came as much from people not involved in the academia, as well as academics, and I would eventually become very well acquainted with comments on 'the meaninglessness' of my work as opposed to theirs, and the selfishness of people like me 'who don't contribute anything'. Furthermore, from people within the humanities, I would hear things like 'I wish I did an easy PhD like yours just to get the title', among other antagonistic and derisive utterances. I often go back to re-watching Gómez-Peña's performance playing with the word and notion of the 'academia'.[4] I can't stop myself from doing something lesser while risking sounding like Gus Portokalos: 'Academia' from the Greek Ακαδημία from ἑκάς (= μακριά) και το δᾶμος ή δῆμος (= λαός). So 'academia' literally meant that which is far away from the people. Upon a first reading, one thinks of ivory towers, but it could also be that the academia is pushed or pushes one to the outskirts, to the margins of 'normal' life. While balancing being in (as a researcher) and out (as an artist) of the academia and confronted with the above comments, performance, and thoughts I was frequently reminded of Tom Holert's text 'Artistic Research: Anatomy Of An Ascent' and the tension between attitudes such as Gruppe Spur's and Asger Jorn's, that is the attempt to distance art from scientific knowledge and ultimately stupidity by insisting art is premised on instinct more than anything else vs. demanding the same possibilities that scientific researchers have at their disposal, that is demanding entrance into a productive economy often in Fordist terms.

While the academia is undoubtedly an antagonistic environment, there is a special kind of contempt for those working towards a practice-based doctorate. While the initial reaction is often to justify one's work and the merit of it, ultimately it might be doubling down that gets the point across better. And so in this project, I move in and out of academic jargon, linguistics, and theory, as I do with references to artworks (those of others and those I created), expressing feelings and thoughts, admitting to uncertainty, employing humour, and often self-deprecation. Most importantly, I include filtering through knowledge from the Periphery combined with

Anglo / Euro / US-centric thinkers and concepts in order to insist that multiple voices are necessary in an ongoing conversation. Epistemologies that are unconventional (even if they have been institutionalised in some ways over the past decades) and critical political prisms are perfectly legitimate partners and contributors in a conversation whether that conversation takes place in a classroom, a bench, an auditorium, a beach, on chairs or on the floor, wearing ties, leather chaps, or feather boas.

My interest in language peeked when coming across Kaliarnta and then consequently the terrain of lavender linguistics. However, sub-cultural communication codes were always something I have engaged with. In particular, slangs, which focus on not only who understands—but more importantly— who does not. This interest speaks to my idiosyncrasy and my need for opacity and hiding. It further evokes playfulness and childishness, making a 'mess' of language, being inappropriate, and upsetting hierarchies. I had focused on space and queerness during my master's, and later I wanted to further explore those realms in connection to temporality through language. My research objectives revolve around locating linguistically constructed queer spaces and queer temporalities, the ways in which language forms ephemeral spaces of safety and connecting, and how (much like the pleasures and desires that have prompted it), language itself generates pleasures.

The closet for me has been a shelter, a refuge, a home, a friend. It has been my happy place for decades. I'm not arguing here for a μουσειακή preservation of the closet filled with nostalgia, but for allowing it to exist and be relevant as a potentiality for those who want it, for those who need it, and for those who can't afford to be left without it. However, for the most part, I am not referring to the closet as the secret space one hides in, but rather a complex spatiotemporal event all of us are forced to come out of, thus activating or affirming its existence in the first place. I'm also interested in the set of attributes assigned to operating within a particular social sphere, one which no matter how loosely conceptualised it may be, it is always connected to the (false) dichotomy of in / out. I understand the closet as an example of minority, showcasing how heterocissexist privilege works, most visibly around issues of who speaks out without fear of repercussions, who can touch whom, and who is allowed to connect with whom. The closet and the above concerns have over the years shaped my politics and helped me filter things better and listen more. I'm writing this with Pulse, Άρωμα, Paris is Burning, Τρολ, Στέκι, Stonewall, Istanbul Onur Yürüyüşü, Gaycation S1 E3 on my mind ...

My work (I refer here to all aspects of my work as I do not wish to separate 'written' and 'practical' work) is an assemblage of different languages, and slangs, lowbrow pop cultural references, and 'highbrow' theory, misunderstandings, pretentiousness, and insecurities. I owe a lot to Gloria Anzaldúa and her generous way of expressing herself, which helps me express mine by overcoming shame and feelings of inadequacy. I try to own up to the fact that what I did / do is research while also struggling to recognise the ills of such a term and its history. Aspects of exploring (as a term featured in this book's title) are mostly related to queer understandings of knowledge-acquisition and child-like curiosity. I further try to be honest about the contradictory elements my work entails, some of which I see as failures to be consistent, others I embrace matter-of-factly. In the following chapters, I employ an academic style, diaristic entries, excerpts from performances, and artist statements. Sometimes they fuse together, others they stick out like sore thumbs. Όλα καλά είναι. I chiefly use British English orthography because it feels more familiar to me. I do not italicise 'foreign' words, as in this work I did not use any such words. English is not my first language, though it has become my primary one, and I don't consider my made-up words much different than the corruptions, fusions, neologisms, observed in the slangs. I knew from the beginning that there would be moments that a native English-speaking reader / participant would find annoying or confusing, and I don't see that as a bad thing for my work overall. I can, however, see how these are uncomfortable feelings to have and understand the need to address them. I make words up, I try to sound 'academic' and allow my work to show merit and originality, and I also use slangs, talk to myself, and write of my blushing when I go into something way over my head. I translate selectively and inconsistently because this works for me.

I want to connect queerness with opacity, minority, and alternative ways of relating (through language) and ultimately make a claim for the closet, as a space of resistance, self-care, community-forming, as a heterotopic and heterochronic space of creativity, as a potentiality. Not as a demand, but as a possibility. I want to offer a reparative reading of, or listening to, the closet. A reparative reading based on a paranoid reading, in that I deal with the aspects of the closet that are deemed problematic and those views that demand the closet to only be a space of oppression and shame that one should come out of. Instead, through a reparative reading of that paranoid reading of the closet, I see a closet that opens up potentialities. Given the closet's heterosynchronicity, or alternative temporality, I would not want to say that it is a 'looking backwards', or even a 'feeling backwards', but neither is it a looking forward. It is instead a looking and feeling connected to being, resisting, making up shit on the fly, enjoying oneself, enjoying (with) others. It is a potential for the moments of tiredness, happiness, sadness, illness, affirmation, depression, affective bondings, anxiety, rejection, organising, why not even navel-gazing, pausing, breathing, withstanding, and standing with.

I further wanted to bring together the various slangs I had come across—as most publications had dealt with them in-depth from within the field of linguistics and rarely viewed them in conjunction to one another—under the scope of postcolonial theory, tactics of resistance, and the right to opacity. My work draws heavily on linguistics, and queer and postcolonial theory and intends to offer an exploration of the closet as a producer of language, not merely as a linguistic product itself. Additionally, I wanted to do so by employing art as a performative research tool and performative aesthetics as an expressive means.

My aim throughout this project has been to produce a well-rounded theorisation of the closet by way of linguistics and a bridge it with postcolonialism and decoloniality. The questions that shaped my research had to do with the function of the slangs and an overview of the social ontologies that the speakers represent and perform. Next, I wanted to address questions on tactics of concealment for reasons of survival and resistance. To paraphrase Nicholas De Villiers, what would a non-revelatory speech sound like? Which tactics of survival and resistance are employed through the slangs? I further aimed at tracing how oral tradition (in the case of the slangs) relates to other linguistic productions (i.e. literature) and how the notion of 'minor literature' can help deepen the understanding of the tactics mentioned above. Finally, noticing a pattern in the frequent use of familial terminology (and their semantic alterations) through the improvisation of the slangs, I ask: 'How does familial terminology contour the social milieu of the speakers?' And 'what would an improvised queer home sound like?'

To this aim, I have laid out this book as follows; In chapter one, I lay the groundwork on the formation of the proverbial closet. I briefly refer to its history, the way metaphors—in particular, spatial metaphors—function, and then move on to theorise the closet drawing from Sara Ahmed, Judith Butler, Nicholas De Villiers, Édouard Glissant, and Eve Kosofsky Sedgwick.

Then I go on to introduce the slangs which I see as cultural productions of the closet and the broader fields of lavender and queer linguistics. Finally, I analyse the performativity of the slangs in connection to camp and drag performances and connect it with my own attempt at performing the closet. This proved a much more arduous than initially imagined task, as the relationships between words, inhabitants, ontologies, and observational methods became murkier. As Stuart Hall wrote, 'as the relationship between the sign and its referent becomes less clear-cut, the meaning begins to slip and slide away from us into uncertainty. Meaning is no longer transparently passing from one person to another'.[5] And it was this opacity that both confused me and allowed me to move more freely.

In the second chapter, I posit the closet as a place surrounded by opacity and further delve into the slangs, the social critiques, and political stances they convey. I am referring to the sense of humour and creativity they entail, and I then examine their opacity as a tactic of survival and resistance.[6] I thus attempt to give a reading of queer theory and postcolonial theory that brings them together through similar tactics of resistance and survival beyond opacity and talk about silence, passivity, and detour. The visual politics that opacity activates, the aural politics of silence, the spatial references of detour, and the gender politics of passivity are all brought together with a variety of examples from artists, activists, cultural producers, affective and sexual workers from different times and places. Muñoz's disidentifications lays the groundwork for these performative tactics.

Chapter three is dedicated to the notion of minor literature and becoming-minor, two concepts developed by Deleuze and Guattari. I create parallels between what they call 'minor literature' and the slangs, and by so doing I undertake a reading of the slangs as innately revolutionary, merging boundaries, borders, and minorities, and ultimately I assert that the slangs are a case of minor literature. Relatedly I write about orality concerning other literary formats of cultural production and use Simon O'Sullivan's application of the deleuzoguattarian notion of minor literature on artistic practice to introduce the street art component of my project. Throughout my work I use the terms 'minority' and 'minoritarian' much like Muñoz does, to refer to queers and other subjects who 'due to antagonisms within the social such as race, class, and sex, are debased within the majoritarian public sphere'[7] and not in numerical or sociologically statistical terms.

In the final chapter, I theorise the closet as a potentially improvisational room of one's own, and use linguistics to frame it as such. I understand the closet as a potentiality, especially for those who can't afford a home, or a 'home', a family whether it be a family of origin or a family of choice, or a community. I read through familial terms in particular from Kaliarnta and Polari and while steering clear of theorisations on 'alternative families', 'rainbow families', 'gay marriage', and such, I try to trace an understanding of homeliness and belonging that is not toxic or bound to capitalist, repronormative, generational, chronopolitical notions of relating. In this chapter, my contradictions become more apparent as I attempt to incorporate elements from the negativist turn of queer theory while allowing for a futurity and a potentiality of comfort, safety, and self-care that take into consideration dis_abilities, racial politics, class, age, and pleasures. It is here that Muñoz's work guides me as I focus on the 'on and against' nature of the slangs (particularly in their capacity to reformulate kinship) and how they erode the dominant regime from the inside while simultaneously working towards a queer counterpublics. This chapter has always taken a path different to the other three. Some pointed out its failure. I have reworked it many times, and I understand their critique. However, I want it to stay. Even if it hasn't quite come together yet, I still think there is space for it.

The working title of this project (The Chronicles of the Closet: Opacity, Minority, Improvisation) was a direct reference to *The Chronicles of Narnia: The Lion, the Witch and the Wardrobe* the first film based on the Narnia book series that were adapted for TV, stage, and film. Besides the apparent pop-cultural nature of the proverbial closet and the slangs and the series of high-fantasy novels by C. S. Lewis, it was the existence of a magical closet that I found particularly fitting. In the novels, the closet leads to an alternative parallel cosmos where time and space are skewed in a universe populated by all sorts of creatures. There, the children protagonists find themselves helping them fight oppression, acquiring different subjectivities and social ontologies while doing so. The elements that composed the title (and which remain) are a bit different though. Opacity not only describes aspects of the closet's function but, more importantly, is a postcolonial loan. Minority is a term that addresses asymmetrical power dynamics but primarily connotes linguistics and addresses literature and orality. Improvisation refers to the creative tactics of survival and resistance and those aspects of queerness that make do with what they have.

Methodology, Methods, Aesthetics

I situate my research among poststructuralist, queer, and postcolonial theories, while allowing for room that enables the necessary fluidity, instability, and always-becoming nature of the term 'queer' even if that might at times work at odds with queer theory. In order to build on that framing, I must mention the importance of lavender linguistics in this project, even if structuralist notions often penetrate linguistics of all kinds. I see parts of my work as autoethnographic, and I draw from feminisms in order to—together with queer theory—challenge normative understandings and oppressive regimes (the closet being often seen exclusively as one, but also the innate ambivalence of the notions of home, belonging, or familiality) often incorporating personal experiences, and interweaving the social with the personal between the various components of my work. As such, it is precisely this upsetting of the distinction between the insider's and the outsider's point of view that 'allows for the emergence of theory from both "within" and "without".'[8]

By default, since there is a discussion of non-normativity or anti-normativity and non-normative sexualities, orientations, and genders, together with the social constructions behind them, the work of Michel Foucault acts as groundwork. Similarly, Foucault is a guiding force behind ideas of truth. It might seem inconsistent with current times to embrace opacity and challenge the value of truth. In an era of post-truth politics and right-wing populism rising partly because of such tactics weaponised by bad actors, it might even seem dangerous. The truth which I mention throughout this project is a philosophical, Modernist idea of an axiomatic, single, transcendent truth. And it is challenged by a constructivist, Foucauldian understanding of truth that leans heavily on postcolonialism to make sense of the world. As such, I use opacity as a method deriving directly from Glissant's postcolonial analysis on creolised languages and the right not to be understood, and apply it to my findings on the slangs, listening to them like another minor literature. In Deleuze and Guattari's concept of 'minor literature' and 'becoming minor' I see parallels with the background, function, and collectivity of queer slangs. Furthermore, I use Sara Ahmed's theories on happiness to analyse moments of rejoice, safety, connection, belonging, and ultimately happiness, that derive from the production of oral/aural safer spaces and a restructuring of social hierarchies that shake kyriarchy, and view the speakers as willful subjects, whose willfulness opens up potentialities.

While working on this project, I was incredibly concerned with working with opacity, respecting cultures I do not belong in, or practices I do not participate in. This preoccupation resulted in an almost a priori apologetic stance and a penetration of my own opacity in many respects. This project thus turned out to be a diary of sorts in which I step out of my comfort zone several times. Perhaps this was my way of feeling out opacity, tracing it, and recognising it at the moments when it was disrupted.

I wish in this work to embrace a 'queer' that is inconsistent, that may—and perhaps, must—elude me, that is plural, and opaque. My methods include textual analysis, archival research, interviews, and audiovisual materials. Whether these practices are in some way themselves queer, I am not sure, and I am even less sure if they would have to abide by a certain understanding of queerness to be legitimised as methods of (artistic) research on these topics. That is not to say that this project will use this positioning as an alibi to any epistemological 'failures' claiming them as intentional, instead it simply means that I want to face my contradictions and question my methods, feeling it is not unscientific, anti-academic, or poorly theorised research, if a research allows for failure (especially as Jack Halberstam proposes it). A failure that opens up alternatives, that questions normative understandings of success, linear ideas of temporality, possession or the self and includes textual analysis on popular/lowbrow culture, and perhaps even touches upon Elspeth Probyn's *Outside Belongings* and Lauren Berlant's *Cruel Optimism*. I use Kath Browne and Catherine J. Nash's *Queer Methods and Methodologies* as a guide to many of the questions I encountered during every stage of this process, and I choose to adopt their openness in defining terms, and admitting to not having answers, even when that is what may be expected. I try to embrace their openness and generosity in framing research, queerness, and academic writing, as they suggest 'despite being able to recite a somewhat cogent and coherent pedigree for "queer" scholarship, what we mean by queer, we argue, is and should remain unclear, fluid and multiple.'[9]

In my work I was often oriented towards how the concept of opacity and its decolonial connotations encourage moments of queerness in artistic practice as well as the ways an epistemological framework that does not only revolve around the Western canon contribute to a re-reading of queerness and what this has to offer as a tool for research. In this project, I want to fight against my own and academia's need for consistency, reaffirmation of positions, and 'sound' επιχειρηματολογία. I want instead to allow for thoughts that have not (and may never) reach(ed) conclusion, trains of thoughts that have derailed, and an overall openness to what Halberstam calls 'the queer art of failure', thus exploring territories that are forbidden, stupid, wrong, bad, or simply not academic (enough). I want to share ideas that I realised were contradictory, but still feel they have something to offer if shared, and I want to open myself up to perhaps even harsher criticism for admitting I do not have the answers but have more questions. I guess that could place my work within Halberstam's 'scavenger methodology' of picking up different pieces and putting them together. Even though this is not a hard sciences' research aiming to provide definitive answers and conclusive replicable results, there is still the need to make some sense, which I hope I will do in the majority of this body of work, while allowing for creative failure. Ann Cvetkovich quotes Lynda Barry (whose work is a messy bricolage of texts, images, comics, and biographical notes), when she asks: 'Is this good? Does this suck? I'm not sure when these two questions became the only two questions I had about my work, or when making pictures and stories turned into something I called 'my work'—I just know I'd stopped enjoying it and instead began to dread it.'[10] Ultimately this is a project of and on vulnerability. I explore topics that range from pleasure to trauma, from desire to survival, and I do so by exposing a lot of myself, which I am incredibly uncomfortable with, but I see as important. Especially in order to allow for points of entry for the reader / participant.

As mentioned, performativity and performance are essential components of this project, both in its content and its format. Apart from performances, 'stage instructions' or recollections, other elements such as different scripts appear, words or entire sentences disappear, and the project gradually becomes undone.

I position myself and this project, by extension, in what I would call a queer off-centre critique / position. Not 'queer-of-centre', meaning in the margins of the centre but 'off-centre', as in external to the centre, of the periphery. Είμαι μια ανώμαλη εκλεπτισμένη βάρβαρη ρε παιδί μου. I adopt a certain queer, but, at the same time, I stand opposite it viewing it as too 'modern'. There's the Anglo / Western / European part of me that feels at home with it, and then the Balkan part of me that retreats to more locally relevant terms and taxonomies such as τζίβα ή πλακομουνού. There's the Anglo part that wants to get to the bottom of things and present a respectable (by whom?) literary project and then there's the Balkan έλα μωρέ τώρα μη ψάχνεσαι / τρώγεσαι, όλα καλά είναι. Even these antitheses have a place here even though it might make me seem as undecided, trying to please everyone, or prove that I have thought of everything that could be thrown at me.

In this book, I refer to several projects of various formats and media, (a five minute video titled *Lipstick*, 2013), and the video installation this resulted in (*Closet Case Studies #1*, 2013), a re-formatting of the video installation shown during a one-day event in Vienna's MUMOK that was part of Springerin's 'Chronic Times' issue (Winter 2014). The projects mentioned above dealt with the links between the physical and the proverbial closet, zooming in on objects and materialities they both contain as a connecting thread. These objects relate to desires and play with the opacity and / or visibility of the closets they are placed in. Later on, my preoccupation with text and textual analysis led me to produce a performed speech piece (*Closet Case Studies #2*, 2014). Behind a closed door for the duration of a three-hour-plus event, I spoke to one person at a time about my closet(s), isolation, abuse, creativity, and oppression. Wanting to work with archival materials relating to the slangs, I used bits of *Round the Horne*, a BBC radio show that aired in the late '60s and featured a comical flamboyant duo of out-of-work actors speaking Polari.[11] The initial idea was to present it as a black video employing visuality to accent the opacity of the original format, but given that many people had a hard time understanding their (British) accents, I decided to subtitle it. Not wanting to flatten out the effect of not fully understanding the accents nor some Polari instances myself, I opted for not forcing a clear and accurate subtitling, but include blanks where I could not understand what they said. My research continued and included a series of stencils / unsolicited public art interventions and finally a performance, an oral history of the projects and ideas that would lead to the production of this book and which accompanies or introduces each chapter. A discussion / picnic followed the performance which was another way to disrupt the formality of the Q&A format and instead propose a setting where we are all seated, οκλαδόν, in a loose circle on blankets, sharing and passing food around.

Around that time, I started writing and shaping the backbone of the dissertation-turned-book where I would tackle the closet in an all-around manner. No, I would only focus on linguistics. But what about capitalism? Back and forth. And sideways. Mainly sideways. What I thought would be the more linear part of the projects proved to be the messiest and most chaotic. And worst of all, I loved it! I was once again reminded that 'Writing is a corporeal activity. We work ideas through our bodies; we write through our bodies, hoping to get into the bodies of our readers. We study and write about society not as an abstraction but as composed of actual bodies in proximity to other bodies."[12] Not in the least because of the many physical strains, injuries, migraines that did not allow me to write whenever I wanted, but also because trying to bypass them (by experimenting with speech recognition software and failing), once again highlighted the manual labour of the task.

Soon after I became aware of my need to express myself in whatever way available without taking into consideration each interlocutor's knowledge. I started producing brief texts, sentences, phrases expressing my feelings and thoughts related to various parts of my personal/professional life.

There is a discrepancy between an always becoming/improvisational production of the self and the repeated moments in which I speak from the 'I' position. This discrepancy is often articulated through voicing the shift in opinions, the change in foci, and the critique of past moments or decisions. I don't use the first-person narrative to establish a continuous and consistent self; rather I do it to allow for a vulnerable, work-in-progress, opinionated, and undecided self to appear. By using autoethnography I go through my insecurities, decision-making process, and unveil my doubts. I see this book as one of my research methods, as part of the artistic research process itself and not merely as a dissemination tool for results and answers. Throughout my work I 'position autoethnography as a queer research method, one that works against canonical methodological traditions and "disciplining, normalizing, social forces"'[13] as Stacy Holman Jones and Tony E. Adams state in their inspiring essay, arguing that autoethnography is a queer method by virtue of allowing:

> a person to document perpetual journeys of self-understanding, allows her or him to produce queer texts. A queer autoethnography also encourages us to think through and out of our categories for interaction and to take advantage of language's failure to capture or contain 'selves', ways of relating and subjugated knowledges.[14]

My methodological position being situated in the intersection of queer and postcolonial theory examined through linguistics, results in the use of methods that foreground the personal, the affective, the ever-changing, and the fluid. This is reflected in the tools themselves, which include non-traditional scholarly methods of research or result dissemination, and in the conceptual and purposeful project design. I use storytelling, interviews, conferences, textual analysis, lexicography, personal experience, sketches, assemblages, mappings, photos, videos, installations, and public interventions. In line with working methodologically with 'queer' and periférica knowledge, I found what Craig Gingrich-Philbrook calls 'lost arts, hidden experiences' an interesting reading on how autoethnography can be read as queer in a way that emphasises decoloniality. He suggests that telling stories of subjugated knowledges—stories of pleasure, gratification and intimacy—offers one possibility for writing against and out of the bind of sacrificing multitudinous artistry for clear, unequivocal knowledge.[15] I would further like to mention the parallels that Holman Jones and Adams create between the shared affinities of autoethnography and queer theory by quoting them directly:

> Autoethnography and queer theory are both also often criticized for being too much and too little – too much personal mess, too much theoretical jargon, too elitist, too sentimental, too removed, too difficult, too easy, too white, too Western, too colonialist, too indigenous. Yet at the same time, too little artistry, too little theorizing, too little connection between the personal and political, too impractical, too little fieldwork, too few real-world applications.[16]

It is precisely in this reading of queerness and autoethnography where a paranoid reading and a reparative reading converge and the ethics of a queer project are unravelled; I am too much and too little, and I attempt a reading towards a metaphorical structure of oppression that is both paranoid and reparative, expressing myself through means that are too artistic and not creative enough, and from positions that are simultaneously too Central and too provincial, too Anglo αλλά και με μπόλικα Βαλκάνια.

It was also important for me to locate my interest in who speaks those languages and who, or what, they are recognised as. I opted for a first-person narration to foreground my own experiences, incorporating the element of emotion against the imperative for 'objectivity', and scientificity. At the same time, I talk about a framing of selfhood that is fluid and shifting, as such the person writing might not be entirely the same person with the one that made the art projects mentioned. The first person voice historicises both the moments of the creative process and the person's thoughts that went into it and indicates the moments where these diverge. The framing of who the author is focuses on subjectivities that themselves would require further framing as they too can be seen as shifting, culturally and historically specific forms of identifying such as migrant, woman, queer, artist. 'Queer theory revels in language's failure, assuming that words can never definitively represent phenomena or stand in for things themselves', write Holman Jones and Adams adding that autoethnography as a queer method takes a stand on poetics of change.[17] Similarly, I chose to switch between tenses. Initially, it happened by accident / mistake; when it was pointed out to me I began to rake through trying to make the text temporally uniform. Endlich, I decided to go back and allow myself to go back and forth.[18] I found this to be fairer to the closet and the conditions of its existence, fitting to the autoethnographic (mis)historisation of queer linguistics and transcending places and times where these have been practised.

I wanted to share those first-person (singular but often plural) avowals and communicate them, spread them in public and alter public space in an ephemeral way, leaving traces that others might find funny, empowering, or haunting. So I turned this idioglossic diary of sorts into stencils and spread them around different cities and towns in Europe. Anzaldúa was a valuable source of inspiration along the lines of occupying liminal spaces, thinking and expressing oneself in various codes, and producing texts that are not penetrable, accessible, or transparent to and by all.[19] I leave it to each reader / participant to decide on whether to look things up, embrace them, or dismiss them altogether. I also understand how it may cause a break in reading, become frustrating, or activate feelings of hurt entitlement. All three are welcome.

This is a never-ending project, and I would like to share it with you in hopes of learning from the conversations that will follow ...

'And so the first video was shot. White frame with a tube of red lipstick standing a bit off-centre. White noise. Then suddenly a loud noise begins, and soon the lipstick's tip begins to melt. The perfect, unused lipstick becomes soft and assumes phallic/clitoric shapes. Then gradually melts away completely, leaving streams of red colour on the white surrounding. Strangely aromatic. Unusable. Messy. Phallic, blood, period, gender blah blah blah. That resulted in a series of videos based on the same premise: objects related to both the proverbial and the physical closet being deconstructed by household objects and my hands, which often remained out of frame. A bit too much on the nose. I know. Oh! By the way, prior to this, I experimented with some spatial installations with smoke (ideally in the end mist) lights and lasers, all very disappointing and failing miserably to become something I would eventually dare to share with anyone.

The other videos depicted other items which can be found in closets or are often closeted in relation to gender identities, sexualities, sexual orientations and sub-cultures, and desires of all sorts. They were all close-ups, in white backgrounds, not revealing much about the setting. The next one was of a leather black belt being perforated into uselessness with a hole punch. I had never used the tool before, so I hadn't realised the amount of strength required for so many holes in a row. It took seventeen minutes, and by the end, one can see that my pace is slowing down and I'm using both hands to clench the plier tool. The belt was from the 'men's section', as was the next item, a flannel shirt. I wanted to have it laying down on an ironing board, place an iron on it and have it burn through, leaving a big gaping hole. Next was a whip; a cat-o-nine tails whip being chopped into bits with a butcher's clover. Then posters of semi-nude bodies being unstuck from my teenage closet and shred to pieces, a pair of pink suspenders (braces) cut *shows how* with a pair of scissors. Imagine all of them in close-ups, with their respective sounds playing simultaneously, once in a while one of them would fade into black and loop as their durations were different. The process of finding, purchasing and then destroying the objects was a tricky one, which caused me to consider my own gender and conditioning towards mending, maintaining, caring, rather than destroying or acting out. Giving myself license to do so, under the guise of Kunst was liberating and even somewhat therapeutic, creating new associations between closetedness, commodification, and expression. That was Closet Case Studies #1.
long pause

Soon we would have a public presentation, and the spatial arrangement of the works became an important component in their contextualisation. It was in Vienna's Museum of Contemporary Art. Imagine there were six of these big black old-school hentarex monitors in a line, like this *gets up and shows spatial arrangement* facing the corner, thus forcing the audience to physically corner themselves in order to see the work. Several of the monitors malfunctioned until twenty minutes prior to the opening, which was stressful since my project would go first in the sequence of 'performances' we had planned. Anyway, the audience was facing towards the entrance of the space also, which for the duration of the work (about seventeen minutes) was empty.

The entire room had gravitated to the corner, and I was taking pictures of their glaring faces, which was really interesting along the lines of in / out and minority / majority dichotomies, but more importantly, it caused me to consider the visibility / transparency element. They were all facing me, but they were not looking at me, and so I felt a bizarre sense of hiding(?) in plain sight.'

long pause

The Chronicles of the Closet

> And to imagine a language means to imagine a form of life.
> Ludwig Wittgenstein, *Philosophical Investigations*

Μια φορά κι έναν καιρό ...¹

With the proverbial closet acting as the starting and centre point around which this project revolves, this chapter explores the expression it is often placed within—'come out of the closet',—its sociopolitical context and its linguistic history. While this has already been done by various researchers,² I find it imperative in tracing the production process of this linguistically formed space and laying the groundwork for the coming chapters. The cultural significance of this Anglo expression is also examined through its global permeation and its various adaptations. I further theorise the closet as a space shrouded in opacity, trying to focus on the opportunities opacity affords while keeping away from bad / good dichotomies that have populated much of the discussion around the closet. Moving on from the construction of social spaces through language (and linguistic metaphors at that), I present my findings in the linguistic productions that these social spaces in turn generate, and introduce the eleven slang varieties that friends, acquaintances, and researchers around the world were generous enough to share with me. I find myself interested in the performativity that comes with the delivery of the slangs, their embodiment, and potential for belonging, and so I chose to close this chapter with elements from a performance I presented based on my own experience with the closet at the time.

'Closet' is a late 14th-century word, from Old French, meaning a 'small enclosure, private room'.³ The Bible mentions the Latin *cubiculum* 'bedchamber, bedroom', Greek tamieion 'chamber, inner chamber, secret room'; thus originally in English 'a private room for study or prayer'. The modern sense of it meaning a 'small side-room for storage' is first recorded in the 1610s.[4] Closets as standard mass-produced household furnishings to store clothes, linen, shoes, and other items became popular in the 20th century and as Brown points out, 'The timing of the metaphor can be linked to the rising popularity of its material signifier in domestic space.'[5] A quick research of the usage of the term between 1800 and 2008 shows a tremendous and consistent increase after 1960.[6] Apart from containing the aforementioned items a closet has been known to act as a hiding place for objects their owners intend to keep secret, concealed, or protected from unwelcome eyes, as well as a hideaway while playing hide-and-seek.[7] Much like the legendary wardrobe of the Chronicles of Narnia, it can prove to be more than a hideaway and turn into a (back) door to something else, to a whole different world—or a world-view.

Beyond the obvious simultaneity of the proverbial closet with the Fordist closet,[8] there seems to be another point where the linguistic and the physical closet converge, and that is in the assemblage of objects they store; objects that do not only relate to both but do so in terms of performativity and subversiveness, playing around the fine line between visibility and opacity. Aside from one's everyday / work clothes, closets can conceal attire related to desire and pleasure; clothes and accessories that for a variety of reasons may not be (allowed to be) visible. Clothes from sections in clothing stores that might cause the salesperson to indicate that you may be shopping in the wrong section («Αυτό είναι ανδρικό αλλά αν θέλετε είναι και γιούνισεξ, όχι σαν τα άλλα»), or cause them to pause when you ask to try them on, forever shattering their assumption that you intended those items as gifts for someone else, whose body might seem more fitting or appropriate, according to the labels and the occasional salesperson. Closets also store boxes full of (still or moving) images, or objects that evoke or respond to certain kinds of desire, and are not to be found by others. They also provide a home for toys to be played with only by certain bodies and at specific times. All those objects relate differently to gender performances, non-repronormative sexual practices, and romantic feelings, often subverting their intended use (by the industry that produces and markets them). They can share this private space with items that while facilitating performances, simultaneously do so under different terms: compliance, and the creation of a cloak of invisibility so to speak.

Going back to the linguistic origins, it seems the phrase is a combination of an expressive loan from the phrase to 'come out' referring to young débutantes of the late eighteenth century and their introduction to their social circle upon reaching adulthood (or what was considered marriageable age)[9], and the furnishing item of the closet in which things are stored and kept away from sight. Coming out, usually in the form of a variety of social events, was the occasion when young British upper-class women[10] were presented by their families to the monarch—and the rest of the society by extension—in order to be introduced to potential husbands of similar social standing.[11] There are no markings of where one comes out of in that case, but rather the focus is on where it is they move towards; married and familial life, and a certain visibility in said elite circles. This paradigm entails clear socio-financial connotations with upper-class, cisgender, white nobility to be introduced to heterosexual marriage. The closet has been featured in other expressions relating to secrecy, hiding, and non-disclosure of certain information as in the expression '(one) keeps skeletons in the closet' meaning that one is hiding something shameful about themselves or their past. It also looks like this is not the only closet within LGBTQ+ culture (at least in a British linguistic context). 'Cottaging' (a British term referring to sexual encounters between strangers in public bathrooms) also creates a link between deviant sexual orientations, sexualities and sexual practices and the closet through the term 'WC' an abbreviation for 'water closet', another British term to refer to the bathroom.[12]

The phrase 'come out of the closet' or 'come out' in direct relation to non-heterosexual / non-normative individuals disclosing their sexualities (primarily gay men) was not used until the '50s or '60s. As Chauncey writes, prior to that time, homosexual men who were becoming part of the homosexual society were said to be 'coming in' said society.[13] At that time, such a declaration bore the meaning of joining a community and being welcomed in it (the 'Gay World' as it was called), rather than disclosing one's sexualities or orientation to a number of individuals in said person's life. As a matter of fact it was more common for people to lead double lives, and therefore move in and out of those two circles (or worlds) constantly.[14] 'Coming out' in exactly the same meaning as used in connection with young debutantes was only used by/for gay men in the drag balls that took place in several large US cities before World War II.[15] In the years following WWII the closet came to signify the space of isolation, secrecy, and suppression that a person of non-normative sexual orientations, sexualities, and/or gender identities (from now on referred to as LGBTQ+)[16] undisclosed to others, was occupying. Since then it has become a commonplace expression to refer to someone who decides to openly state their non-normative sexualities/orientations/gender(s), but also other non-normative qualities that may not have to do with such categories (mental health, substance abuse, emotional and/or physical abuse, eating disorders, religious/spiritual affiliation or lack thereof, and others).

With the closet and coming out of it acting as metaphors, I would like to briefly mention the roots of the term as well as how metaphors function grammatically and cognitively. The term 'metaphor' comes from the Greek 'metaferein' (μεταφέρειν) meaning to 'transfer, carry over; change, alter; to use a word in a strange sense',[17] a notional relation particularly interesting in the instance of the metaphor of the closet. It entails ideas of movement, change, and making language strange. It brings to mind Sedgwick when she remarks, 'queer is a continuing moment, movement, motive—recurrent, eddying, troublant.'[18] I looked into existing work related to metaphors and the ways in which they may shape our understanding of space and time. One prominent researcher on such topics from the field of psychology, Lera Boroditsky, observes that '[t]he job of the metaphor is to provide relational structure to an abstract domain by importing it (by analogy) from a more concrete domain'. The closet, imported from home life, creates an analogous situation between someone exiting a confined space and carries that relationship into the realm of symbolism. However, it also goes a bit further, in that a spatial structure is used to indicate not simply a temporal relation, but a complex spatiotemporal one.[19] Further, the expression indicates movement (coming out) and the position of the speaker (out of the closet). It is never 'going out' or 'getting out' to indicate the position of the speaker as inside the closet, which is interesting in its own right in who speaks or how/where the speakers position themselves.

It is this shaping of abstract thought that leads me to ask further: If the closet is constructed by language, how does its presence affect language in turn? How is the closet('s construction) visualised? I approached these questions through artistic practice in the works *Closet Case Studies #1* and *#2*. I used spatial arrangements to direct how bodies occupy space, thus visualising separation, restriction in physical space, and isolation. In *Closet Case Studies #2*, in particular, I did not only utilise a restricted and restrictive space but language as well, employing my voice to narrate and share closetedness with the audience. I used a spatial arrangement that in a literal manner represented the closet (unlike in *Closet Case Studies #1*), and used orality as the tool that creates spaces and affirms proximities of bodies to rethink the affectual relationship between tongues and pleasures, using slangs and sharing emotions. The spatial schemes we seem to base such spatiotemporally-related metaphors on, draw from spatial arrangements and movements. Thinking of movement brings us to the topic of displacement; from the inside of the closet to the space outside of it. Whether there is an equivalent to an ego-moving schema or a time-moving one, concerning the duration of occupancy or the actual performative of exiting the closet is an open question with answers that I have come to see as not necessarily mutually exclusive.

My research into how this term / notion is translated or transferred into non-English linguistic realms has disclosed a rather interesting social and geographic permeation of the phrase / term. The expression (either in its entirety or the isolated 'coming out' component alone) is used in six continents, in three different ways: there are languages that have adopted the English expression (using it with Latin / English characters when written down), those who have transliterated it to their domestic script, and those who have translated it altogether, or use a similar domestic one. Of course, there are also places, cultures, and languages in which the closet is not an existing concept as such. The degree of popularity varies, and often the expression is used interchangeably with a domestic / local one. In Italian, for example, despite having a native equivalent (uscir fuori),[20] the English expression is more popular. This further seems to be the case in several other languages such as Polish, Czech, Slovak, Romanian, Greek, and Slovene (also used is 'razkritje' meaning disclosure).[21]

Transliteration in the national script seems to be another option we find, especially in Slavic languages utilizing the Cyrillic alphabet like Bulgarian ('каминг-аут',) Russian ('Káминг-áут', 'кáмин-áут', 'кáминг áут' or 'каминáут', 'выйти из шкафа',) and Serbian ('Каминг аут' or 'аутовање').[22] And finally there are the literal translations in languages like Spanish with the expression 'salir del armario' (often 'salir del clóset' in S. America), or Catalan ('sortida de l'armari',) Portuguese (BR and PT 'sair do armário', although in Brazilian Portuguese the English expression is more often used), French 'sortir du placard', Dutch 'uit de kast komen', Welsh ('dod allan' [does not include the word closet]), Norwegian ('komme ut av skapet',) Georgian

('ჭაზობა ამჯით' coming out), Indonesian ('Keluar [dari lemari]'), Japanese ('カミングアウト'), Korean ('벽장 밖으로 나오다' gush out of the closet, or ' 커밍아웃' coming out), 'יָצָא מִן הָאָרוֹן' in Hebrew, and even found its way into Esperanto ('Elŝrankiĝo' [does not include the word closet]). Other languages seem to have equivalent phrases like the Turkish 'açılmak' which translates as 'opening up / being open',[23] or the not-so-popular 'come out of one's shell' in Greek («βγαίνω απ' το καβούκι μου»).[24]

Coming out, and the ontologies[25] claimed while doing so, are admittedly as much of a modernist twentieth century concept as is the closet. It is directly connected to understandings of knowledge, truth, and of a unified, consistent self. It is primarily a Western concept, despite the extensive permeation that has followed. As Ali Ahmadi argues in his theorisation of homosexuality, outing, and the Iranian society, same-sex sexual practices are rather commonplace among youth, seen as a fun way to subvert conservative traditionalist politics, but also for married men (here married is by default understood as 'man married to a woman') and do not seem to be connected in any way to identity. He mentions Pardis Mahdavi's 'Passionate Uprisings: Young People, Sexuality and Politics in Post-Revolutionary Iran'[26] and the insight it offers into how these types of sexual practices are bringing a 'sexual revolution' in an otherwise conservative society.[27] There seems to be a discrepancy between the rigidity of social ontologies and sexual practices particularly in non-Western settings, which allows for fluidity and an embracing of desires as long as those do not constitute identities or challenge the repronormative order. This seems to have been the case with Greek society in decades past, as is indicated by interviewees in the film *Kaliarnta*, as well as some descriptors for those engaging in same-sex sexual practices in the slang itself. In various settings, it might be / have been acceptable for men to engage in sexual practices with other men (in the setting of the hamam for instance), but not to express romantic desires towards that gender, or as extending beyond the sexual realm and the locus of the sexual encounter.

To speak of coming out and gender more specifically, I would like to briefly offer an overview of gender categories and their social status in relation to their capacity at upholding gender-related restrictions or not. Even in societies where the binary is disrupted by introducing more genders, the rules that contour them often seem as rigid as binary heteronormativity's. For example Hijras, in India and Pakistan, are individuals that were assigned male at birth, who come out as Hijras, express their gender in an effeminate manner, and are understood to be attracted to men. It is generally frowned upon to not go through the nirvan (the procedure during which the penis and scrotum are removed without anaesthesia), and it is also frowned upon to be attracted to women or other Hijras.

The Muxe in Mexico also follow a tradition of male-assigned children growing up to be women who have relationships with men.[28] According to Stephen Lynn some Muxe marry women and have biological children, while others date men (who are called 'mayate').[29] In both societies, these individuals are referred to as 'a third gender' and while Hijras ignore the caste system in their community, they are relegated to the realm of working-class/poor citizens. Similarly, Muxe are often relegated to the domestic and the care of elderly parents and often belong to the poorer class. In some areas however Muxe enjoy acceptance and visibility (e.g. several Muxe have been involved in local politics, performance artist Lukas Avendaño whose performance 'La manda (No soy persona, soy Mariposa)' [The command (I am not a person, I'm a Butterfly = faggot)] deals with such issues as gender, sexualities, and religion openly).[30]

Likewise the Samoan fa'afafine, as a third gender, 'have sexual relationships almost exclusively with men who do not identify as fa'afafine, and sometimes with women, but apparently not with other fa'afafine' and the Tahitian māhū observe the same restrictions as cis women.[31]

The Bugis people in Indonesia recognize five genders. 'In South Sulawesi', writes Graham, 'notions of gender are constituted through a variety of intersecting factors, including biological sex, spirituality, sense of self, roles, behaviours, occupation, dress, sexuality, government and religious ideology and subjectivity.'[32] Graham reports on the calabai who are assigned male at birth and don't aspire to be men, the calalai, who are assigned female at birth and assume masculine roles, the bissu who are androgynous shamans, the oroané who are similar to cis men, and the makkunrai who are similar to cis women.

In Thailand, the conceptualisation of gender happens along similar lines that involve spirituality, religion, corporeality, and behaviour. What is especially interesting in these conceptualisations of genders is the overlapping of gender, sexuality, and behaviour that goes beyond the normative Eurochristian model and includes assignments of fertility, relation to celestial bodies, role within the community or reference to specific tasks or talents (e.g. shamans), and elements of cultural position. Nevertheless, at the same time, we see a set of rules that mark a lack of social mobility and restrictions in choices directly related to gender.

Περί Νισεστόκουτου

Coming out as an act reduced to a binarism and related to a notion of the self that is clear, stable, consistent, and 'truthful' is simplistic and at odds with queerness. It is premised on oppositions of in/out, woman/man, or homo/hetero following a binary reading of relationality. What I see as in line with queerness is opacity, a notion related to postcolonial politics, and one that allows for fluidity evades clear-cut statements and goes against the demand of identification on such terms. I understand the closet as a fluid non-binary situation. More precisely, I understand it as an always already liminal spatiotemporal situation with no concrete or visible borders. A situation that can potentially entail all of us, for different amounts of time, while possibly simultaneously allowing us to be out of it. It remains unclear when someone enters the closet for the very first time, or if the closet builds itself around the person, the same way agency is debatable in the outing process. Does the person take the step or steps out or does the closet simply vanish, thus exposing them? Along the lines of Sedgwick's dismantling of the homo/hetero binary, a theorising of the closet as a shifting, fluid, and opaque device is, I think, pertinent.

Opacity as the condition of lack of transparency is a concept Édouard Glissant developed borrowing from visuality to think of orality and resistance. Queers, through their slang creations, have been using language—a system regulated by literary, national, ethnic authorities, often ridiculing those excluded by it (as illiterate, uneducated, uncivilized)—against the very authorities that stipulate it. By using neologisms, semantically altered words, and corrupted linguistic loans, this type of performative speech foregrounds the tension between entitlement and solidarity, various types of intersecting exclusions and inclusions, the minor, the major, and everything in between. Through the humour that queer slangs activate, brief instances of pleasure momentarily shift social hierarchies. Opacity is evident in queer's fluidity, its resistance to clear delineation, its willfulness to become transparent through constancy; this is why queer subjects have used the tactic in their struggle to resist and survive. Glissant saw this as an example of employing opacity (ununderstandability in this case) to avoid being transparent to their oppressors, to carry meaning back and forth between colonised people while excluding the white man. Not only were they then able to communicate more safely, but they were also able to mock the 'master'. I do not only see the closet as opaque in the way it sustains the unclarity of who is in or out (as what), but more importantly, I see in its linguistic creations a similar attempt to evade transparency. I further use such tactics in my everyday life and work—this text being one such example—to overcome shame, to connect and to actively produce moments of exclusion as a response to microaggressions and oppression.

I read the closet as a situation that anyone can find themselves in but individuals who identify as LGBTQ+ might be more often associated with, spend more time or energy in, and have a more visible or audible relation with. I do not understand the closet in absolute terms or good/bad dichotomies, and I share understandings of the closet as a potential that everyone and anyone can find themselves in; a situation veiled in opacity. An opacity that is generated by assumptions, indirect questions or open-ended answers, an opacity produced by suspicion rather than knowledge, and hypotheses rather than statements. The ever-present demand to come out of the closet is specifically activated in order to shatter this unbearable—for some—opacity that surrounds it. Let me digress for a moment, and comment on the positionality of the uttered 'invitation' to 'come out of the closet'. It is never 'go out of the closet'. The demand always comes from those who currently do not, or never have, or do not think they ever have or will ever occupied it. The asymmetry of power here is telling.

But, back to my main point on visuality and visibility's background. Ingrained in Modern Western thought are ideas of truth, which often go hand in hand with ideas of confession and admission. Foucault presents confession as a demand since the Middle Ages that serves a variety of institutions and authorities, and its function is pertinent to the closet in forcing individuals to confess desires, pleasures, and the ontologies these (supposedly need to) signify. He writes that 'sexual interdictions are constantly connected with the obligation to tell the truth about oneself',[33] and ultimately contends that this practice—connected to surveillance and power—is intended to eventually impose a homogenising normativity by punishing deviants. When Foucault talks about confession in relation to the modern idea of the Self he refers to an undoing of the opacity that shrouds the Self otherwise. Or better yet, the Other. The Self is seen as transparent, truthful, honest. The Other is opaque, needs to come clean, to confess, to be(come) understandable; penetrable even. This association of the closet with opacity is what prompts me to not only claim it as a valid potentiality but also argue that it is not against queerness, just against certain ideas of what queerness should be. I see queerness, especially given its theoretical ancestors, as heavily based on self and collective care. In that sense opacity, as a protective mechanism, as a tactic of survival, of dealing with mental difficulties, of feeling uneasy with transparency, confession, and an idea of a fixed and consistent truth, is very much in line with queerness. I want to suggest a reparative reading of the closet that perhaps sees the closet as the antithesis of the panopticon. The closet as an apparatus that disrupts surveillance and the discipline that follows it. An event that disrupts normativity and negates categorisation along clear lines and binarisms.

In the coming chapters, I suggest that the closet can be a potentiality, especially for those who are underprivileged in several axes and cannot afford (forced) visibility. In times and places where being deviant (or considered as such) could and can bring along forced medical torture, loss of employment or housing, chemical castration, imprisonment, forced labour, sexual violence ('corrective' rape), death brought on by the state, family of origin, or religious authorities and emotional and/or physical violence, finding ways to communicate and connect safely becomes vital. Having spaces to express oneself, act on one's desires, and feel safe, is what the closet might also have to offer apart from an ideological opposition to binarisms, clarity, and control.

Much like the asymmetry of the homosexual/heterosexual binary, the in/out binary indicates a position of power, freedom, openness vs. a position of inferiority, fear, shame, hiding, and much like the impossibility and restrictions (and inevitable failure) of the first binary, this seems to be the case with the latter as well. The closet can be seen as a backward move, but why not feel a bit backwards as Heather Love has so eloquently put it? I prefer to think of the closet as beyond binaries, and to, as De Villiers says, 'examine queer strategies and processes that might overcome the vicious circularity of the dialectic of the closet.'[34] Thinking of shame and fear, I want the notion of «γκέτο»,[35] «κύκλωμα», «συνάφι» to be incorporated into the closet. The closet signifies (by way of opacity) and can include anything that is not white, from the Centre, repronormative, cisheterosexist, privileged and is thus potentially a spatiotemporality of queerness, that is asked or expected to make a statement of otherness. The closet can be a space of and for queerness, a time when queerness is safe.

Going back to the relation between language and concepts, I think of Derrida's 'différance' and how Butler (introducing his Grammatology) frames a queer understanding of binaries that is so germane in thinking about the closet and writes:

> Those pairings that so pervasively govern our thinking would include inside/outside, nature/culture, mind/body, but also present/past. Those binaries are produced and maintained by excluding a set of differences that cannot appear within that relationship and that are effectively suppressed by those operations of différance that secure the binary frame. These differences are supplements, remainders, ruins, barred from entry by a reigning discursive field, indefinitely deferred. And if the binary framing decides in advance what can be said to exist, what kind of concept or referent belongs to the realm of what is, then there is no reference to what is outside the field constituted by this positing, exclusionary procedure.[36]

As Sedwick says, not coming out—not negating the closet, I would add—is usually associated with some sort of silence. Silence is again a way of expressing oneself that is not common in the West but valued, for instance, in native American cultures. While it is seen as passive, cryptic, withholding and in a negative light in Occidental societies, it is seen as a practice of quiet evaluation of a situation, one's right, and often responsibility not to speak (out) unless they are certain they have something to say and they want to say it. Glissant remarks, 'Quechua: Amerindians of South America known for their obstinate silence.' He doesn't really elaborate, and I asked my colleague Sandra Monterroso whose Mayan heritage and research focus offer her an insight into such practices. She responded that for the Mayan culture thinking, reflecting, admiring are actions, like silence, and that when people are in balance, they are quiet, which Western culture perceives as passivity when it is not. Communication, she says, doesn't only happen in terms of speaking, but through dreams, thinking, contemplating. At the end of her reply she writes, 'In Abya Yala this can help us to 'good living'/'byen vivir'. Balance is very important.'[37] Anzaldúa's thoughts on the notion of silence, quiet, and survival come to mind once again:

> *Los Chicanos*, how patient we seem, how very patient. There is the quiet of the Indian about us. We know how to survive. When other races have given

up their tongue, we've kept ours [...] Stubborn, persevering, impenetrable as stone, yet possessing a malleability that renders us unbreakable, we, the *mestizas* and *mestizos*, will remain. (emphases in original)[38]

Having previously theorised the closet as a liminal space with unclear boundaries, Anzaldúa's notion of mestizas as   , between cultures, where language is concocted, and subjectivities are re-figured, feels extremely fitting. It adds to the notion of being a (cultural) migrant, using language to find shelter, using language as a survival tactic, improvising oneself.

Drawing from Sedgwick and having been socialized and educated in a post-structuralist educational environment, I do see the binaries of hetero/homo as restricting and doomed to fail in describing such complex ways of relating and the desires that lead to those relations. Unlike Sedgwick though, I do not see the closet as 'the defining structure for gay oppression'[39] and on the contrary, believe that the closet is something that can potentially allow people to escape the very surveillance Sedgwick accused the closet of. What I see as oppressive is the constant demand to come out of it, for it is a demand that additionally implies an expectation to know oneself in order to be able to use the right signifiers while coming out. By using or activating the closet's opacity, one can fly under the radar of society's need to police people's attractions, desires, and acts. The opacity surrounding the closet allows for a re-thinking of dichotomies and a more fluid and adjustable understanding of subjectivities. I also have to acknowledge at this point neologisms in queer linguistics that have only come about recently, and incorporate much more nuanced conceptualisations of desires, practices, relationships, and self-identifiers such as demisexual,[40] lithromantic,[41] skolioromantic,[42] desisexual,[43] androromantic, gynesexual,[44] sapiosexual, zucchini[45] etc. that were not around at the time Sedgwick wrote her iconic texts. These open up a much more complex conceptual space where intersections are of utter importance, which the binary hetero/homo and woman/man fail to incorporate, or even conceptualise.

With such a fluid and unfinished definition of the closet, and the references to potential harm, I would like to move on to how the closet, in turn, produces language. I would like to shift the focus to how the closet's linguistic productions (re)affirm the social space the closet navigates, how/if it relates to the creatively abstract nature (physis?) of the closet, and how its locality might affect said social space.

This linguistic production takes the form of slangs (argots, or cants), or dialects, falling under the broader category of lavender linguistics,[46] and they seem to have existed in geographically and culturally unrelated areas. They do not constitute languages per se in the sense that they do not have distinct grammar and syntax, although in some cases they do have a vocabulary extensive enough to allow one to speak exclusively in them. Falling under the overlapping space of slangs and argots, these idioms, seem to have specific geographic radiuses and are produced and used by particular social groups, which would qualify them to be additionally described as sociolects.[47] The slangs are primarily a feature της εργατικής τάξης και του πρεκαριάτου, μάλλον τελικά του πουσταριάτου, something I see as an affirmation of the potential of the closet as a space of belonging, healing, and occupying. As I explain further below, these creations are a necessity, a survival tool, and have been authored by working-class people, or people whose lives are situated in precarity not only in terms of employment and class, but also age, dis_ability, and ethnicity/nationality. According to Ildikó Gy. Zoltán 'Self-defense, defiance, opposition and mutiny can all be included in the emotional charge of slang usage, in which case we can also speak about it as anti-language depending on how sharply it may turn against the standards and norms it invariably finds ridiculously restrictive.'[48] As I will analyse further down, the slangs indicate opposition to the status quo, as well as a seemingly contradictory adoption of some of the normative mores. Through this synthesis, they divulge the specifics of the social milieux the speakers occupy. While Zoltán refers to them as 'anti-languages' in the sense of their counter-cultural stance and critique of the norms, other linguists (such as Canakis in sub-chapter «ΛΕΞΙΚΟ») use the term to refer to their function on the premise of who does *not* understand, rather than who understands or speaks it. By so doing the focus is shifted to those left outside, those excluded in that reversal of societal norms, the 'normals', τους «φυσιολογικούς», the breeders, the heteros, the cis. While that might momentarily once again bring the privileged or majoritarian figures to the foreground, by so doing it also simultaneously allows for opacity to enshroud the social make-up of the speakers.

When I first began to explore the possibilities the closet offers, I thought of the closet as an apparatus, as a complex structure that consumes and produces space and time. Working further on the slangs that this device creates,

I have come to think of them as a separate set of apparatuses, mechanisms of communication, subjectification, and belonging. Agamben, who also considers language an apparatus, suitably expands the class of Foucauldian apparatuses to include:

> writing, literature, philosophy, agriculture, cigarettes, navigation, computers, cellular telephones and—why not—language itself, which is perhaps the most ancient of apparatuses—one in which thousands and thousands of years ago a primate inadvertently let himself be captured, probably without realizing the consequences that he was about to face.[49]

Another element that accents the social regulation of the closet as a space of cultural production and of embracing difference is the new potentialities it affords the speakers of the slangs. As Stephanie Rudwick remarks:

> [M]ost informants described what they considered their 'coming-out' as the period when most of the isiNgqumo acquisition took place. Some interviewees also claimed that this period was also the time when they started to think of their own homosexuality as a 'gift'. They claimed to have talents none of their siblings have, such as, for instance, an impeccable sense of good style, exceptional cooking skills, social competence, and, importantly in the context of isiNgqumo, great capacity of being articulate.[50]

Once again deviancy opens up an array of possibilities to express oneself and find pleasures that go beyond the originary desires that led to the ontological categories thought of as deviant in the first place.

Άει μωρή καλιαρντή!

I already knew Καλιαρντά and Polari from associating with the local LGBTQ+ communities while living in Greece and England, respectively. After conducting research (aka asking around) to find out if the phenomenon has been more extensive and appeared elsewhere I came across Bajubá or Pajubá in Brazil, Swardspeak in the Philippines, Bahasa Binan in Indonesia, IsiNgqumo and Gayl or Gail in South Africa, Hijra Farsi in India, Ókhchit (אוחנית) in Israel, Gayspeak in the English-speaking world, and Lubunca in Turkey.

In the coming chapters I aim to analyze them through a descriptivist prism in terms of their vocabulary and the social critique they apply, and share how getting to know them more, and eventually thinking in their terms, has informed my life and practice especially ever since I started living abroad.

Kaliarnta, the idiom primarily spoken by 'cinaedi' or 'homosexuals' (according to Petropoulos)[51] within Greece, was thought to have come into existence in the late '20s or '30s, but now seems to have been around much earlier having had a brief glossary documented in a 1904 publication.[52] The main reason for its existence is to provide a safe(r) exchange of information between the speakers and render them practically invisible (or rather undecipherable) to outsiders. Kaliarnta employs Greek, English, French, Italian, Turkish, Albanian and Romani words,[53] altering them sometimes beyond recognition, resemanticising Greek words, while also using plenty of neologisms. Furthermore, it incorporates a small number of slang words from other Greek subcultures like the one of manges, or that of rembetes.

The dictionary is rather extensive with Elias Petropoulos documenting around 6,000 words during the time he conducted the research for his book Kaliarnta (1971), which is the only book to document the idiom and as the author himself states is the product of 'amateur research'.[54] According to Petropoulos—who immersed himself in the subculture as an outsider and remained critical of the speakers, indeed often queerphobic—most cinaedi use about five hundred words, while there are others that can fluently speak using several thousand, a richer lexicon referred to as 'Ντούρα Καλιαρντά' (Hard Kaliarnta), or 'Βαθιά Λατινικά' (Deep Latin), or 'Ετρούσκα' (Etruscan) among other terms.[55] As an additional security measure, Kaliarnta is spoken fast and with accompanying gestures that create the corresponding contexts. Kaliarnta was/is perhaps primarily spoken by the most vulnerable subgroups of the community, the (primarily cross-dressing / τραβεστί,[56] trans*) sex workers. Kaliarnta is seen as the quintessence of camp performance, which itself is often referred to as a method of resistance that, according to David Halperin, resists the power of the system from within.[57] Moe Meyer maintains that:

> What "queer" signals is an ontological challenge that displaces bourgeois notions of the Self as unique, abiding, and continuous while substituting instead a concept of the Self as performative, improvisational, discontinuous and processually constituted by repetitive and stylized acts.[58]

The connections this reference creates between non-uniqueness, rejection, non-continuity, queer, and camp are particularly telling of how the tactic performs the subjectivity, or how the subjectivity becomes performed and enters the sphere of visual politics. Both 'queer' and 'camp' act willfully towards stable categories and instead opt for their undoing through frivolity, humour, and creativity. In that sense, they negate the Modernist/Western idea of the Self.

Polari, according to researcher Paul Baker is:

> a secret form of language used mainly by gay men and lesbians in London and other cities in the UK during the twentieth century. Derived in part from the slang lexicons of numerous stigmatised and itinerant groups, Polari was particularly popular among actors and gay men in the Merchant Navy. Initially used in order to maintain secrecy, Polari was also a means of socialising, acting out camp performances and reconstructing a shared gay identity and world-view among its speakers.[59]

It is composed of a few hundred terms and includes Romani, Yiddish, and Mediterranean Lingua Franca elements. Polari became known to a broad public through *Round the Horne*, a BBC radio show that aired between 1965 and 1968, and has since been used in several cultural productions such as puppet theatre (*Punch and Judy*) TV (*Queer As Folk*, [US]) and music (Morrisey's 1992 'Piccadilly Palare', David Bowie's 2016 'Girl Loves Me'). It includes heavy influences from Cant, the secret idiom used by criminals in Britain between the sixteenth and eighteenth centuries.[60]

Pajubá (or Bajubá), the Brazilian counterpart of Kaliarnta and Polari, is spoken among quia and travesti people, bichas, and Candomblé practitioners. The vocabulary (a mixture of several African languages, based on a Portuguese syntax), seems to have been initially used by the holy fathers of the religion and subsequently by sexual dissidents. It grew primarily in areas with heavy African presence and thusly apart from Yoruba has traces of Fon and Ewe, (both part of the Gbe cluster of languages), and Kikongo, Umbundu, and Kimbundu (Bantu languages).[61] My friend Pêdra tells me over facebook that she first heard about these words in the Umbanda's terreiro (spiritual place of umbanda afro-brazilian religion)[sic] in her childhood and then when she started to know gays, in 1990, she was 12 years old and the gays, between 25 and 40 years old.[62] Reporting on Pajubá speakers and issues pertaining to the intersection of race and sexuality for a large number of them Lewis, quoting Wolfe, maintains that they come together in speaking this slang and that they do so in order to 'avoid both civil and police surveillance.'[63] 'This argot, tellingly, is becoming popular among those who celebrate the revival of regional and Afro-centered identity discourse, one that is not enmeshed in Brazilianness but in the experiences of marginalized sectors and those who confront criminalization in day-to-day existence', writes Lewis elsewhere.[64]

In the Philippines, an argot or cant that derived from Englog (Tagalog-English code-switching) and incorporates Spanish elements as well (also known as 'Bekimon' or 'gay lingo') is used by 'gay and transvestite men' since at least the '70s (the era of martial law in the country).[65] What affected the sprouting of these terms and communication modes could be attributed to the power exerted against free speech. The argot, Swardspeak, is on that regard also an underground movement. It destroys the clout of power being brandished to minorities, oppressing those who would speak truth to power, and gagging the Filipinos, preventing them from communicating efficiently and freely. Swardspeak is pronounced by Filipinos similar to swards-PEH-ahk.[66] Another source claims that Swardspeak also uses Cebuano, Japanese, Sanskrit, and other languages, as well as names of celebrities and trademark brands.[67]

Among those speaking Swardspeak are Baklâs, a community similar to the Hijras in that ideas of gender and sexual orientation are often seen as going hand-in-hand, unlike Western conceptualisations of gender identity and sexualities. Baklâs are also referred to as bayot (Cebuano) or agi (Hiligaynon), and according to Michael L. Tan the term refers to a person who was assigned male at birth, but usually, has adopted feminine mannerisms and attire.[68] In Catacutan's words, 'Swardspeak rebels against the norm of syntactic rules but gives heavy emphasis on semantics through shared consciousness and knowledge but more importantly, unconventional pragmatics.' [...] 'It is also a battle against the norm or the status quo. It does not adhere to strict form, nor does it squarely follow structures which other forms of languages have.'[69] In the decades following the 1986 revolution, two TV shows catered to gayspeak (Giovanni Calvo's *Katok mga Misis* and Out) both of which had segments dedicated to explaining the meanings and etymologies of terms.[70] Further, recently facebook pages and YouTube accounts devoted to a Swardspeak dictionary appeared, some of them reaching substantial popularity;[71] all of which resulted in both shattering the opacity and generating new audiences and new terms along the way.

Bahasa Binan (or Bahasa Béncong, or Bahasa Gay, or Bahasa Gaul) (meaning the language of the homosexuals)[72] is a dialect spoken by the gay community in Indonesia. It has several regular patterns of word formation and is documented in both writing and speech. This idiom also resemanticises everyday words, and also uses prefixes, suffixes, and replacements to bring drastic changes in how a sentence sounds.[73] Similar to Swardspeak, Bahasa Gay uses the national language (bahasa Indonesia), English, brand names or celebrity names (like 'Brad Pitt' for berapa [meaning how much]), and syllabic substitution.[74] Regarding its composite nature concerning the available national languages Leap claims, 'to my knowledge bahasa *gay* terms are never formed from Arabic or Sanskrit loanwords, despite their frequency in contemporary Indonesian. This likely reflects the close relationship between *gay* subjectivities and the mass media rather than Islam or the historical links between Indonesia and India.'[75] (emphasis in original) The same author also states that the idiom can be found in all of the archipelago. Boellstorff maintains that the use of such a translocal language affirms that one has a place.[76] He further claims that this place is the nation, and this is where my understanding differs from his.

I understand these registers as having more in connection to fantastic communities and support networks whose frameworks are fluid and ever-changing. Further,—based on the vocabularies that I can access—the idea of the nation (i.e. the nation-state) is one that is fiercely mocked, and participation in it does not seem to be an appealing idea for the speakers. Perhaps this is a good point to think further of these communities as fantastic and how they may differ from Anderson's 'imagined communities' by which he mainly refers to the nation-state. My understanding of the imaginary communities the languages construct (based on a mutual understanding of being excluded from something based on gender, sexualities, and sexual orientations in particular) is that, unlike Anderson's imagined community of the nation, they are constantly negotiated and performed and members are keenly aware of that. Members of these communities, having experienced marginalisation, mockery, lack of civil rights, and precarity are not so willing to embrace the idea of a (national) community worth dying for. While they do embrace belonging to communities and forms of collectivity, at the same time, their life experiences remind them that self-preservation and self-care are essential, thus giving those communities a sense of conditional membership and a strong sense of valuing the individual and their experiences as well. The slangs further negate a single dominant channel of communication; they even negate the authority of the national language. Not by the extensive ξενομανία[77] of recent years (where anything and everything non-Greek / non-Balkan) is good and superior, but by equally corrupting them and eventually re-appropriating them.

Indicative of the segregationist politics of the country, in South Africa there are two of those varieties along racial lines, speaking volumes to the racial, class, and gender politics in place. IsiNgqumo is a Zulu and Bantu-based idiom of black South Africans, mainly used in townships. According to Hugh McLean and Linda Ngcobo:

> It is difficult to pinpoint the time or specific event marking the emergence of a gay movement in black townships. It probably came about in recent years, due to a combination of events and factors. For younger gays, the recent gay pride marches and the existence of a gay character on Dynasty are usually cited as the events marking the emergence of this movement. For older gays it was the Soweto uprising of 1976.[78]

The same researchers report that, 'isinqumo without the "g" means "decisions", and the skesanas say that the parole got its name because one must take a decision to use it' which foregrounds issues of agency, need, and decision-making in naming, labeling, and belonging. In their paper 'abangibhamayo bathi ngimnandi' (which means 'Those who fuck me say I'm tasty') the authors introduce the terms 'skesana' (a boy who likes to be fucked, someone who adopts a female persona and performs 'girly' mannerisms, habits, tasks),[79] 'injonga' (the active partners of the skesanas, they can be boys or men, and whom skesanas regard as straight even if they acknowledge openly that they like having sex with men),[80] 'pantsula' (the "accidental" homosexual, a person who has sex with what he believes to be a hermaphrodite [sic] or with someone who pretends, or who he pretends, is female)[81] and 'imbube' ('someone who goes fifty-fifty').[82] They further discuss the gendered aspects of those roles and their performances in Durban and Soweto, and touch upon the topic of closetedness and the respective societies in the townships. On the topic of IsiNgqumo's corrupted Zulu linguistic origins, they maintain that:

The fact that most of the words are derived from Zulu point to *isingqumo's* origins among Durban *skesanas*. This would seem to indicate that a gay sub-culture was more developed in Durban from earlier on. On the other hand, it could be related to the intensely patriarchal nature of Zulu society and the greater need for secrecy. Many Soweto *skesanas* will insist that Durban *skesanas* are 'more closeted' than other gays.[83] (emphasis in original)

Cage reports that it first emerged in the South African mines among mine workers and their boy-wives. Rudwick says some of her informants have confirmed this happened but does not necessarily mean the idiom began there. She quotes Louw who 'describes how Mkhumbane became known for its public male-male wedding activities and in this context refers to isiNgqumo as a homosexual argot derived from the isiZulu word ukungqumuza meaning 'to speak quietly so that others about do not hear of important matters.'[84] Rudwick notices that affluent Zulu gays employ English as a main medium of communication; this is also the case with many heterosexual 'upper-middle' class Zulu people.[85] At the same time, isiNgqumo speakers make little to no use of English and instead rely almost exclusively on a Zulu lexicon, indicating the strong bonds with traditional Zulu culture.[86] Due to the patriarchal nature of Zulu culture though, it seems that the speakers re-interpret many things, including gender roles and relations, in the framework of IsiNgqumo.[87]

Gayle (or Gail) (also initially 'Moffietaal', Afrikaans for 'homosexual language') is the second such slang used in South Africa, which, based on English and Afrikaans, circulates mainly among white / Afrikaans-speaking gay men. 'Gayle' was reportedly the word used for 'chat / to chat' in Moffietaal in the '50s, and then ended up replacing the name of the slang altogether.[88] Cage claims the slang was initially used by South Africans of colour and was then appropriated by white South Africans.[89] He adds that while the first gay bar opened in the late '40s, it catered mainly to well-heeled, English-speaking gays and so the majority of gay men remained on the streets.[90] Unlike the use of IsiNgqumo, the frequent use of Gayle in recent years has declined as a mechanism to conceal 'gay identities' (Cage's phrasing), but it still functions as a community-forming tactic. Its relation to camp and exaggerated performative creativity might be a reason for that.[91] The sociopolitical situation that prompted the creation and use of such slang was, of course, the strict legal regime deriving from colonisation and South African law. Rooted in Roman-

Dutch law, in which 'unnatural practices' between men were criminalised, South African law did the same.[92] Cage maintains that initially, the svartgevaar left gays alone despite the legislation. However, in 1966 the police started becoming concerned by the pienkgevaar. Soon both 'threats' were seen as equally dangerous and went hand-in-hand (non-procreative gays were not contributing to the white population to combat the 'black threat').[93] In 2015 Capetonian rapper Dope Saint Jude created 'Keep in Touch',[94] a song (and subsequent music video) with Angel-Ho that uses Gayle and provides commentary on issues of gender, race, and class.

In the English-speaking world (primarily the US, and to a smaller extent loan-words in Australia, New Zealand, and South Africa) there is the loosely defined 'Gayspeak' which may have come into being during the lavender scare of the '50s. Though many lexicographers have managed to document terms, it seems that it relies heavily on English to exist and carry meaning, not merely in terms of structure, grammar, or syntax, but utilising official English words in their original form. It is of course still connected to camp performativity and elements, and has made its way into mainstream language with terms such as 'queen', 'butch', 'breeder', 'top / bottom / verse', 'bear', and 'twink'. In New Zealand male sex workers, mainly working in the areas of the harbours borrowed lemmata from Polari via the Merchant Navy in the '50s[95] which then melded into a lexicon of 'male prostitutes' [Ings' phrasing] that had already evidenced several definable strains of metaphor.[96] Ings observes, 'Historically, the language of the male prostitute borrows heavily from boob (prison) slang, bogspeak, Polari, cant, Maori, and the working language of the tima mole (ship boys).'[97] *Round the Horne* was also broadcast by Radio New Zealand on Saturday nights in 1968-70.[98] As with many of the other slangs, this one also exhibits a large preoccupation with issues of the law, the police, and illegal activities. Ings documents a number of terms for the police by the '60s such as 'Vivian Vice', 'Nelly-law', 'Dolly Handbag', 'Alice', 'Dora-D', 'Hilda-Handcuff', 'Lily-lunchbox', 'Jennifer-Justice', 'Hilda Box-rot', 'Petunia Pig', 'Tilly Tight-twat', 'Cherie Cunstable', and, my personal favourite, 'Our Lady of the Golden Brooch'[99] managing to at once feminise the force, correlate one law-enforcing authority with another (church), and reduce the all-powerful badge into a mere accessory.

The famous Hijras in India and some areas of Pakistan speak Hijra Farsi,[100] a sociolect based on Hindustani (the lingua franca of North India and Pakistan) on Urdu structure. Since the partition of India in the late '40s it has incorporated several local linguistic varieties such as Punjabi, Seraiki, and Sindhi.[101] Using the Indian Hijras' public verbal displays as an example of how they claim public space, Kira Hall observes:

> In order to make any sense of the hijra's seemingly innocuous and nonsensical utterance, the passer-by must enter into what he believes to be the hijra's frame of reference, a linguistic space involving sexual innuendo, crudity, and gender fluidity. Yet by doing so, the hearer must also admit to himself that he in many ways inhabits that same space."[102]

Hall understands that the Hijras, like other self-effeminised speakers, enfranchise themselves by creatively upturning gendered preconceptions. She further elaborates, 'Through this verbal play, then, the hijras, who have a precarious status in the Indian social matrix, are able to compensate for their own lack of social prestige by assuming linguistic control of the immediate interaction, creating alternative sociosexual spaces in a dichotomously gendered geography.'[103] McBeth also maintains that for the Hijras public life is a queer stage, and their performance is significant when 'normal' people begin to reconsider the societal roles they take for granted.[104] Hall also comments on Hijras' lineage that according to them dates back to the eunuchs of the medieval Mughal courts.[105] Hijra Farsi is the only one of those sociolects I have been able to find for which academia grants the status of a language and not simply a collection of code-words. Anahita Mukherji writes in the Times of India, 'academic research validates the claim that Hijra Farsi is indeed a language and not simply a collection of secret code-words'. Prof. Muhammad Safeer Awan and Muhammad Sheeraz, researchers who studied the language spoken amongst Pakistan's Hijra community, show that it contains its own unique vocabulary, syntactical and morphological character that differs from other mainstream languages, making Farsi 'as good a language as any other'.[106] With regards to the performativity and the full extent of the embodiment of the language, Hijras have a much referenced characteristic gesture. Nidhi Dugar Kundalia reveals:

> At traffic junctions, or in baby-naming ceremonies, I always wondered about that distinct gesture of the Hijras, of flat palms striking against each other, with the fingers spread limply. A few published papers in journals such as

International Journal of Humanities and Social Science imply that this is an extension of their physiological identity. It means 'I am who I am.'[107]

Elsewhere, activist Laxmi Narayan Tripathi comments, 'There is a sense of instant identification of the community they belong to.' 'Sociologists', reports Kundalia, 'think there are subtle variations in the taal (beat) of the Hijra's clap that, apart from controlling the attention of 'normals', are also used for internal codified messages.'[108] Again colonialism has played a major role in importing a different ethos and framing the national legal system according to—in this case—Victorian / Edwardian British mores. Simran Shaikh, a member of the community, says, 'it was created for the purpose of self-preservation during the British Raj. While literature shows that Hijras occupied a privileged position in ancient India, the British criminalised us and put us behind bars. This language was as a survival mechanism for Hijras.'[109] Ranjeeta Sinha, provides a glimpse into how geographic and ethnic backgrounds shape this language, 'they have two kinds of languages' she states. And she adds: 'Muslim Hijras speak mostly Farsi and Hindu Hijras speak Gupti with regional dialects. So depending on where you are in India, a Hijra could be called hikra, kinnar, safadi or khujda.'[110]

In Istanbul, Turkey, (and elsewhere, e.g. Ankara) an argot called Lubunca has been used, and its traces are by far the oldest of any of the others. According to Kontovas:

> While no record of a specifically Queer Turkish slang variety appears before the 1980s, a number of Ottoman lexicographers and proto-ethnographers from the 16th century onward displayed a remarkable interest in sex-related slang, much of which refers to same-sex relations if not specifically labeled as being commonly used by the contemporary Queer population such as it may have been.[111]

According to the blog 'Mavi Boncuk' (describing itself as a 'Cornucopia of Ottomania and Turcomania') Lubunca is a composite of the word 'lubunya' (from Slavic: liubima)[112] which in Lubunca means darling (feminine) and 'ca' meaning 'the way'. According to Nicholas Kontovas again (who wrote his master's thesis on Lubunca):

It is derived from the *Lubunca* word *lubun*, a shortened form of the word *lubunya* 'gay, queer, fairy,' which seems to be derived from the Romani word *lubni* 'female prostitute'. *Lubunca* is also sometimes referred to as *Lubunyaca*. The Turkish suffix *-ca* means (among other things) 'in the style of,' and is frequently used on nouns to denote the language, dialect, or style in which that noun speaks."[113] (emphasis in original)

According to Mavi Boncuk: 'lubunyaca: An argot used by the "lubunyalar" of Istanbul, combines Turkish, Slavic and Romani - Gypsy vocabulary on the base of a largely Turkish grammar."[114] According to Kontovas, Lubunca has Turkish, Romani, French, Greek, Armenian, English, Ladino, Arabic, Bulgarian, Italian, Russian, and Kurmanji roots.[115] Its terms reflect not only gender and sexually connoted words, but quotidian things, crime, as well as lemmata related to beauty, money, fun, ethnicity, and age.[116] Traces of its vocabulary (albeit composed of very different lingual composites) can be found from the 16th century onwards, which further highlights the question of who spoke it and which category / label / word was assigned to them before the invention of the homosexual subject as such. This seems to coincide with several of the other slangs.

Ya'ar lets me know of Ókhchit (אוֹחְצִית) the Israel-based slang that has elements of Iraqi and Moroccan Arabic with Persian influences, as well as influences from European languages such as English and French. Additionally, much like the other slangs, it contains distorted Hebrew words and a high prevalence of humourous elements. 'Okhcht' means 'sister' in Arabic, Ya'ar tells me, and 'okhcha' indicates an effeminate gay man.[117] He informs me that, consistently with many of the other slangs, the feminisation is a tactic present here as well, and with Hebrew being a highly gendered language, there is plenty of room for that. Ókhchit seems to have started in the '70s and developed in the '80s in dating advertisements in gay newspapers[118] as well as in the Tel Aviv club scene of the '90s, Liat tells me.[119] At the end of the '90s, Ronen Pe'eri published a dictionary in the gay newspaper *Pink Time*. I have not been able to get specific information about the demographics that spoke / speak the slang. An illustrated online dictionary that Liat shared with me and which was created for the purpose of 'introducing gay slang to straight people and strengthening the bonds between the two communities' according to the illustrator Nir Biton, appeared online in 2009.[120]

Although all of the above categories are in one way or another marginal, perhaps illegal, with intense minoritarian traits, and although socialization between them could explain this transcultural permeation of terms, it also clearly indicates the significance of intersectionality. This quick run-through of who creates/speaks those registers proves—beyond the obvious diversity of the descriptors of the interlocutors in terms of desires—the intricate extent intersectionality has played in the sharing and usage of them. The lack of socially waterproof spaces is clearly illustrated here with the loan words from other subcultures, the foreign loans, the marine-related jargon (sabir), and further the way it was shared among religious practitioners, sex workers, actors, circus performers, and eventually spilt into the mainstream.

Εσύ μωρή, που κάθεσαι; - Situating the Denizens

The overview of the slangs I provide here uses terms from the original sources as well as my own descriptors. This might seem inconsistent, but I decided to, firstly, keep the terms as they were in the original texts in order to avoid drawing conclusions or applying a localisational logic on them, and secondly, to use the terms 'queer', 'queerness', and 'queering' in order to refer to any of the speakers of those slangs despite the fact that it is a rather contemporary (and in some way Western/Anglo/North) aiming at activating its fluidity and potential for inclusiveness this umbrella term stands for. I found it to be the most fitting wording in encompassing social categories, identities, subjectivities, subcultures, or simply participants in certain sexual acts or desires, in comparison with any other terms that are by definition more fixed, less inclusive, and have unambiguous class/race/ability identifiers or connotations. I do not wish to erase the terms otherwise used as they are valuable sources of conceptual and semantic information and highlight the immense intellectual diversity of the speakers.

Parallel to that, and since I am not a member of most of these groups, I want to frame things through the methodological lens chosen for this project, especially since I'm advocating for a 'queer' that is not restricted by its Western/Anglo roots. The use of different terms and 'queer' in particular as a catch-all term to describe the slangs does not imply a fixed and/or bidirectional relationship between the closet and the potential denizens. Not every person identifying as queer or feeling queer was, is, or will be in the closet, and not every person that has been, is, or will be in the closet identifies as, is, or feels queer. And with a preoccupation on language comes the topic of naming those who speak. As Kulick writes this is an 'unavoidable and ultimately unresolvable problem'[121] and as he continues 'In a constructionist vein, we can explore how certain linguistic practices performatively materialize speakers as gay or lesbian.'[122] Much like the several spatio-temporal paradoxes that surround the closet, the languages that could be its product seem to predate it in some instances. Furthermore, who speaks or spoke these languages long before the emergence of any contemporary understanding of certain concepts (such as 'homosexuality', 'the homosexual', and notions such as 'trans*' or 'queer') becomes an even more important topic to keep in mind in light of queer modes of communication. As Koch writes, perhaps we cannot even talk about a 'homosexual language' as there is no monolithic gay experience.[123]

Queer / Lavender Linguistics

Lavender linguistics is broadly defined as the language used by LGBTQ+ speakers and includes spoken and written language, pronunciation, and speech patterns (such as intonation and lisping).[124] Does the '+' at the end of the initialism indicate a broader understanding and inclusion of non-Western / Northern subjectivities, and social ontologies related to genders and sexualities as well as spiritual practices etc. (e.g. Hijras in India and Pakistan, skesanas in South Africa, faggots in the US, poofs in the UK, qvir in Russia, quia, bichas, and travesti in Brazil, πούστηδες, μπινέδες, τσόλια, τρανς, τζίβες, πλακομουνούδες, και κωλομπαράδες στην Ελλάδα, two-spirit persons in the Americas, faʻafafine in Samoa, fakaleiti in Tonga, mahu wahine in Hawaii, mahu vahine in Tahiti, whakawahine in New Zealand Māori, and akavaʻine [Cook Islands Māori], bissu, calabai, and calalai in Bugis, kathoey or katoey in Thailand, ashtime of Maale culture in Southern Ethiopia, mashoga of Swahili-speaking areas of the Kenyan coast, mangaiko among the Mbo people of the Democratic Republic of the Congo, palaoʻana in the Chamorro language in Micronesia, koekchuch [extinct] in Siberia, mak nyah in Malaysia, winkte [also spelled wįntke] of the Lakota people, mukhannathun and mutarijjalun in the Arab world)? For this project, I want to assume it does.

Contemporary queer linguistics, partly thanks to the advent of the internet, social media, fora, and wikis, has attempted to create neologisms (often based on Latin and Greek components) that offer visibility and representation to ever-developing subjectivities in relation to romantic or sexual orientations, or lack thereof, preferences that anchor to characteristics other than gender etc. This is not meant as a secretive project of an extensive vocabulary that escapes scrutiny, but rather as a project for accurate representation of communities and individuals demanding the right to be referred to and described accurately and in a positive or at least neutral light, especially by those outside their communities. Additionally queer linguistics employs the tactic of reclaiming (formerly) pejorative terms used by outsiders to insult members of the group. The word 'reclaim' itself is particularly interesting in this context as it comes from the Latin reclamare meaning 'cry out against'.[125]

There are diverse approaches to the topic of language, with equally diverse understandings of who the speakers are (extending from essentialism to poststructural politics, and from Foucauldian ontological aspects to identitarian ones). Likewise, there is a big debate about which exact category these linguistic creations ultimately fall under (as seen above I opted for maintaining the characterisation of the sources in an attempt to exhibit the diversity and various positionings of linguists, anthropologists, speakers, folklorists, sociologists, lexicographers, and others with an interest and contribution to the topic). Attempts to create a consistent, linear, and comprehensive category that encompasses all have naturally failed, but some offer interesting contributions to the discussion nonetheless. Kulick further positions himself in the field by saying:

> One problem to which I return repeatedly is the belief in much work that gay and lesbian language is somehow grounded in gay and lesbian identities and instantiated in the speech of people who self-identify as gay and lesbian. This assumption confuses symbolic and empirical categories, it reduces sexuality to sexual identity, and it steers research away from examining the ways in which the characteristics seen as queer are linguistic resources available to everybody to use, regardless of their sexual orientation.[126]

I must admit that while researching these languages, anti-languages, slangs, idioms, sociolects, cants, argots, registers, I came across equally as many descriptors for their speakers. Ultimately what binds those languages are not specific identities, subjectivities, professions, race, or class positionings, but desires and acts of reclaiming agency. Consequently although I do transfer the terms used by the respective researchers of each paper / register I would like to clarify that I bring them all together in this project due to this common underlying denominator that is deviant desires whether they be in terms of sexual orientations, sexualities, genders, or sexual or romantic affinities and practices. Kulick, reporting on the names of such slangs (restricted to English speakers) mentions:

> Gayspeak (Hayes 1981b, Cox & Fay 1994), lgb talk [for 'lesbian/bisexual/gay' (Zwicky 1997)], Gay male language, gay and lesbian language, gay male speech (Barrett 1997:185,192,194), lesbian speech (Moonwomon-Baird 1997:203), Gay speech (Zeve 1993), lesbian language (Queen 1997:233), lavender language (Leck 1995:327, Leap 1995), gay English (Goodwin 1991), Gay English (Leap 1996, 1997), queerspeak (Livia & Hall 1997a), and my personal favorite—Faglish (Rodgers 1972:94).[127]

Kulick finally concludes very poignantly that 'the object under focus here does not, in fact, exist. There is no such thing as gay or lesbian language.'[128] An overview of the field of lavender linguistics shows that this research area draws not only from linguistics but also queer theory to understand the speakers as creators with agency. As Penelope Eckert observes 'The emphasis on stylistic practice in the third wave places speakers not as passive and stable carriers of dialect, but as stylistic agents, tailoring linguistic styles in ongoing and lifelong projects of self-construction and differentiation.'[129] Lavender linguistics further focuses on the construction of social categories through language/s rather than how language/s already reflect/s them.

There have been countless discussions about 'sounding gay' within and beyond LGBTQ+ communities, a number of studies, and many jokes (mainly at the expense of people who 'sound gay' or use 'gay talk'). Ron Smyth, a linguist, talks about the phenomenon of 'gay voice' in terms of microvariations. He lists several things that gay men supposedly do (clearer and longer vowels, clearer Ls and longer Ss, overarticulation of the Ps, Ts, and Ks) the combination of which leads to the phenomenon read as 'gay voice' or 'sounding gay'.[130] The gay 'lisp' is a bit of a misnomer, usually referring to a sibilant 'S'.[131] Munson says the 'gay lisp' doesn't exist. A true frontal lisp happens when people say 'sink' when they want to say 'think', and a lateral lisp is what Sid, the sloth in 'Ice Age', has.[132] William Leap, a major contributor to the field, and the person that has mostly been associated with the coining or mainstreaming of the term 'lavender linguistics', has provided insight into what these idioms or speech performatives constitute, but like others has not pointed out what makes them particularly gay. As mentioned, other groups, social categories, sub-cultures have developed slangs, cants, argots, all of which use semantically altered words, incorporate word games, foreign loan-words etc., and have done so similarly for reasons of protection, cohesion, and group membership. As Kulick comments. 'Hence, a circular argument emerges. If we ask "What is Gay English," the answer is "English spoken by gay men." What makes it gay? The fact that gay men speak it. Why do gay men speak it? Because they are gay men. And so on, round and round.'[133]

When it comes to coding and shrouding prec(ar)ious content related to sexual minorities with secrecy, I have to mention Anne Lister. Lister, also called Gentleman Jack by her fellow citizens, was an AFAB gender-nonconforming person in Georgian England. Lister had several relationships with women (being wealthy and well-educated did not hurt I'm sure). Given the disapproval (to say the least) of such gender nonconformity and sexual activity at the time, Lister communicated with one of their lovers and also kept their own diary in a code they had created specifically for the purpose (the code included Greek and mathematical symbols). The diaries are detailed accounts of their romantic and sexual relationships and the code was not deciphered until much later and went on to become part of UNESCO's Memory of the World Programme.[134]

Another characteristic located in many (if not all) of the slangs mentioned above, and a popular way of addressing interlocutors within queer contexts, is the feminisation of pronouns and descriptors (nouns, adjectives, epithets). Livia, pointing out a tactic of reclaiming pejorative ways of addressing others and their essence, perhaps throwing some shock value in the pot as well, writes:

> The very fact of referring to another man in the feminine, even if the speaker never uses the feminine designators in reference to himself, indicates participation in the countercultural, antiheterosexual discourse mode. Speakers thereby underline their own alliance with the sissy, the nelly, the drag queen, and in fact create this alliance by their use of the feminine gender.[135]

In what is, to my knowledge, the first documentation of Kaliarnta, the phenomenon of feminisation is explicitly addressed providing specific examples of feminised names as well as ways to address each other. Here is an excerpt from the aforementioned 1904 satyrical newspaper that presents Kaliarnta and introduces some of the speakers:

> In the 1904–12–09 issue you can read the names of 'the Group of Twelve in Peiraeus':
>
> Αλεκάκι, Μανωλάκι, Γαλατού, Χαραλαμπάκι, Ρόφα, Σαλεπιντζού, Ροδίτισσα, Αντωνία, Καμπουρίτσα, Καμπερούλα (ναύτης), Οδοντοϊατρός, Παπλωματού, Μπουντούρης (ναύτης), Πετρού
>
> Little Alex [neut], Little Manolis [neut], Milkmaid, Little Haralambos [neut], Rofa [Sucker?] [fem], Saloop-Seller [fem], Rhodian Woman, Antonia, Little Hunchback [fem], Little Kambera [fem] (a sailor), Dentist [masc], Duvet-Seller [fem], Boudouris (a sailor) [masc], Petra [fem]
>
> [...] They call one another 'sister' (αδελφή) [...] The members of the Group Of Twelve have become completely feminised; they speak as women, they behave as women, they walk as women, they dress indoors as women, and they swear at each other as women, using [expressions like] μωρή παληοβρώμα 'you damned hussy'.[136]

The slangs discussed are assemblages, composites of various languages, dialects, and neologisms. They are also always fluid, bringing heterogeneous bodies into proximity.[137] Drawing from Deleuze and Guattari and their concept of assemblages, as things that do not have a function, that are not designed to only do one thing, that exchange functioning components in a mix-'n-match fashion, I see assemblage theory as pertinent to understanding the slangs.[138] They further disturb language and disturb normative expectations or the demand for specific visual cues with their mix-'n-match aesthetics. I want to read this disturbance—releasing confusion in public perhaps—as a sign of willfulness and resistance. Ahmed writes:

> Can we learn not to eliminate the signs of disturbance? Disturbance can be creative: not as what we aim for, not as what grounds our action, but as the

effect of action: disturbance as what is created by the very effort of reaching, of reaching up, of reaching out, of reaching for something that is not present, something that appears only as a shimmer, a horizon of possibility.[139]

Lavender linguistics has been featured occasionally in lexicography which has focused on such slangs since the '40s with different descriptors both referencing the linguistic register and the speakers, all of which were, of course, indicative of the wider frame of social, political, medicinal, and legal structures.[140] A brief overview of such publications and their position is vital to contour the sociopolitical frameworks surrounding the slangs. In 1941 the first English-language lexicon under the title *The Language of Homosexuality: An American Glossary* was compiled by folklorist Gershon Legman. He lists three hundred and twenty-nine items, one hundred and thirty-nine of which are identified as exclusively homosexual.[141] Ten years later (1951) Donald Cory (a pseudonym of Edward Sagarin) included a ten-page chapter on language in his book *The Homosexual in America: A Subjective Approach*. His main argument about what he called 'homosexual "cantargot"' was that it had been created because homosexuals were in need of creating terms that did not describe them in a pejorative manner.[142] In 1966 Rose Giallombardo's *Society of Women: A Study of a Women's Prison* provides a lexicon of words used by female inmates documenting two hundred and ninety-eight words; many of them referring to lesbianism and relationships.[143] In 1972 Bruce Rodgers' *The Queen's Vernacular: A Gay Lexicon* documents 'homosexual slang' throughout English-speaking words amounting to 12,000 entries, including terms originating among Black men (from the US South).[144] In 1981 a scholarly volume devoted to 'Gayspeak' was published, focusing on communication with an added emphasis on rhetoric. Parallel to the preoccupation with English slang varieties, Elias Petropoulos published *Kaliarda* in 1971 (in the midst of the military dictatorship regime in Greece), Debby Sahertian published a dictionary of Bahasa Gay titled *Kamus Bahasa Gaul* in 1999,[145] Paul Baker published *Fantabulosa: A Dictionary of Polari and Gay Slang* in 2004, Félix Rodríguez González published his *Diccionario Gay-Lésbico (Vocabulario general y argot de la homosexualidad)* in 2008, and Nicholas Kontovas, presented his master's thesis 'Lubunca: The Historical Development of Istanbul's Queer Slang and a Social-Functional Approach to Diachronic Processes in Language', in the Department of Central Eurasian Studies, Indiana University, Indiana, in December 2012. Between those, there have been numerous publications of essays, conference papers, and online dictionaries on many of the other slangs, especially in recent years. Kulick maintains, 'Although the work done in the 1960s and 1970s still focused mostly on vocabulary, at least the step had been taken toward seeing that vocabulary as embedded in a matrix of affective, social, and political relations and therefore constituting a linguistic code in the more usual sense of the word.'[146]

Regarding neologisms and linguistic creativity as a queer tactic of resistance, survival, defence or even offence, it is necessary to mention the term 'santorum' as a noun which appeared in 2003. Rick Santorum is a US Republican Party Politician with a track record of homophobic and bigoted statements, favouring anti-equality bills, and anti-polygamy and anti-sodomy legislation. In response to his public policies and stance, columnist Dan Savage decided upon a reader's suggestion to proceed to an open vote to assign his (Santorum's) name to a sex act because 'there's no better way to memorialize the Santorum scandal than by attaching his name to a sex act that would make his big, white teeth fall out of his big, empty head.'[147] More than 3,000 suggestions later it was decided by vote that the santorum would be 'that frothy mixture of lube and fecal matter that is sometimes the byproduct of anal sex.'[148] It was followed by such hit popularity that Google's search engine featured it above the politician's website in online searches, with the consequent demands on his side to take the page down, which Google declined. This was, of course, a very public (and deliberately so) campaign which included mainstream media and had the purpose of being circulated so widely it would become a problem for the politician and his career. It is in many ways different to the motivations behind the slangs discussed above; not least because it works against opacity—it actually celebrates the opposite—but because at its very essence such acts serve similar necessities, ίδιες ανάγκες. While some necessities might be similar, this is in some ways the product of a white cis, well-off, gay man with a fraught relationship with the trans community. As Butler comments 'queer' is 'redeployed, twisted, queered from a prior usage and in the direction of urgent and expanding political purposes.'[149] Similarly, the santorum project used language within a minoritarian community to fight against hate speech from a person elected in public office, whose policies affect millions of lives. The term does not seem to have caught on but in the internet era its mark was made by permanently staining the politician's name as it were.

Performance

Through the embodied performances they deliver using the slangs, the speakers activate such elements as camp or drag. They do so by mixing components and defying seriousness while dealing with important issues such as precarity, oppression, and discrimination. The social critique the slangs apply activates racism, sexism, classism, transphobia and homophobia often in order to mock them. Some -isms remain, maybe not as intact as before, but still traceable.[150] Yet, they are challenged nonetheless. I have often been asked about the queer credentials of the slangs given how contradictory the two may be by making use of hierarchical systems evident by the derogatory terms they contain. What I see in the slangs, and what I find both fascinating and queer, is how they refuse sanitisation. By this, I mean that they do not pretend hierarchies are non-existent; nor do they opt for a queerness that is consistent, politically correct, or academic. Instead, their speakers accept hierarchies exist (how could they not? They have felt them on their skins) and often choose to embrace them, not as they are, but as how they feel they should be. They tip them on their heads, not only regarding the already existing social categories, but they go further in inventing new ones and finding a place for them as well. Nobody is shielded from critique, irony, mockery, or defiance. Moreover, their place in hierarchical systems is not a fixed one. The slangs don't reflect subjects that take such hierarchies too seriously. That is not only exhibited in the humour of the terms they use to describe social ontologies but by the easiness with which the hierarchies are re-imagined and flipped. They call up components such as humour and frivolity that go against the standard politically-informed jargon, to make cutting political critique. Gavin Butt, who has worked extensively with lowbrow humour, gossip, and queer seriousness, tells Mathias Danbolt:

> I'm interested in how we habitually—almost ritualistically—contribute value to something in cultural terms by being serious about it. It might be that we do that in terms of writing a scholarly, analytical study of something; it might be that we spend time and effort in reading a work or engaging with it—but we do that almost without thinking. This is what I have called a Foucauldian technology of serious value, that not only produces the objects we take to be worthy of serious attention, but that also posits the appropriate attitudes we should adopt in addressing them.[151]

'Camp taste is, above all, a mode of enjoyment, or appreciation—not judgment. Camp is generous. It wants to enjoy. It only seems like malice, cynicism',[152] writes Sontag, and further down she remarks, 'What it does is find the success in certain passionate failures.'[153] I'm thinking these are the same failures Halberstam speaks of. The failure to perform one's assigned gender in the expected, repronormative manner, the failure to occupy higher steps in the socio-financial ladder, the failure to not be miserable because of one's misery. Drawing from a number of theorisations on camp[154] and experiential knowledge, I must highlight the parallels in the difficulty of defining the terms, and the innate openness it carries to that of the term 'queer'. I see camp as an aesthetic mode of 'translation', one that renders fluidly, misunderstands, and re-signifies. One where meaning is not clear or inherent, but open and often contradictory on a case-by-case setting. In that sense, I see it as in line with opacity. They both de- and reterritorialise standard forms of expression—whether linguistic or otherwise aesthetic—and call out their 'gravity' and plasticity. They further go on to attempt playful interventions which destabilise the notions these forms represent, unsettle the normative order, and become joyful commentaries on the social.

Sontag writes, 'to talk about Camp is therefore to betray it.'[155] The moment the plasticity is called upon and examined as such, it becomes a different product, as if the consensus is disrupted, and the 'being woman', 'playing woman', 'becoming Yuppie', is diminished into 'silly make-belief'. I will take a detour here and come back to betrayal by way of an example. The first gay (maga)zine that circulated in Salonica in 1980 included a polemic against Petropoulos, whose motives the editors saw as suspicious and commercial, due to him being an outsider shedding light on a code that was much needed at the time. The extent to which it was necessary is evident in the magazine's back cover; it featured the Law Regarding Venereal Diseases, which essentially targeted all those not practising procreative sex and was used as a legitimation of the police's brutal operations against 'homosexuals'. I am speaking of the slangs—researching them at that!—with an understanding that that may mean I am betraying them. I might not be a tourist like Petropoulos was, but I am still walking on very thin ice, the thinness of which I often lose track of. I hope I am not going to end up in water way over my head. I hope that my work will open up liminal spaces that defy binaries and by so doing I will escape becoming a bad actor while speaking of/with the slangs. I would have to disagree with Sontag on the apoliticism of camp, as I cannot conceive something as apolitical when it ridicules something serious, trivialises binaries, or magnifies the trivial by using gender as a vehicle. Performances that critique the status quo and offer brief moments of comfort—healing even—to people are anything but apolitical. As Justin Torres wrote on the occasion of the Pulse shooting, 'If you're lucky, there will be drag queens and, if so, almost certainly they will be quick, razor-sharp with their humor, giving you the kind of performances that cut and heal all at once.'[156] 'Isn't that what "reading" is after all?' I thought to myself...

Looking back for instances when camp and/or drag was used in an overtly and directly political manner, I think of the US elections candidate Joan Jettblakk. In a lecture during my time in BCU, Elspeth Kydd spoke of Joan Jettblakk, a black drag queen with working-class teeth (as she put it) running for mayor of Chicago in 1991 (and then for President of the USA in 1992 and 1996).[157] Seeing Gabriel Gomez and Kydd's film *Drag in' for Votes*[158] with Jettblakk many years later was for me another reminder of the direct political power of camp and/or drag performances. 'It is empowering for the community', someone is heard saying in the film. This campaign, run by Queer Nation,[159] in the midst of the AIDS crisis explicitly foregrounded the political potential of tactics of survival and coping, through humour, frivolity, and shock value. The candidate exemplified queerness in ways that went beyond gender performativity and extended to race and class. Rusty Barret observes the 'cooccurrence of linguistically incongruous and socially contradictory forms and registers in the same stretch of discourse' in his essay on the performance of African American drag queens.[160] He thus further highlights the above-mentioned intersections of gender, racial, and class politics within such complex performances that include important political messages through frivolous delivery. He points out the way 'speakers index queerness by skillfully switching between a number of linguistic styles and forms that stereotypically tend to denote other identities, such as those of white women or African-American men', appropriating and merging them in a way that is fluid and transcends strict social confines.

At this point, I would like to point out the connection between the performative nature of the slangs and/or camp and the performativity of the archetypal speech act of coming out in the form of 'I am _____.' This performance is oft expected and sometimes even demanded, by individuals and state alike, and is supposed to clarify, to shed light, to calcify where one stands. To pigeon-hole, to force a migration, to force to 'come clean'. Of course in the true nature of a J. L. Austin performative, it might be a felicitous or an infelicitous one, beyond the felicity or infelicity it might bring for the speaker or their audience at that moment. It might turn out to be affirmed, or not, but luckily—and this is where queerness with its performativity comes in—these are not the only two options, because while the felicity or lack thereof of a performative act exist in a one-or-the-other type of condition, viewed through a queer prism, through non-fixed identifiers, non-essentialist subjectivities, and numerous points in an endless continuum, there are more options, that complicate things, and by doing so offer a sense of liberty. J. L. Austin established kinds of sentences that he sees as having no truth-value (i.e. they are performative and neither true nor false), and instead of carrying forth information, perform an action. This is how I see the 'I am (blank)' utterance. As a sentence that is beyond the true / false dichotomy, and instead falls into the performative, as at that moment one 'becomes' whatever the descriptor that substitutes the blank indicates. Whether that will be the case in the next moment is what could make that statement a happy or an unhappy one, but certainly cannot be thought of within the restraints of a juridicomedicinal logic of truth or falsehood.

Thinking of performative acts that can no longer be thought of as simply true or untrue, we find the speech act of silence as well. Refusing to perform that utterance is already a stance that defies binarisms, and more importantly, ideas of a consistent truth. It is not only the performative utterance of 'I am _____' that I read along J. L. Austin's line of thought, but silence as well. Silence, as an integral part of speech, can also be performative.

Being in the closet is often connoted with not speaking. Not performing the 'I am _____' act, not responding to yes or no questions, showing willfulness when put under pressure. And I would like to argue that this does not necessarily constitute a failure. It is not by default an inability to speak up or to stand up for oneself; it may simply be a choice of not sharing, not giving in, not complying. Happiness, as Locke says, is idiosyncratic, we are made happy by different things.[161] While some may feel happy, fulfilled and liberated by performing those speech acts, others might feel oppressed, powerless or asphyxiated by such demands and expectations, and by the very act as well. This reminds me of composer John Cage, and how he made silence the most recognizable and significant part of his work.[162] By refusing to produce sound he made the lack of it, or rather the lack of orchestrated, organised, predictable sound and the existence of all the other audible elements that we often perceive as silence, the most influential element in his work. He shifted the audience's focus from the performers and their expertise, to what is already there—that which we pay no attention to. He thus challenged sound and music epistemologically. He had people pay to listen to that which they pay no attention to. He forced an entire symphonic orchestra to sit there for almost five minutes, with an audience watching them, listening to the sounds their bodies produce in space. As Jonathan Katz comments, Cage didn't just do that at any random point, he did it at a time when Cold War mentality and McCarthyism were at their peak, and masculinities were at the core of that.[163] His stance was in direct opposition to the Abstract Expressionist ego.[164] Cage, himself in a long-term relationship with another man, and— perhaps by that era's standards—effeminate, was choosing to accentuate silence. He found that not speaking would be heard louder than speaking and making people listen, and, as a composer, he used silence which became his trademark feature. I would argue he also employed opacity, as upon being asked on the nature of his relationship with Merce Cunningham, he would reply that Merce cooks, while he himself does the dishes.[165] I find this act of avoidance, detour, and ultimately, opacity, indicative of the way Cage lived and worked, and a major tactic of survival and coping for queer people. Instead of replying with a relationship term that would describe how he related to Cunningham and by so doing satisfying the inquisitor with a category term, he offered a visual image of two people that collaborate on an everyday task, at once avoiding pretending and also escaping getting in the spotlight of the authorities, while simultaneously possibly speaking in a double entendre.

A Little Outing

Go to the next room.
Push the button on the small lamp on your right.
Walk up the stairs.
Knock on the door and wait.

(1 person)

Before my first performance, I could hear footsteps walking up the apples. Τώρα θα σας μιλήσω πίσω από την κλειστή πόρτα. Καθήστε στο μαξιλαράκι. Με ακούτε; The archetypal performance of outing is usually associated with the expression: 'I am _____', where the blank can be filled with any minoritarian quality (that perhaps has no visible markers), in popular culture we are often confronted with the 'I am gay' utterance. What? Yes. About the closet. The proverbial closet. Not the one you have in your bedroom. Or maybe this one as well. *laughs uncomfortably* This serves the purpose of one disclosing a piece of information (of a varying degree of importance) to someone else. Apart from this primary purpose, it also serves as a 'checking-in' procedure with oneself as I've come to realise in recent years. Every time one makes such a statement, one simultaneously listens to this utterance once again. This instantaneous 'self-monitoring' offered at that moment is a very valuable side-effect of the process. One has the opportunity to monitor their feelings the moment they make that statement, and re-evaluate how they feel over the use of the specific term used. Μπάι, λεσβία, τζίβα, gay, «δεν βάζω ταμπέλες» κλπ. κλπ.

relaxes a bit, reads slower

After having changed the language I used to describe myself in relation to such personal, minoritarian qualities, choosing whichever words felt closer to how I felt at each given moment in time, I stopped doing it altogether. It happened almost without my realising it. After being accepted at the master's programme 'Queer Studies in Arts & Culture' at Birmingham City University, I found that people had already chosen to assume me as (at the very least) 'not straight' upon my introduction to them since one's field of work/studies is usually brought into conversation before one's sexualities. Since I didn't mind not being clearly 'boxed', and having gotten the often awkward part of the outing process out of the equation, I was happy enough not to delve deeper into the mechanics of this. *tries to hear if they are still there*

Sometime later, upon a discussion with people from my fields of interest, I found myself having a—what seemed pointless—discussion over the use of the term 'queer' as a description of one's self, and realised the amount of time I had kept away from such arguments. Arguments over the choice of language to communicate one's subjectivities. At that point, the amount of energy consumed in defending one's identities and/or linguistic choices seemed rather unnecessarily high given my mental health, so I went back to not performing any kind of 'I am _____' utterance. *checks camera*

Several years later, I found myself lost for words when it came to describing myself in such a way, in any terms. My long break from that practice / performance had caused me to miss the opportunity to check in with myself every once in a while, and as a result, I no longer knew what or how I identified as.

The convenient assumption people made of my being gay / lesbian / not-straight had caused me not to know how to describe or communicate parts of me I deemed important. Although it sounds like a major existential crisis could have arisen from that, I felt slightly liberated and took the time to explore this in relation to my work. *starts to feel comfortable* *enjoys herself*

This liberatory instance, combined with a few incidents where I was wrongly presumed as heterosexual (and heteronormative?) and, one or two incidents where I was presumed Austrian(!) led me to feel even more disassociated from any such categorisation.

Something else I should mention is that the timing of my not performing the 'I am _____' utterance that coincides with my first move abroad which was followed by a series of relocations between different countries. At that point, I didn't have a 'home', and the idea of having one was not all that tempting either. That would later change. But the point was that apart from losing the language to describe myself in certain terms, I had spared myself from a geographical point of reference, so when I talk of losing the language, I don't simply refer to the terminology, but the linguistic and cultural context altogether. Soon geography became something I started factoring into my relation to the closet as if the closet was or could be the only 'real' home. Since I constantly moved geographically / physically, the only 'fixed' 'home' I could have would have to be a notional one, not one in tangible space, but one I could somehow carry along in my shifting bases. So I started thinking of the closet in terms of homeliness. The closet not only in relation to (queer) countercultures and a sense of belonging but the closet as a space of secrecy and isolation. As an only child living in the countryside I was always comfortable being by myself, and awfully sceptical when it came to sharing and communicating the things that were very dear to me with others. The closet for me was also a refuge, my own special place that only I knew about and I would evoke it when and where I needed it. And now I was completely exposed.

And that cost me, I found that amount of sharing energy-draining, and there wasn't much I could do to reclaim my secret σπιτάκι. Καθώς έγγραφα αυτές τις γραμμές ήμουν σε μια καλιαρντή σχέση με μια αλμομπαριασμένη καλιαρντή λάλα. Τώρα πια έχω άλλη εγγύτητα με την έννοια του σπιτικού και πολλά άλλαξαν εν τω μεταξύ. Είμαι ασφαλής.

'At that point, I started working further with words, focusing more on the linguistic productions of the closet that take the form of slangs. The need for safety and inner-group communication in circumstances of extreme marginalisation and violence produced these creative ways of coded speech among queers. I knew the Greek and British one, so I started becoming a bit obsessed with them and begun asking around, googling, emailing linguists, authors who had written on similar topics, messaging facebook contacts. More slangs started appearing. Pajubá, spoken by travesti in Brazil. I read through a DIY dictionary found on a blog online with friends from São Paulo. It was so similar to Kaliarnta and Polari, funny, abrasive, creative. Then Lubunca, Nikos kindly shared his thesis with me, and friends in Berlin shared their experience of first coming in contact with Lubunca when they first went to Istanbul to study. Then Swardspeak, IsiNgqumo, Gail, Bahasa Binan, and Gayspeak followed. Later on Ya'ar told me of Okhchit, and I also came across Hijra Farsi. I find them extremely fascinating and looking into them offered me tools to better understand my need for opacity. But I'll get to that in a bit.

For several years I had been feeling I had to switch between different senses of humour and intellectual levels so much, and it was frustrating for the most part. So I started making peace with the fact that I wouldn't speak one consistent language possibly ever again and that was OK. Anzaldúa helped a lot with taming that confusion while allowing it to exist. She and Sara Ahmed helped me keep the tension, the willful moments of disrupting linearity, of wanting to be understood in order to be valued.

Periférica knowledge is not always passed on in hierarchical, didactic ways, nor is it its potential presence in academic institutions that awards it legitimacy. Υποτίθεται υποστηρίζω τη δουλειά μου η καλιαρντή while knowing that I am being assessed, while also going against the formal/ist setting of a Viva. I am mixing French philosophers with slangs from 1930s Greek sex workers, and queer theory with abuse, I am using pop culture while offering Chicago Style references meanwhile καθόμαστε όλοι μαζί, Ντόλες και Καλιαρντές.

I realised my own voice, accent(s), stuttering and stammering needed to become part of this work which dealt with closetedness, privacy, belonging, and (not) fitting in using autoethnography as one of its methods. This is how the Closet Case Studies #2 performance was workshopped. In here. I got this door. *points towards desk* I started cutting it with power tools, the sawdust was covering everything up.

I presented the performance during a group event with my colleagues. I opted to having only one person at a time and make it an intimate sharing moment. I had also prepared slightly different texts so that each person would get to hear different things. The guests were given simple instructions to walk up the stairs, knock on the door, and sit on the pillow. During the performance, I spoke to people sitting on the other side of the door. Their footsteps would approach in the creaky staircase, and then my heart would go wild. *walks up the stairs, allows the creaky noises to muzzle words* I spoke to them about myself, and the closet, my languages, and how I use the slangs even if no one understands, the importance of opacity in my life.

Ήταν σαν να έκανα κάποια παρανομία, μπροστά στις αρχές αλλά χωρίς αυτήκοους μάρτυρες. It was an intense experience, not only because of the dread of sharing with strangers, but also the unexpected emotional ramifications: I felt in my attempt to create a safer space for communicating with the audience, I had forgotten about the aspect of communicating with my colleagues, one of the factors that made this type of event usually so pleasant. I could hear them chatting, and drinking, and laughing downstairs, seeing Hong Kai's posts on facebook, and I had put myself in a pink corridor for over three hours. Having solely focused on the closet as a potential safer space, I had neglected my own moments of discomfort and disconnect. Memories from the past were unexpectedly coming back.'

long pause

Opacity

> Against this reductive transparency, a force of opacity is at work. No longer the opacity that enveloped and reactivated the mystery of filiation but another, considerate of all the threatened and delicious things joining one another (without conjoining, that is, without merging) in the expanse of Relation.
> Édouard Glissant, *Poetics of Relation*

Opacity and the Closet

Here I am exploring the question of what   can do for   . I borrow the term from Édouard Glissant and the framework of postcolonial theory and I want to see how it works within queerness. I understand opacity as a notion that foregrounds visuality[1] not only in the existence of the closet but also in slangs as products of the closet. Exploring this as a tactic of survival brings me to recognise other stances that work in similar ways, albeit relating to audio politics or spatiality / movement. Through this synthesis of lavender linguistics, queer theory, and postcolonial theory, I hope to open up those qualities of 'queer' that might still hold on to whiteness, Westerness, and the Global North, and by highlighting similarities in how precarity is dealt with, offer a more περιφερειακή reading of 'queer'.

The event of the closet with its ambiguity and potential for concealing (yet not constantly, not exactly, and doing so while allowing for a porous shielding) is immersed in opacity. The same quality is found surrounding the slangs analysed earlier. As already established the reasoning behind the creation of these linguistic registers is constant and common: the production of safer spaces of communication and contact between members of marginalised minoritarian groups who have traditionally been persecuted, faced legal punishment, or the threat of medical torture. I am not equating the struggle of those who suffered from the transatlantic slave trade, slavery, John Crow laws, the prison industrial complex etc. with the struggle of non-normative individuals over the centuries. Instead, I want to point out the similarities in terms of creative ways to escape being clearly understood, the need to hold on to something that is one's own, and form or maintain a community of support; all of them can be read as tactics of coping and survival. These communication codes allowed for an easier exchange of   , an exchange that, to some extent, shielded group members from potential aggressors: simultaneously, these languages did not render group members completely invisible. It is precisely this position between visibility and invisibility—   —that interests me and which I would like to explore in relation to the particular political stances of passivity, silence, and detour. David Van Leer, an American scholar who researched queer cultures in the US from the '20s to the '00s, observed that, 'often minorities speak most volubly between the lines, ironically reshaping dialogues the oppressor thinks he controls or even finding new topics and modes of speaking to which the oppressor himself lacks access.'[2]

Language—regulated by the state, taught in educational institutions, and used to discipline, inform, educate, or structurally violate, among other uses—is frequently subverted by minorities in an attempt to bypass authority.[3] In this case, in particular, the 'new topics' and 'modes' Van Leer refers to are perhaps illegal pleasures, embodied performances, irony, and disguised (or not-so-well-disguised) social critique. It is necessary to clarify here that it is not necessarily a characteristic of minorities, but rather of minoritarian social categories, subjectivities, or individuals. This is additionally indicated by the 'Nüshu' language / script, the only recorded 'women only' language / script in Jiangyong County in Hunan province of southern China,[4] the claim being that women don't necessarily constitute a minority, but have minoritarian characteristics in most patriarchal societies. I see this as an écriture féminine of sorts, for lack of a better term and keeping critically in mind the (original?) Westernness and whiteness of the term. I also think of Butler's reading of women as the sex that 'cannot be thought, a linguistic absence and opacity'[5] in connection to women's silencing, lack of participation in the public sphere, in open discussions, and ultimately in literature. Another note I would like to add here regards the aesthetics of the above-mentioned script which seems to be a 'slimmed down' version of the mainstream one, perhaps further indicating by analogy the space afforded to women in the social. This could also be seen as a reversed form of 'manspreading', perhaps something like 'womensqeezing'.

Slangs spoken among those outside the law, outside normative understandings of 'decency', 'properness', 'dignity', outside 'respectable' professions are plenty and found worldwide. Through Anzaldúa I found this poem of Melanie Kaye's:

> My fingers
> move sly against your palm
> Like women everywhere we speak in code...[6]

Slangs have been used by social, ethnic, age-based, and activity-based groups in various periods and cultures. One of the characteristics of those sociolects is that they are frequently expressing cutting critique, that might not only be directed towards the oppressing groups or institutions. In the case of the slangs, I am often asked about their lack of political correctness in relation to a 'queer' that is—or tries to be—politically correct. The slangs are lowbrow, and as much as queer theory wants to be inclusive, it is arguably, by its origin, academic and highbrow. Political correctness is sometimes a privilege and a luxury that some of us get to think in and abide by. It is not accessible to all, and in certain situations, it could be read as, or signify, weakness. In the precarity of some of the environments in which the slangs were created and used in, such characteristics could portray one as an easy target. The slangs produce (or reproduce) hierarchies in an attempt to position the speakers in different places than the bottom of said social hierarchies. These slangs are not of the academia; they are of the brothels, the street corners, and the ships. Of the circus, and of the travelling performers, of the travesti, the λούγκρες, and the poofters.

I am here talking about a 'queer' that includes—or potentially can include if they so choose—those who fall through the cracks between the 'queer', the «πλακομουνού», the 'gay', and the 'faggot', the 'poof', the 'bull-dyke'. Ultimately the slangs are in-line with tactics of survival and resistance like opacity, and as such in an indirect relation to queerness, if queerness does not want to expel its most vulnerable members. Thinking on this I learnt about a generous sense of belonging which includes those in need of inclusion despite the fact that they might (still) be acting in ways seemingly against the very premise that affords them this inclusion. Through further thinking with and in the slangs, I caught myself feeling ,

,

.

. This bubble soon began to trace itself as too white, and too central European. I was missing parts of my Balkanness, the harsh humour that is often medicinal, and this project helped me bring it back with the focus on ephemeral pleasures that one needs in order to keep going. Studying the slangs, and starting to use Kaliarnta again was an exercise in queerness, in being othered, reprimanded for one's tongue, expected to abide by a certain set of standards.

Tensions

'Isn't there also a tension between opacity/detour and queerness?' Renate asks me … Is there? For me queerness is not so much about visibility (as gayness is/was) as it is about opacity. Opacity implies a veiling that allows for change and is therefore non-identitarian. Gayness and mainstream LGBT politics have been about visibility, and their causes (and effects) have been to an extent seemingly always oriented towards normativity. Their visibility was supposed to prove that we are all the same, that 'we are just like you'. Queerness is in line with opacity and detour and does not produce tension with them simply because it survives only through them. Opacity exists in a negation; not only of the 'we are just like you' dogma of homonormativity, but even more profoundly negates being seen, let alone compared and potentially deemed non-dangerous for the status quo.

I do not want to discard the importance of   , and the steps the new civil rights movement has taken thanks to it. When Harvey Milk was calling for coming out to all those surrounding an LGBTQ+ person, he was of course imagining the significant impact that would instantaneously have on hetero/normative people realising the large percentage LGBTQ+ people make up and the proximity to them, something he hoped or assumed would have a direct impression on society at large and a shifting of mentalities and legislation.[7] I maintain that visibility is not for everyone, and not for all times or situations. Those who can afford to and want it for themselves, can exit the closet however often they wish, but before crossing boundaries and applying pressure on others to do the same, we should consider the different abilities, social circumstances, class, age and many other factors that might make it difficult, dangerous, or impossible for some to perform that. Thinking within a queerfeminist framework, self-care, and collective care are important and need to be considered often before other political actions, especially when they equal survival. Furthermore, we should consider the situations when one does not know what to come out as, since things don't operate in strict binaries. Belonging to more than one category is always possible, add to that the fluidity of some or all of these categories would quickly make coming out, as we've known it, redundant or outdated.

Since the social makeup of the communities creating and speaking the slangs is of particular pertinence, it is crucial to note the additional functions of them. While trying to stay safe and communicate, individual subjects are seen as beginning to form a community based on a common culture. In her essay 'Qwir-English Code-Mixing in Germany: Constructing a Rainbow of Identities', Heidi Minning argues that 'the resulting sociopsychological function is one of constructing group membership and a sense of the self as a participant in larger gay and lesbian local and transnational cultures.'[8] I have to point out that I am mildly uncomfortable with the identitarian and limiting nature of the descriptors Minning uses, but simultaneously have to admit that they indeed are representative of the stance many of these slangs have, and so her comment is relevant. 'Indeed, if there is an affirmation of a new community, it is precisely of the always already excluded, a bastard community of the sick and the frail, a hybrid and mutant collectivity always in progress, always open to any and everyone' writes O'Sullivan in his 'Notes Towards a Minor Art Practice'.[9] I especially like the mention to sickness and frailness and will write more about it, in particular in connection to disability and ableism later on. While the languages were not intended as works of art, they are—much like political art—socially engaged (and creative) ways of communication and speaking against the status quo.

ΛΕΞΙΚΟ

My knowledge of Kaliarnta begun by associating with older gay men in my late teens. We used a few words among Greek when in front of unfamiliar people, especially in the metro or other crowded spaces which would be hard to get away from if a homophobic incident took place. I remember using them when police officers were in the vicinity, especially in Exarchia (Athens' leftist/anarchist district) the surrounding areas of which was often brimming with cops. Later on, I got to have the first glimpse at Elias Petropoulos' dictionary through a mislabeled word document a friend emailed me. Upon opening it I found a transcript of the entire dictionary (bar the introduction text). He later told me he had been typing chunks of it every day in order to eventually toss the actual physical book so his parents wouldn't find it and confront him. He was in his late teens at that point, planning to become associated with the gay community once he was eighteen (the legal age of consent for same-sex practices between men in Greece at that time was seventeen, for different-sex practices fifteen, lesbians did not register as sexual actors enough to be regulated) and what he was doing I can only describe as culturally preparing and educating himself for his coming into the 'Gay World' or what he thought was the 'Gay World'. I got to know Polari from friends in Britain when I lived there (though I knew of it from Paul Baker's dictionary before then), and Pajubá from friends when living in Germany. The remainder, as mentioned, I found through research, emailing linguists, asking artists, activists, and acquaintances abroad.

The slangs with vocabularies ranging from 600 words (as is the case of Polari) to more than 6,000 documented words (as in Kaliarnta), or 12,000 words (as in Gayspeak) and different life spans (400+ years in the case of Lubunca's lingual ancestors, or thirty years in the case of IsiNgqumo), constitute mini-universes where their users freely circulate and through which they are able to connect. They do not only include terms to describe the particular practices/interests of the ingroups, which might be dangerous to describe in a non-coded way publicly. They also include words or phrases to describe everyday household objects, professions, toponyms, and activities. They are patchworks of several other languages, including etymologically untraceable neologisms, word games, backslang, and other (contemporaneous or earlier) slangs from sub-cultures like circus performers and actors, thieves, substance users, and others.[10] The multicultural linguistic loans seem to indicate a certain degree of mobility on the part of the speakers, who appear to have come in contact with foreigners beyond their immediate border neighbours, by befriending migrants, or through working at sea, or through unsuccessful attempts to find better employment options abroad, but also due to dealing with sailors and seamen as sex-workers themselves. Further, as Paul Baker says, we shouldn't throw out the possibility of the use of foreign languages as a way of coming across as more sophisticated and well-travelled.[11] Costas Canakis, a linguist at the University of Aegean, claims the slangs are anti-languages, their main objective being not understanding rather than understanding. It's about who doesn't understand rather than who does. He further states that Kaliarnta embodies an aspect of childhood-ness (as children talk and communicate with each other in ways that escape adults), and consequently sees it as 'overthrowing' hierarchies and binarisms such as 'educated/knowledgeable/scholarly vs slut/pleb'.[12] Perhaps because it is a language that is secretive and does not abide by a fixed set of rules, and perhaps because it reflects the diverse positions of the speakers, it allows for this disrupting of binarisms. This does not mean that binary terms are not used; it means that they are situated differently in the social, not necessarily as oppositional, not as fixed.

Social Queetique - χαχα. χα.

As I can only fully access Kaliarnta and to a certain extent Polari, and much less Pajubá, I have relied heavily on the analyses of others. One of the things I have noticed in my firsthand experience with the slangs—apart from the above-mentioned lack of political correctness (or any sense of self-censorship for that matter)—is the vast number of pejorative terms used for both those who are socially looked down on by society (including the speakers themselves) and their oppressors alike.[13] This seems to indicate a certain adoption of the mores of the general population, in addition to their own, no matter how contradictory the two may be.[14] For instance, the words for an effeminate homosexual or the receptive partner in penetrative sex are always pejorative, and the same cannot be said of the terms for the insertive partner. The word 'Kaliarnta' (καλιαρντά) itself has only negative meanings: 'mean, ugly, weird', with the verb 'kaliardevo' (καλιαρντεύω) meaning to speak ill of someone.[15]

In addition, there are pejorative terms for other groups that seem to already be looked down on by Greek society, and for whom there already exist several offensive terms, like for the out-of-towners, the obese, the old, the non-able-bodied, the not conventionally beautiful, and of course women. The inclusion of those terms outlines the classist, fatphobic, ageist, lookist, and sexist tones in the social milieu of the interlocutors. But as already mentioned the element of frivolity and the offensive-against-all διάθεση hue the words differently than in mainstream society. Simultaneously, there are plenty of derogatory terms for legal, religious, and political authorities. This points to the counter-cultural elements of the subcultures using the slangs. Arguably this could be the result of constant friction with such authorities, further indicating the co-existence of contradictory—one could even argue mutually exclusive—mores. Regarding the playful nature of such registers and their critique of the mainstream, Hayes writes that 'trivialization of the world, because social Gayspeak is often frivolous, comic, precious, or fleeting, amounts to a trivialization through parody of the dominant culture.'[16] This, as Kulick notices, contains direct parallels with Butlerian ideas of camp (and) performativity. For Butler, the legitimisation of certain bodies, binaries, and attributes goes hand in hand with others being considered 'false, unreal, and unintelligible.'[17]

It seems that by allowing for a mockery of those seen as oppressors, or by placing themselves somewhere other than the lowest position in the social ladder, queers can afford fleeting moments of pleasure that derive from their deviances and their organising through them. While such linguistic registers bring down certain hierarchies or affirm an understanding of things beyond binaries, they also act in very hierarchical ways, often violently so, either affirming mainstream values or substituting them for their own. Δεν κρύβουν τις πληγές, γράφει ο Πετρόπουλος.[18] So beyond the importance of a safer space, and the practicalities of communication between precariously-living subjects, another element of these languages—one that takes the cake and dismisses political correctness—is the proximity they produce between the speaker, and most importantly the moments of humour and joy they allow for. Canakis highlights the higher rate of humorous terms and notions in Kaliarnta than in Greek.[19] For instance, brief moments of pleasure among fellow deviant subjects seem to be the case with much of Kaliarnta and the way it is used, which (for the purposes of this project) remains untranslatable. I can only hypothesise that this might well be the case for some of the other slangs as well, and take the word of the speakers and researchers whenever they mention that.

Elizabeth Freeman suggests that we might be able to glimpse in our archives 'historically specific forms of pleasure' that have not been institutionalized, and a deeper look at queer languages can definitely provide a confirmation of that.[20] Sara Ahmed states, 'To be happily queer might mean being happy to be the cause of unhappiness (at least in the sense that one agrees to be the cause of unhappiness, even if one is not made happy by causing unhappiness), as well as to be happy with where we get to if we go beyond the straight lines of happiness scripts.'[21] The cause of unhappiness (perversion, sexual/social deviance, gender non-conformity) becomes the way off the prescribed lines of straightness. Creations deriving from that, indulge in many forms of pleasure including joy, humour, socialising through laughter, and mocking others as well as oneself.

Kaliarnta, as mentioned, manages to make a somewhat humorous social critique with terms reflecting a certain regard towards institutional religion, other peoples, politicians, and tourists with words like 'Vatican' (Βατικανό) to mean a gay men's brothel; a word referring to London that translates as 'faggville'/'sisterville' (αδερφοχώρι); 'Moutsemeni' (Μουτσεμένη), a word referring to the Virgin Mary as having been naively tricked; 'smartasses' gangbang' (φαεινοπαρτούζα), referring to a political party; and the Acropolis being referred to as 'tourist trap' (τουριστόφακα).[22]

Kaliarnta didn't only serve to comment on religious authorities and beliefs, as Paola Revenioti narrates an experience from the past where she attended a Greek orthodox service in Kaliarnta, with the two αδελφές priests saying—in Kaliarnta—'Που τζινάβουνε τώρα οι πουρές;' ('How would these old folks even understand?').[23] Taking advantage of the inability of church-goers to understand the ancient Greek text, the queer(?) priests, substituted it for Kaliarnta, and obviously managed to pass it to a largely conservative audience. One that had strongly objected to the scriptures being translated into modern Greek, as that would constitute blasphemy—let alone having the scriptures translated in a queer slang. Kaliarnta managed to become part of the ritualised, pure, and self-righteous performance of a mass in a space strictly segregated by gender, and an ideology of strict rules and regulations on bodies, genders, and desires. This gave the priests the chance to activate a subversive form of pleasure, simultaneously exposing their congregation's pretend connection with the scriptures and lack of attention to the service itself. Perhaps some of them noticed something was different but decided not to speak out, most would not have noticed, and somehow I cannot help but think this allowed the moment to feel more empowering to the priests, at that moment their performance being understood by nobody but them and Paola. While that might or might not be considered a camp performance, it does include a certain performance of something that is not authentic, combined with a sense of mockery.

This reminds me of Elizabeth Freeman's comment on drag, camp, and other types of bodily humour. She writes that 'queer camp, perhaps especially the form known as drag, effects precisely this kind of cultural work in somatic form, summoning an obsolete gendered disposition and juxtaposing it with the dominant one.'[24] At that moment the priest was performing in a minoritarian language, juxtaposing it not only with the dominant one of ancient Greek, but with the dominant tradition of Greek-Orthodox Christianity and its direct connection to nationalism and normativity in the Greek context. He did so using a vehicle accessible to him by his deviancy. Thinking further on embodiment and humour and tools often utilised by the speakers, sarcasm comes to mind. 'Sarcasm' derives from the Greek 'σαρκάζω' from the root 'σαρξ' meaning 'flesh'.[25] It is by default a term akin to the body. The body and its potential to maul and be mauled. By words. 'Polari', Baker writes with regards to the elements of humour and playfulness:

> is playful, quick and clever—a constantly evolving language of fast put-downs, ironic self-parody and theatrical exaggeration. The lexicographer, Eric Partridge, once referred to Polari as a 'Cinderella among languages', but I [i.e. Baker] prefer to think of it as one of the Ugly Sisters: brash, funny and with all the best lines in the show[26]

something that resonates with Kaliarnta's very name already referring to such a position.

Another element found in many of the slangs and beyond, as mentioned earlier, is the interlocutors' use of feminine pronouns and articles to refer to any and every gender, thus using the feminine where most people would opt for the 'all inclusive' masculine. This creates a feminisation of language and (audible) space, and an opacification of the gender of the person on topic. Use of that device is different from contemporary critiques related to gender politics, where major publications may assign feminine pronouns to nouns such a 'the visitor', 'the reader' etc., or activist discussions and attempts to use symbols like the 'at' symbol (@) for instance in Greek, or the letter 'x' in

Spanish as suffixes of gender sensitive pronouns / nouns / adjectives, or the underscore (_) or asterisk (*) in German as a bridge between the male and female endings in order to provide inclusivity. The 'gay she'—as it has been termed—was instead a politically substantial move, without necessarily intending to be one. Its intention was to mock the way certain people were seen as effeminate, due to mannerisms, or desires, and the idea that femininity can only be connoted with softness, sneakiness, weakness, superficiality, and a passive role in sexual games. By doing so, the speakers exhibit both knowledge of, and immunity towards, this externally imposed classification; instead opting to activate mockery, joy, and owning of their ways of being. The Greek / Kaliarnta word 'μωρή', or 'παλιοβρώμα' (as indicated in the Fleeting Flirt Periodical's report) the Português brasileiro / Pajubá 'bicha' or 'bixa', the Spanish 'perra', or even the Anglo 'bitch' are all used to address others within the group, as a pet name, but also to attack others within or beyond the group. They are all feminine (and pejorative, which provides another clue in tactics of re-appropriating words, or using them inconsistently, and thus upsetting linguistic standards). Baker reminds us of another example, when the 'she' 'refer[s] to heterosexual men, sometimes deliberately in order to deliberately [sic] undermine a case of self-assured masculinity'[27] thus diversifying its impact in the public realm by a number of ways. I see the above tendencies (self-critique, -isms, normative and alternative mores hand in hand with feminine pronouns and name-calling) as part of the tradition of drag. Let me explain further. The slangs, and delivering utterances in them, might not necessarily happen with the help of accessories or embodied aspects that are usually associated with drag, but they activate a frivolity, a not-taking-things-too-seriously (including oneself) that is integral to survival in difficult circumstances.

However such social critique is not unique to queer slangs; it is a phenomenon common among subcultural languages, the same is true for hobo slang, spiv cant, μάγκικα, ντόρτικα, teen slangs (perhaps of pertinence here is Kebabnorsk) and other such idioms. Paul Baker writes that in '"anti-languages" the social values of words and phrases tend to be more emphasized than in mainstream languages', a phenomenon termed 'sociolinguistic coding orientation',[28] while Nicholas Kontovas points out that the slang of marginal groups betrays an alternative sociolinguistic market, in which the value of markers from the majority market is neither intrinsically positive not negative, but reassessed based on an alternative habitus which is particular to the field in which that group interacts.[29] Both Baker and Kontovas point to the specificities of the social universes these languages produce, which much like the words themselves are borrowed, re-appropriated, and creatively adjusted to reflect the ever-changing needs and positions of the speakers. The speakers—marginalised—reflect their points of view and critique of the system that refuses them certain sets of rights, opportunities, and restricts any ideas of upward social mobility. The lemmata manifest how the mainstream is evaluated through the words that make it, the ways in which they are transformed, and the connotations they carry. Referring to a different community of made-outsiders Glissant speaks to the creative process and the necessity behind it, 'Everywhere that the obligation to get around the rule of silence existed a literature was created that has no "natural" continuity, if one may put it that way, but, rather, bursts forth in snatches and fragments. The storyteller is a handyman, the djobbeur of the collective soul.'[30] I will focus more on the topic of literature in the following chapter, for now I would like to foreground the successful function of the slangs and their fundamental relation to opacity.

As already mentioned opacity is a state that allows for things not to be visible, yet might not completely conceal its object of protection. The in-betweenness of visibility/audibility of the performed slang and the ununderstandingness, is what activates opacity. At the same time, the slangs can only exist within it.[31] While primarily discussing the notion of opacity in terms of audibility, Renate Lorenz reminds us that it is primarily a 'category of active visualization, of a visualization however, that is rendered unintelligible, beyond understanding'[32] and it is this unintelligibility that makes this tactic so relevant to both visual and audio politics. Opacity, as Glissant used it, was based primarily in the communication/language creations of the colonised peoples to evade being understood by the colonisers. He talks about how the native is rendered opaque to/by the coloniser as the latter fails to understand them, whether they speak in their native tongue or in a creolised language, one that while incorporating elements from the language of the oppressor—in Glissant's case French—remains a puzzle as it refuses to fully conform with grammatical, syntactical, or lexical rules of the 'standard' language.[33]

Opacity, Detour, Silence

To conclude the above discussion, subjects do not become invisible when talking in these languages; they can actually attract more interest from the public. Yet, simultaneously, the content of their discussions remains somewhat sealed and opaque. It is through this practice, which is not vocal (although it is verbal) and which does not actively disrupt the status quo (and yet builds an alternative social space), that opacity is generated as a political action. Further, it is through a practice that was only intended to provide safer communication, joy, and community membership, that opacity is activated, and an inadvertent hit is managed. I see this as a detour. I am borrowing the term 'detour' from postcolonial theory again; it is a term used by Glissant to indicate the inadvertence of the resulting political aspects of a tactic, and primary focus on the needs of those oppressed. As such, I find it carries similarities to passivity as another tactic of resistance employed by enslaved people, women, and LGBTQ+ populations in a variety of ways. I see detour (often connected with passivity) as a political stance that is, on the one hand, unintentional yet still has effects beyond the terrain which it was generated within, in a gradual manner. On the other hand, it refrains from being loud, aggressive, or destructive. I think of Halberstam here, who, while analysing the film *Chicken Run* writes:

> Ginger says, for example, 'We either die free chickens, or we die trying.' Babs asks naïvely, 'Are those the only choices?' Like Babs, and indeed like Spivak and Mahmood, I am proposing that feminists refuse the choices as offered—freedom in liberal terms or death—in order to think about a shadow archive of resistance, one that does not speak in the language of action and momentum but instead articulates itself in terms of evacuation, *refusal, passivity, unbecoming, unbeing*.[34] (emphasis added)

Halberstam places these tactics in the hands of feminists. I would argue that these tactics (of refusal, passivity, unbecoming, and unbeing), have been used by diverse groups of oppressed and vilified people. I find the term 'unbeing' particularly interesting in terms of the visual politics of opacity, as though one ceases to exist simply by not allowing for transparency, merely by refusing to use the acceptable—mandatory even—ways of relating, communicating, being. And again here, refusal and passivity are not synonymous with inactivity or idleness. On the contrary, people (and chickens) are going against what is expected from them, when what is expected from them is compliance with an exploitative system (often based on biological determinism), and oppression.

The voices of those speaking the slangs claim an agency that is otherwise lost or stripped off of them on an institutional level. They are kept in positions of little or no power of determining and changing things for themselves. They are without papers, unemployed, 'unqualified', they don't perform the expected gender roles, they are homeless. Yet they use an institution (that of language), and subvert it, producing, as Halberstam says, 'a new grammar and a new voice, a passive voice for the necessities of a different kind of struggle, and anarchistic one.'[35] I see passivity as an important component of such resistance. I perceive it as a key queer mode of resistance, especially concerning bodily and sexual politics, as well as visual politics. Passivity as a sexual practice, was often the indicating factor of a pathology, a diagnosis of homosexuality, and an accusation of not performing a certain kind of masculinity, or—what's worse—performing femininity! The attitudes towards the partners based on their sexual roles are telling. An active/insertive partner, at least according to an adumbration offered by Kaliarnta and accounts of speakers from past decades, was identified as 'κωλομπαράς' and not seen as homosexual or gay. The passive/receptive partner (who was seen both as 'queer' and often more of a 'woman') carried a significant stigma, leaving queers who wore it in their sleeves constantly forced to defend themselves. As already mentioned in Chapter one, similar constructions appear in India and Pakistan, as well as South Africa. Queer men have long been taunted and ostracised for not performing certain aggressive behaviours and thus being seen as passive, as not manly enough, and ultimately as closer to resembling women (who are seen as passive by default). I see passivity as interconnected and overlapping with opacity and detour in the case of the slangs. Baker's definition of 'passive' includes the adjectives 'quiet and effeminate',[36] 'quiet' being another term I understand as related to not being vocal, but again, not necessarily giving in. McLean and Ngcobo assert that '[s]ociety insists that women should be passive. Ironically skesanas often have to dominate to assert their own "passivity"',[37] because as men, or men*, or 'men', skesanas' passivity is not a given, and is something that has to be(come) actively established. Ann Cvetkovich and Karin Michalski also hint at the alternative (activist) potential of passivity in their short film 'The Alphabet of Feeling Bad':

P is for Passivity,
which is another feeling that shouldn't be
easily dismissed.
We are often told that in order to be good activists we
have to get rid of our passivity.
What if radical Passivity were also a way to
get things done?[38]

What if this radicalism is not a call to arms, but tongues? What if we activate the element of surprise and instead of 'corrupting the[ir] youth'[39] and 'turning the[ir] wives into feminists, witches, and lesbians',[40] we corrupt their language? Instead of a direct hit, we manage confusion. Britton writes:

> If the enemy cannot be attacked directly, the confusion is such that opposition is not coherent and organized; it is not even entirely conscious. Thus, the detour is itself marked with the alienation it is trying to combat. It is both an evasion of the real situation and an obstinate effort to find a way round it.[41]

By manipulating language for their safety, minorities deliver an indirect hit to the values of normative society by playfully ruining their institutions with mockery and finding humour in their own hardships. It is their own interest they have in mind when doing so. It is about their safer communication, the creation or maintenance of a support system, and ultimately the pleasure it produces to laugh at your enemy and yourself as well. 'Isn't it the sharing of feelings of pleasure and distress which binds a community together — when (in so far as it is feasible) the whole citizen body feels more or less the same pleasure or distress at the same gains and losses' asks Ahmed, quoting Plato.[42]

Humour, laughter, trauma, and desires seem to go hand in hand τόσο στις αργκώ και σε άλλες δημιουργικές εκφράσεις της κουιρ ζωής όσο και στην καθημερινότητα της κουιρ κοινότητας. Γέλως (Gelos), the Greek God of laughter was pictured either as a member of Dionysos' ensemble, or, more pertinently, as one of the divide gifts of Aphrodite to humans, the other two being Desire and Pleasure. Humour is activated in order to deal with trauma, adversity, loss in ways that are specific to queer life. Hannah Gadsby's *Nanette* is a brilliant example, not least because of its genre-crossing content and delivery, but by the buzz it caused due to its very nature (the mixing of humour and the standup comedy format as a vehicle to discuss among other topics abuse, male privilege, violence, and the power of heteropatriarchy). Netflix's distribution reached demographics that would not have been among the audience that normally would populate the seats of a theatre for a masculine-of-centre queer woman. Drae Campbell, who hosts TELL, a New York-based queer storytelling show and the longest-running program at the Bureau of General Services, Queer Division, a queer bookstore and event venue comments that there's a specific way in which queer folks are trained to use humour that makes traditional stand-up an awkward fit at best. She says:

> There is queer storytelling in stand-up, but what Gadsby said specifically is, I took my trauma and I sealed it in jokes. And so I think that when you're a person who has a story to tell and you look at what's [available] in the world, you go, 'Oh well, I guess I'll do stand-up.' And you have to sort of fit what your life is into this fucked up system in which the only way to get out there is to seal up your little traumas and make them into jokes. And that's the way it always was.[43]

It is tongues that manage community binding through a sharing of the difficulties of the margins, making do with what little one has, and still finding the mental and emotional strength to creatively allow oneself to have fun.

Opacity and Postcolonial Critique

Perhaps opacity should be used in the plural, as Glissant writes, 'the right to opacity that is not enclosure within an impenetrable autarchy but subsistence within an irreducible singularity. Opacities can coexist and converge, weaving fabrics. To understand these truly one must focus on the texture of the weave and not on the nature of its components.'[44] Opacity is something that is already multiple and against the singularity of clarity and transparency. He talks about the juxtaposition of opacity (as barbaric)[45] and   (as the ideal), and demands opacity as a right which led to him being confronted with indignant exclamations and questions like 'How can you communicate with what you don't understand?'[46] The confusion (and even rage) that these ways of inner-group communications cause is hardly due to one's genuine intention to communicate, but rather a fearful response to a shattering of the usual entitlement to accessing everything. Glissant makes a call for opacities to be preserved and obscurity in translation to be created and calls for a discrediting of vehicular sabirs which would allow beyond group communication. He further states, 'The framework is not made of transparency; and it is not enough to assert one's right to linguistic difference or, conversely, to interlexicality, to be sure of realizing them.'[47] Ideas of penetrability and full accessibility to a system within a group one does not belong to are inherent to colonial mentalities, and transparency is indeed a Western / European / Northern demand.[48]

Reflecting on the subversive power of language, Fanon writes that 'to speak a language is to take on a world, a culture'[49] and he further comments on the close watch teachers kept over children to make sure they did not use Creole.[50] Instead, they had to learn to be 'civilised', and thus accessible, clear, and reducible. 'To speak' he writes, 'means to be in a position to use a certain syntax, to grasp the morphology of this or that language, but it means above all to assume a culture, to support the weight of a civilization.'[51] I would like to focus on the first part of this statement, the one about syntax and morphology, and by introducing linguistic imperialism make a connection with another postcolonial thinker, Anzaldúa, and her notion of 'linguistic terrorism'. The way colonised peoples were expected—forced—to speak 'properly' was a way to cut them from their culture, social cohesion, way of thinking and of rendering them transparent, understandable, and reducible. It was an aggressive—barbaric one could say—way of lifting the veil of unknowability that covered them on behalf of the colonisers. Like Fanon, Anzaldúa highlights the significance that language and linguistic manipulation have in the formation of communities brought together by oppression and trauma.

As a Nepantlera who has worked on language and colonialism, Anzaldúa sees the identifiers that 'out' her as a way to help them (her) not get 'erased, omitted, or killed', thus creating an outing of necessity. And yet not an outing that submits to the demand for transparency on behalf of the dominant culture, because at the same time she uses non-standard English and speaks Spanish with a non-standard accent and numerous variations of both languages in her work. By so doing, she consciously decides to make her work visibly inaccessible, frustrating or confusing (and ultimately partially exclusive) to her audience. In this contradicting space of visible inaccessibility, I read Anzaldúa as activating opacity. Given her position on language and identity, this is an opacity that begins in linguistics only to be extended to the Self as a whole. Anzaldúa speaks about not letting go of one's native tongue (that happens not to be the standard, mainstream, or majoritarian variety) in order to have a linguistic home of sorts, something she always felt she lacked. The slangs I talk about here have the same goal; that of producing a proverbial home, but may lack a clear and linear link to the past. While traces of their origins—or the origins of some of their lemmata—seem to have a history that goes back several centuries, they lack the consistency and clarity of the identities Anzaldúa speaks of, and the continuity of the terms used to describe them. The social categories now theorised under the broad LGBTQ+ umbrella, have been distinct and diverse, and for the most part, lacked the signifier of ethnicity that runs through Anzaldúa's described social ontologies.

Another influential postcolonial theorist, Spivak, focuses more as Britton sums it up, 'on the subaltern's inability to "speak" the dominant discourse whereas Glissant focuses more on the dominant discourse's inability to "understand" the subaltern',[52] and the subaltern's right not to be understood, I would add. Both are different facets of the same issue of the violent and uneven dynamics between the dominant group and a subordinate group, through a problematisation of language as a representation of this asymmetrical relation. Spivak—and Anzaldúa—speak of the forcefulness of speaking in a language different to the one that one thinks in, detached from their culture, and imposed upon, and the simultaneous devaluing of one's own language and culture. Glissant focuses on the social space this creates (or can potentially create) for the minoritarian group. By taking advantage of their original, ancestral languages, mixing them with the oppressors', and ultimately not being understood, they produce spaces of resistance.[53]

Following on Anzaldúa and thinking further on the hierarchies and exclusionary systems language produces, opacity in the slangs is employed to turn those exact characteristics of language on their heads, thus activating them while giving power to the oppressed, to the minoritarians, to the disenfranchised. The demand and expectation of clarity and strict consistency of language that Anzaldúa calls 'linguistic terrorism' is shattered by the opacity of the unintelligibility of the slangs. Another element that slang varieties, native tongues, and other—unintelligible to the master—ways of communication turn on its head is the barbarism that the interlocutors have been accused of.[54] Barbarism comes once again through the oppressor's demand for full transparency. 'Widespread consent to specific opacities is the most straightforward equivalent of nonbarbarism. We clamor for the right to opacity for everyone'[55] writes Glissant. Since beginning this project I have faced many people who were utterly puzzled and often antagonised me for speaking of the benefits of opacity. No matter how patiently I explain of the reasons I personally became a speaker of slangs and why they matter to me and people like me, I often fail to convince them of opacity's importance. It happened time and again, as a comment, or review on a publication of mine, after lectures, or in informal conversations. Those who have a hard time seeing opacity's function are always white Central / Northern Europeans or white North Americans.

In opacity 'aspects of one's own self are always opaque to oneself, let alone to another, and allowing oneself the space for unknowable complexities is not only an act of interpersonal generosity but also a necessary corrective to the assumption that rigorous research questions will always yield the most accurate knowledge'[56] Jeannine Murray-Román concludes, reminding us again of the absoluteness of the traces of modernity still thriving in the field of (academic / scientific) research. Murray-Román further conceptualises the term regarding the oppositional relation of Eurocentrism, stating that opacity 'names an alternative to Eurocentric methodologies of acquiring data and demanding complete transparency from its objects of analysis.'[57] In relation to one's own opacity to oneself, but also the respect of the opacity of others ('interpersonal generosity') Murray-Román's thoughts connect to another theorist's work on fluidity, that of Agamben and his concept of 'whateverbeing'. 'Relation and Opacity, like Agamben's whateverbeing, undergird forms of personhood defined by their fluid interplay', summarises Murray-Román.[58]

I especially like these analyses of opacity as they shift the focus from the external relation (i.e. how one is seen by the oppressor) to an internal one, of how one sees oneself, and how one defies or rejects the modernist project's need for constantly shedding light on and dissecting everything. It allows for being comfortable not *despite* not knowing, but *while* not knowing all about one's self, and perhaps even extends a notion of self-care and being kind to one's self, in that you don't have to constantly scrutinise the Self in order for it to be legitimised. According to Britton 'opacity is based neither on opposition nor on identification.'[59] She additionally notes the similarities between Glissant's 'community', and 'relation' and Jean-Luc Nancy's 'being singular-plural' and observes, 'in the first place, both insist on the primacy of the plural: the collective dimension of being is not something added to an originary individual subject, but is itself originary. [...] At the same time both writers refuse to conceive of this "primordial plurality" as a fusion based on closure and sameness.'[60] It is as if opacity in its limiting of seeing or reading clearly, in its ununderstandability, accommodates for multiplicities, liminalities, and even movements to happen.

bell hooks reflects on how she imagines the moment in which the Africans realised the language of the oppressor could be claimed. In her own words, 'I imagine them also realizing that this language would need to be possessed, taken, claimed as a space of resistance. I imagine that the moment they realized the oppressor's language, seized and spoken by the tongues of the colonized, could be a space of bonding was joyous.' This joy, the joy of figuring a way out of an oppressive regime, a moment of realisation that there are still tactics of resistance, and the awareness that with creativity a new form of communication will evolve, one that excludes the oppressor, is how I imagine the beginnings of the slangs. I imagine this joy as the absurd aftermath of a police beating, an illegal detainment, while wandering the streets in lack of a home, or being laughed at by a teacher, john, or colleague. I imagine it as coming through moments in which creativity as a form of necessity takes over, new names for the oppressors are created, and gradually, the sharing of them generates more terms. The generating of new terms which come back to some of the original creators further confirm the width of the community and the sense of camaraderie brings further joy. 'Possessing a shared language, black folks could find again a way to make community, and a means to create the political solidarity necessary to resist'[61] concludes hooks. She further writes:

> The power of this speech is not simply that it enables resistance to white supremacy, but that it also forges a space for alternative cultural production and alternative epistemologies—different ways of thinking and knowing that were crucial to creating a counter-hegemonic worldview. [...] That power resides in the capacity of black vernacular to intervene on the boundaries and limitations of standard English.[62]

It is the need for and simultaneously the function of opacity that allows for this alternative cultural production to take place, for, without it, the exposure and self-censorship imposed would render it useless. It is precisely this veiling or unintelligibility—perhaps even the undervaluedness of the slangs that makes them unworthy of deciphering—that establishes the spaces of alternative, minoritarian, sub-cultural elements that critique the status quo, and in some ways embrace some kinds of anti-normative views creating futurities that are so necessary for some in order to keep on living.

When African people ended up in the Americas, having been abducted, ripped from their communities, familiar surroundings, and cultures, they were forced to adopt the oppressor's language in order to communicate between them. As hooks writes in the words of Adrienne Rich 'this is the oppressor's language yet I need it to talk to you.'[63] But the oppressed didn't adopt the oppressor's language as they were expected to. They instead corrupted it, altered it, adapted it, communicating in parallel ways among them, creating poetry, music, narratives the oppressor did not have full access to, a stance for which would be discriminated against as Black Vernacular is often looked down on, uncovering an array of classist and racist sentiments. However, when hooks remembers Rich's lyric, she thinks of Standard English, the language of conquest and domination. When I think of how I use English to work and socialise, I think of my version of English, one with a funny accent the Brits sometimes have a hard time with (yet have mostly remained polite), one that includes cussing in Greek, pet names for friends in Kaliarnta and Pajubá, and jokes that no one understands. Bad jokes too, but I am here referring to the ones that fly over people's heads. In the context of the academia, or an artistic / academic publication, it is the lingua franca (much to Glissant's disapproval of such creations), but also the language that some of us have had a harder time getting their points across in, causing me to both sympathise with them and get frustrated by them, forcing me to face my own linguistic imperialism or linguistic terrorism. I further had to confront my linguistic self-terrorism in the case of speaking German, as I didn't want to sound 'silly', or 'childish'. This occurred to me after realising the different social standing I could have as an English-speaking tourist versus a (struggling) migrant from the European South that tries to speak German. This resulted in me giving up on German many times, and deciding it was better (easier) to occupy spheres populated by other bixas periféricas. Anzaldúa remembers how simply saying her name was seen as inconsistent with the proper English she had to speak, and while this is true for many of us, she was further corrected on her own name. I have stopped correcting people trying to pronounce my last name, and recently noticed I pronounce it in a 'German way' too, in order to be understood without having to resort to spelling every time, or even worse the stereotypically othering responses my reply to 'where are you from?' usually carries. Britton writes, 'accepting the Other's opacity means also accepting that there are no truths that apply universally or permanently. Relation and opacity work together to resist the reductiveness of humanism.'[64] 'Ah Greek! But it'z a beautiful place, or?'

While depriving people of their own language is admittedly not premised on the same place as in a non-ethnic setting such as the one queer slangs have operated has been, the function of reclaiming a language that seems too restricting and most of all accessible by the oppressor is present in African Vernaculars, Tex Mex, and queer slangs alike. The slangs' level of opacity has mainly prevented people from demeaning them, but that has not been the case for AAVE, Chicano Spanish, or Native American tongues. Speaking of the pain this creates Anzaldúa writes, 'so, if you want to really hurt me, talk badly about my language.'[65] 'I am my language' she further states. In 'being one's language', actions of solidarity and community are produced, with language functioning as a link between the speakers, as a delineation of one community in relation to another, and as a tie to the hinterland. Britton adds—referencing Glissant's 'Caribbean Discourse'—'that opacity is not simply a practical, rational strategy on the part of the colonized, but a constituent of their collective unconscious.'[66] Further, relating to peoples that have no such 'hinterland' and for whom linguistic opacity has to be produced from a different starting point—albeit from similar needs and with similar intents—Britton writes, 'opacity cannot mean simply hiding, because there is—culturally as well as literally—nowhere to hide. Opacity therefore has to be produced as an *unintelligible* presence from within the *visible* presence of the colonized'[67] (emphases in original). She positions the production and function of opacity, not in some cut-off regions of the social, but precisely within it.

Glissant speaks to the innate Westernness of the idea of transparency and the upsetting of hierarchies an acceptance of differences causes. In further defining the opaque he states that 'The opaque is not the obscure, though it is possible for it to be so and be accepted as such. It is that which cannot be reduced, which is the most perennial guarantee of participation and confluence'[68] and ultimately (going back to the self once again) concludes that opacity is not only produced in relation to others, but it is an already internal relation as some parts of ourselves remain opaque to us as well. This admission I find very relieving and when thinking of communication, codes, slangs, and language I feel it is a way of embracing confusion, miscommunication and allowing for an otherness to be present without interrogation. It makes me feel more comfortable in the uncomfortability of a 'convoluted text', and opens up a space of understanding without necessarily να αποκωδικοποιεί every single word, every single line. It also acts as a reminder that I can take in a text and give it time to act, and expand in me, and that not everything has to be clear, diaphanous, and consumed then and there, but instead give it/myself time to establish an open-ended relation without force or specific demands, even within academia. It embraces a politics of tenderness and   .

Halberstam uses another term to talk about queer strategies of 'reading as well as a way of being in the world', which he calls 'queer darkness', and understands darkness as the 'terrain of the failed and the miserable.'[69] He does not go much further with the visual politics related to the term, at least not in relation to orality, speech, language. Despite that, the *Queer Art of Failure* definitely provides additional angles toward viewing unintelligibility as one of the ways failure is produced, both as a consequence of, and as a generator of queerness. Furthermore, Halberstam embraces failure as a valuable opening up of alterity and possibility. This opening up—an opening up related to failure—offers the liberating potential of tactics devoted to shuttering consistency, modern ideas of the Self, and success. In shuttering these in this liberatory move, one shutters transparency and allows for opacity, which activates freedom. Another element opacity contains by default, and fosters by practice, is the agency of the subject. The presence of opacity allows the individual shrouded in it or activating it to choose if, when, and how to disrupt it. The same piece of information is very differently shared when offered than when it is asked, or worse, demanded and expected. Jean Genet speaks of the feeling of disgust Sartre's book caused him, explaining that while he strips himself in his books, having someone else do that for him is a violation. In his words, 'in all my books I strip myself but at the same time I disguise myself with words, choices, attitudes, magic.'[70] He clearly expressed his agency through deciding when and how to disguise himself and when to expose himself, and along with it, his tactics of using language in ways that might even be magical. I want to suggest that there is an inherent connection between queerness, language, and opacity, in the ways language is opacified to conceal non-normativity or negate normativity altogether, the ways queerness skews language to sustain said opacity and the social spaces it produces, the way opacity allows for queerness to even be envisioned and practised, and the way queerness looks for alternative modes of expression and sharing that are not inscribed in clear, standard, intelligible content.

> Silence was not only a symptom of oppression, it was also, I want to argue, a chosen mode of resistance. This silence is not the passive stratagem of a closeted homosexual unwilling and unable to declare his identity within a hostile culture. On the contrary, it got them noticed. Indeed, in recuperating silence, absence, negation and other forms of anti-expressionism as a means of what I will characterise as a specifically queer resistance during the Cold War, we will find that it shares more than may at first seem evident with the-anything-but-silent cultural resistances of the '60s.[71]

The above is what Jonathan D. Katz wrote on the relation between silence and—what I will view more broadly as—queerness. He calls attention to forms of 'anti-expressionism' (silence, absence, negation) within a time of expressionist aesthetics which he calls 'queer resistance'. It is not only queer because it may have been employed by queer subjects, but primarily I see it as queer because of its counter-cultural value. At an era when Pollock and his contemporaries splashed colour on canvasses, others did not have the privilege to express themselves in such ways. Not only willful in participating, but willful to express themselves in any material, vocal, or visible manner they reach for the gaps, the pauses, the opaque, the absent and synthesise bodies of work that speak to their life stance. They focus on those things that are not allowed to be said out loud and then centre on the technology of the unspoken. Kulick makes a germane comment on how we learn about what must remain unspoken and unspeakable as children, and more importantly, how repression is fundamental for language. He writes, 'repression is not beyond or outside language but is, instead, the constitutive resource of language; and', he adds, 'repression is an interactional achievement'.[72]

I would now like to explore further the idea of silence, especially the ways it has been used by marginal communities, as well as in the arts, in hostile sociopolitical regimes by queer(?) artists. In doing so, I want to define silence, not as the complete lack of speaking or producing sounds, but being perceived as so doing. I am interested here in an understanding of silence that is performative and escapes the authorities, censorship mechanisms, and eventually escapes the normative altogether. I want to ask: 'what does queer silence sound or look like?' Having framed passivity and detour as tactics that are active and have the potential to undermine normativity, I would like to add silence to that group of tactics that find ways to subvert normativity, produce alternative counter-hegemonic readings of the world, and initiate moments of pleasure or happiness for those that by navigating them manage to mock their oppressors and forge creative ways of resistance.

Katz, in his article 'Performative Silence and the Politics of Passivity' asks the question, ' ... what does queer speaking that doesn't in fact depend on the old fashioned gay and lesbian identities we were trying to get away from look like?'[73] I am not certain the slangs manage—at least not all of them, not all of the time—to escape these old-fashioned identities, but in some ways they do manage to subvert the norms (and that may include gay and lesbian identifiers) enough to produce a queer speech that both queers the here and now and creates a vision—to use another visual term—of what a future in queerness may be like, or sound like; a counterpublic in Muñoz's terms. Later Katz, answering his previous question, suggests that this type of queer speaking does not involve speaking at all. He is referring to 'silence, a specularized, performative silence—a form of political engagement now distinctly undervalued, if not actively frowned upon in our post-Stonewall political context.'[74] He connects silence (not an enforced silence, but rather a silence that one is free to choose and perform) with passivity while making clear that neither of them is a form of giving in. They are instead, within his work, modalities that open up a space between what is said and what is meant, offering another kind of speaking, one that does not by default identify the speaker / performer. As he says, silence 'can tell a story without words but, as a readerly relation, silence is recognized, not written or spoken, understood, not declared. It manifests resistance, but does not articulate the positions or identity from which that resistance comes.' I see elements of such a silence in the slangs and think a connection between the two is not necessarily one of mutual exclusivity or contradiction. A refusal to speak in an understandable tongue works in much the same way, whether one speaks gibberish, or does not speak at all. It goes hand in hand with the refusal to give one's 'real name' to the police who are questioning or detaining them, not giving the names of those one was cottaging with, doing business behind the bushes or in the public restrooms with. To connect silence and this instance of audio politics with the previous explorations of visuality in the form of opacity, Katz maintains that, 'silence offers no naturalized or transparent foothold, no steady or solid framework substituted for the position under pressure. Rather, silence stands in perpetual alterity, appended to its target but capable of shifting shape and adopting new characteristics.'[75] Performative silence as a queer tactic can be seen in the character of Quiet Ann in the TV series *Claws*. Ann, a butch queer Latina, who after a stint in prison for aggravated assault (the details of which as of the finale of season 2 we don't yet know) disses her academic career and her bourgeois life to work (partly as protector) in a nail salon in a strip mall of Manatee County, FL, USA. Quiet Ann is an interesting take on silence and performativity. She is often silent without being closeted. She keeps silent often as a tactic of keeping safe. We don't know much about her as she prefers to keep quiet and take things in. She is perceptive, caring, and highly aware of her friends' feelings and any imminent danger. The only time we hear her voice extensively is through getting to listen to her inner voice in the episode titled 'Scream' in which the inner voice is followed by a cathartic moment of Ann giving her friends, brother, parents, and former partner a piece of her mind.

Foucault has also spoken of the importance of silence which is similar to the things actually said,[76] and De Villiers comments on Foucault's own tactic of opacity which he calls 'hiding it while revealing it' referring I suppose to Foucault's stance of not talking about himself, whilst through his foci on sexualities, homosexuality, BDSM, cruising, and other practices also revealing something. This opacity I will also connect with the visual politics of Pride Parades further down. De Villiers uses the term 'queer opacity' to refer to the 'possibility of nonmeaning and nonknowledge'[77] which reminds me of another term Foucault uses, this of méconnaissance which is translated as 'misunderstanding', but its actual literal meaning is 'misknowledge',[78] which I find extremely appropriate for queer speech. It holds the notion of knowledge, which is what the dominant group always occupies, or thinks they occupy exclusively, and ads the prefix 'mis-' which interestingly can add the notion of something ill, wrong, mistaken, wrong, or failed.[79] That in turn derives from the Proto-Germanic *missa- meaning 'divergent, astray'[80] which brings to mind the etymological traces of 'queer' meaning 'oblique, off-center'.⁸¹ I like the idea of an 'off-centre knowledge'. For me, it relates not necessarily to something that has shifted, but something that was never part of the Centre to begin with, something that was always of the Periphery. So back to bixas periféricas we arrive. Back to an opaque way of (mis?)communication through detours, silences, and passivities. A communication of a people that create their own literature to protect themselves. Adrienne Rich, writes on the topic of the intentionality of silence:

> Silence can be a plan
> rigorously executed
>
> the blueprint of a life
>
> it is a presence
> it has a history a form
>
> Do not confuse it
> with any kind of absence⁸²

In another text where Katz focuses on 'passive resistance' using the examples of Cold War Era 'gay artists' [his words] he writes, 'the gay men who supplanted Abstract Expressionist art at the end of the fifties employed the same strategies gay men had long used in order to escape detection and punishment within a homophobic culture; strategies born of the closet such as silence, dissimulation, masks and personae.' He speaks about the subtle tactics they employed and remarks how 'instead of making statements, these queer artists marked out their resistance through nuanced allusion and the manipulation of things.' In a manner similar to opaque speech and the production of slangs, they work with not saying, but implying, not accepting modes of expression, but altering them. These tactics resulted in the production of works like John Cage's '4'33"' a music piece which comprises entirely rests, Rauschenberg's White Paintings and 'Erased De Kooning' which is a blank canvas, Warhol's 'Invisible Sculpture' being a pedestal with nothing atop of it. Some of them (again according to Katz) also developed 'famously opaque artistic personas' (Johns, Warhol) and I would have to mention here Warhol's appearance on the Merv Griffin Show in 1965 (S3 E18) during which he mostly chews gum, responds monosyllabically, and mainly speaks through his friend and show guest Edie Sedgwick; he whispers in her ear and then she replies to Merv Griffin on his behalf. Upon first appearing on the show he refuses to speak altogether. Sedgwick explains that Warhol will be whispering things to her, and she will share them with host and audience. In the process, this transforms into elusive yeses and nos from Warhol and a lot of gum chewing and silences.

Another example of creativity, one that amalgamates different elements and exemplifies passivity and a very particular kind of performative silence is Cavafy, an Alexandrian Hellenic poet famous worldwide for his idiorhythmic style. In his erotic poems (his poems generally are relegated to three categories, the other two being historic and philosophical) he often avoids using pronouns but other times it becomes clear that he remembers a past or creates a future antérieur in which he admired or even enjoyed young men with red lips, messy hair, and beautiful faces. He even writes in his poem «Όταν διεγείρονται» (1916) of his effort to half-hide these erotic visions in his poetry:

Προσπάθησε να τα φυλάξεις, ποιητή,
όσο κι αν είναι λίγα αυτά που σταματιούνται.
Του ερωτισμού σου τα οράματα.
Βάλ' τα, μισοκρυμμένα, μες τες φράσεις σου.
Προσπάθησε να τα κρατήσεις, ποιητή,
όταν διεγείρονται μες το μυαλό σου
την νύχτα, ή μες την λάμψι του μεσημεριού[83]

Cavafy fused in his short poems Katharevousa and Demotic Greek and often included rhyme only to indicate irony making his works very difficult to translate. In his poems, he blends aspects of history (or scenaria that he draws based on historical figures) with elements of desires and (unsatiated) pleasures.

In trying to sociotemporally situate the production of those artists and their stance Katz claims that 'being able to use what others called "passivity" as a mode of resistance keyed to the pragmatics of survival in a hostile culture', and I would have to agree with him. By performing an opaque persona, a music piece where the orchestra only rests, or by refusing to paint or sculpt in order to be allowed to exhibit, these artists are speaking volumes to the general homophobic, anti-communist, anti-intellectual, post-Fordist, Taylorist mentality of the times. Warhol's persona mixing camp performances with elements of theatricality, Cage's reluctance to be transparent about the nature of his relationship with Cunningham, and Foucault's 'hiding it while revealing it' are only further indications that they employed silence, opacity and passivity not merely as an artistic practice but as a tactic of survival.[84] Warhol Museum's archivist John Smith mentions that writer Truman Capote once referred to Warhol as a 'Sphinx without a riddle'.[85] I find this description telling of a relation to truth that is perceived as holding on to a mystery, or hiding something under wraps, just because one does not perform 'truth' in the expected way. Meanwhile, they might not be hiding anything. The sheer fact is that there might or might not be something hidden; at least not in the sense that that something has to comply with expectations of 'somethingness'. Either way, this is beyond the point, and any attempt to unravel the mystery is always already failed.

I would like to take a detour here. I have been bridging postcolonial thoughts with queerness, through similarities in ways of resisting and creating using notions from Glissant, Ahmed, Fanon, Anzaldúa, Muñoz, and Spivak, among others. I use examples from theory and all sorts of cultural production and even though my focus is in the Periphery, some of my examples of such practices are often by cis, white, Anglo men. There are voices in the contemporary arts' and creative media scene from BPoC from all over the world, yet they are not as visible since the field is still predominantly white, and cis, and male. There are important BPoC creatives (many from the Periphery) that embody queerness in more nuanced ways, often also using locally and culturally relevant terms to identify with. To claim that there are no alternatives to those cis, white, male figures in bibliography would be factually wrong. There is a culture of erasure of people in the intersections of multiple axes of oppression that is pervasive in politics, arts, activism. It seems that the 'opaque personae' of BPoC, women, trans* folk, non-academically educated, poor people is lumped up into a mass of 'opaque peoples', individual achievements and personalities often erased. As I am the product of my upbringing and education I often scavange pieces of knowledge from sources that include 'opaque personae' as well as representatives of a certain canon.

Let us return to the theorisation of silence and the ever-present riddle that Other bodies are assumed to hide. Silence in this sense fights precisely against assumptionist tendencies; it can be activated either because and from within the closet, or in the way of negating it altogether. It shutters binarisms, it annoys those who 'just need to know', and most importantly empowers one not to proceed to any statements they do not feel like making. Being silent, after all, does not imply being silenced.[86] 'In a post-closet context, the speech act of silence—as Eve Segdwick once put it—just might prove to be a route towards the possibility of a queer liberation not structured according to a residual gay/lesbian identificatory remnant, nor an oppositional matrix of homo and hetero, but towards precisely the fluidity the performative implies'[87] reminds us Katz. Though I do not think we are in a post-closet context in the sense that I framed it earlier, I agree with Sedgwick that such speech acts deconstruct or point out the non-binary nature of oppositional, simplistic matrices.

The slangs, whether seen as a kind of   , or whether they employ silence, are premised on implication and innuendo through non-linear, often absurd connotations to produce meaning. Katz writes, 'unspeech or a performative silence produces, importantly, not a set of queer readings but rather a process of queering meaning.'[88] While partly true, with regards to the process of queering meaning, I find this account ignores the premised on creativity, fluidity, improvisation, and subversiveness nature of the process of queer reading. Slangs, lacking regulatory authority and constantly shifting to continue to enable opacity, rely as much on the creativity of the speakers as they do on the creativity of the listeners. Otherwise, they fail. (Of course, there are plenty of moments of 'failure', which I am certain contribute to the introduction of new terms). However let us remember that the central reason behind the slangs' existence is the production of safer spaces; when you inform someone of the arrival of the authorities, they had better be on the same page.

Katz mentions a text published by sociologist Erving Goffman which describes the strategies [sic] that inmates in mental or correctional institutions employed in order to combat the almost complete loss of agency in the framework of institutions that regulated and controlled all aspects of their lives. In Katz's words:

> Goffman concluded that the loss of personal autonomy in such places engendered strategies for survival like role playing, dissimulating, hiding, self-silencing, and denying—thus documenting on the micro scale the sociological tendencies of the closet among individuals who were not necessarily gay.[89]

In creating this connection between non-normative subjectivities and individuals that are considered a threat to themselves, but most importantly to society, Katz makes a very strong point on the tactics of survival utilised by deviants of all sorts, and further connects the loanwords that slangs incorporated which did not revolve around sexualities. This demonstrates perfectly not only the intersectionality indicated by the slangs as mentioned above, but the strong political connections between the closet, surveillance, queerness, and crip theory; the connections with the latter I will explore in more detail in chapter four.

Another aspect that resonates with the closet is this of liminality, and / or unclear and inconsistent borders / boundaries / partitions, and a disruption of normative understandings of borderlines, and in / out dichotomies. I would like to add an idea borrowed from Foucault who argues that 'There is not one but many silences, and they are an integral part of the strategies that underlie and permeate discourses.'[90] Additionally, I find, there are no exact, traceable, or clear limits between silence and the lack of. Much like the closet, silence and its audio politics disrupt shallow dualisms, they lurk somewhere and somewhen that is not easy to pinpoint, that is fluid and refuses categorisation. Again, I have to refer to Katz as he very poignantly writes:

> [silence] is queer because it engenders disruption without polarity, producing an unstable and always fluid hermeneutic opacity that both denies the recolonizing power of the oppositional (the ability of the opponent to co-op the excluded) and the power of the opposed to claim a position from which to speak.[91]

Relatedly, as Derrida maintains, silence, as the source of all language, is not a negation of speech; it is what allows speech to exist in the first place, and subversively using silence—performative silence—offers the possibility of a speech that is disturbing normative, classist, and racist assumptions on language and power.

Detour

According to Britton detour translates as 'diversion', 'defencive strategy', 'ploy'. I find it if not more applicable to the slangs than the closet per se, at least inasmuch as 'ploy' is concerned. I see silence, passivity, opacity, and detour, as tactics of resistance and survival, in particular in a queer context, the frameworks of which are not always clearly defined and overlapping is bound to happen. Britton defines opacity as an 'above all ethical value and a political right', and sees it as overlapping with detour with the latter being 'more tactical and ambiguous'. And this is where I see it overlapping with passivity, because its confrontation is one that gets around rather than tackling an obstacle head-on, and it 'arises as a response to a situation of disguised rather than overt oppression and struggle.'[92] It is this indirect approach both in dealing with oppression and the indirectness of dealing with the oppressor per se, that provides the overlapping ground between passivity (as an unintended subverting of the status quo) and detour (doing so, but doing so by indirect actions whose primary purpose is to facilitate the needs of the oppressed). An example Glissant uses to show how creolization manages to mock the dominant language is telling of the creativity of the people beyond orality. Britton refers to an example of Glissant's regarding stickers issued by the road safety association writing '"NE ROULEZ PAS TROP PRÈS" (DON'T DRIVE TOO CLOSE)' and talks about how Martinicans intervened in this French state-issued instruction by altering the words, and/or rearranging letters with the use of scissors. The variations included Martinican French phonetic spelling 'PA ROULE TRO PRE', the complete opposite 'ROULEZ', and even 'ROULEZ PAPA!'[93] Glissant sees this tactic as a telling example of the ambiguity of the relationship between French and Creole.

Much like the oral pliancy of the slangs, the above practice is equally playful and subversive and shows a willfulness in following the rules of the oppressor. Also similarly to the slangs, it could be seen as not necessarily 'tactical', but a tactic nonetheless, acts that are intentional in one aspect but manage to unintentionally be subversive in another. Sara Ahmed, writing on willfulness observes, 'We know from our shared collective histories of struggle that many acts of resistance are not intentional acts: to think these histories through willfulness risks making an intentional subject into the subject that matters.'[94]

'A rebellious action does not always feel intentional. If our tongues can acquire will by speaking without consent, then we can be willful without being intentional'[95] suggests Ahmed. Could this unintentionality be what makes the slangs work on an additional political level? I definitely see their unintentionality to become the subversive political apparatuses they have become as what has allowed them to maintain such a strong humourous quality. Some intentional tactics can also manifest detour, silence, or opacity. Intentional detours can be the topic changes, opaque answers, or 'false' answers in response to penetrating questions, in an attempt to avoid giving a clear and concise answer that one would feel exposed by. These 'false' answers I would place under the performative silence category. Along with evasiveness, they can allow one not to give information they don't want to share, and most importantly, not give in to the pressure of a person that at that moment violates them.

Thinking of visibility and visuality in the framework of opacity, I would like to draw another parallel to the closet and its relation to hiding, concealing, and visual politics. I want to mention here physical and textile-related manifestations of opacity and the right to negate what the demand for transparency stands for. One has to think of the niqab and the hijab and the discussions relating to their oppressive or emancipatory potential. Because I am uncertain of my place in this as a secular outsider from a non-Muslim background, I will only try to transfer the ideas of others that I find resonate with the closet and the opacity of the slangs, and avoid making claims as the specifics of the cultures, persons, or politics of talking about hijabi and niqabi women* without them. I am still uncertain about approaching this topic here, but at the same time it exemplifies a disruption of transparency and reductiveness that certain people and institutions in the West seem to find unbearable which makes it relevant to the politics of opaque Others.

The people wearing/using the niqab (usually identifying as women) are often seen in the West as hidden away due to patriarchal structures that shame women for their potential as sexual beings and conceal them to keep men in line. The niqab is read as anti-feminist and oppressive by default, often erasing the voices of those who wear it, disregarding their feelings, their politics, and experiences. The wearers are read through occidental ideas of truth, enlightenment, and exposure while notions of privacy, ideology, feelings of safety, and one's choice to do with their body and clothes as they wish, are often rubbed out. There are women who publicly speak about their conscious choice to wear a traditional garment that hides a significant part of their body and has a dark colour (often black). These women frequently speak from a feminist and queer position,[96] and explain why they don't see this practice as antithetical to their feminist/queer ideology, on the contrary, they view it in line with it, as a free choice and an emancipatory practice (in particular from the male gaze). Much like the closet, it allows for the person's agency and the right to choose, it is about boundaries, and respecting those boundaries against modernist ideas with regards to confession, openness, and a stance of answering and admitting, and instead opting for a type of resistance.[97]

For some feminists the hijab is also seen as a negation of commercial imperatives that support consumer culture[98] much like not partaking in events, markets, or rituals that do precisely that (Gay Pride events that have increasingly become an endless free ad space, gay cruises and travel agencies, and of course gay wedding ceremonies, party-planning, and adoption agencies). Like queerness opts out of those cultural settings, the politics of concealment allow for the same opting out. I particularly like Suzanna Milevska's reading of the veil as an event that as such challenges normative ideas of the temporal.[99] I also think of other forms of veiling, like the hood/hoodie and the scarf/bandana, the reasons for their use, and the laws that ban them in public space,[100] often similar to those banning the hijab/niqab. Veiling, whether in its literal sense (veiling of the face or body) or in its metaphorical sense (of the Self) is as much a temporal practice as it is a spatial and corporeal one. It is speaking without expressing, without surrendering to demands of full and consistent exposure. In Derrida's words, 'to avoid speaking, to delay the moment when one will have to say something and perhaps acknowledge, surrender, impart a secret, one amplifies the digressions.'[101] I think of Comandanta Ramona, and Subcommandante Marcos of the Zapatistas, making the ski mask, their pseudonyms, and ultimately their anonymity/metonymity part of the political struggle they wage against colonial regimes, exploitation, and structural violence. It is precisely the existence of this opacity, this veil, that allows them to exist in the symbolic level. 'Once the mask is gone, so is Marcos', he said in an interview.[102]

The notion of camouflage comes up time and again when discussing practices of resistance and concealment, hiding, opacity, and veiling in specific. Bhabha writes:

> In Fanon's essay 'Algeria Unveiled' the colonizer's attempt to unveil the Algerian woman does not simply turn the veil into a symbol of resistance; it becomes a technique of camouflage, a means of struggle—the veil conceals bombs. The veil that once secured the boundary of the home—the limits of woman—now masks the woman in her revolutionary activity, linking the

Arab city and the French quarter, transgressing the familial and colonial boundary.[103]

Remaining opaque about one's subjectivities, especially those that focus on sexualities, and sexual orientation (always in the form of orientation towards a certain gender) in a time when this is often demanded, is similarly a concealment of resistance, a resistance to reduction, classification, diagnostication, and ultimately a resistance to allowing one to claim they can know you. Ahmed reads the veil as charged with willfulness, and writes, 'the veil becomes a willful part, a part that refuses to take part in national culture, a stubborn attachment to an assimilable difference',[104] and further maintains that 'perhaps the Muslim woman herself becomes both will-full and will-less. No wonder her body has become monstrous in the secular imaginary.' She goes on to state that she understands willfulness as an affective judgement,[105] which resonates with the use of the tactics of resistance/survival discussed here. It additionally links with Foucauldian ideas of power relations and surveillance and allowing one to keep their image from the gaze of the inspecting public.

Furthering the associations with other postcolonial thinkers beyond Glissant, Fanon talks about the frustration the veil(ed woman) causes to the coloniser. Both events make understanding conditional, and this frustrates those who have been used to always having full agency over themselves and control over penetrating others. It changes the rules of the game for them, a game they are used to playing by making up their own rules (on the fly). Tactics like the closet, the veil, or the balaclava are not only questioning the (unwanted) gaze, and categorisation, while disrupting transparency. They are also actively looking back from a safer place, while gaining power by removing one's own image from the potential of being looked at, being identified, pigeonholed, or reduced to a single category. 'A being radically devoid [or appearing to be so, I would add] of any representable identity would be absolutely irrelevant to the State', writes Agamben in his book *The Coming Community*,[106] and Britton thinks of opacity, which sometimes takes the form of simple concealment, as a strategy of protection: hiding from the oppressor. Agamben further mentions a letter from Robert Walser to Max Rychner in which Walser expresses his 'fascination of not uttering something absolutely'. I find this relative reading of expression as the mathematical equivalent of the visual term that is opacity. As an author whose work took place in regional dialect, Walser, who wrote in Swiss-German and in a tiny script which was called 'Mikrogramme' expressed this fascination of his in a letter to a friend. The fact that Walser lived with mental illness and worked in a liminal language makes me see this fascination of his through the prism of such tactics of concealment and producing alternative spaces of communication, safer spaces of comfort. This digression will make more sense in the coming chapter.

I have written and re-written parts of this work and I am still certain that the contradictory elements of standing for opacity and trying to figure things out are still in here, others more obvious (to the author) than others. But I also realised that I am the product of such politics; of both political stances, raised in a middle-class family where curiosity was encouraged, in a culture that prides itself for the love of knowledge and wisdom it so 'generously' gave the world, and working and conducting this project within an academic institution. At the same time, having grown up a queer kid, with anxiety and other health issues, in a tiny place surrounded by the sea made me not only activate opacities when and where I could, but also appreciate the need of others to maintain theirs. Later on, my health problems would multiply, the precarious working conditions would intensify the health problems, and being a migrant only added to the everyday mental gymnastics.

And this brings me to the here and now, writing this semi-autobio- / ethno-graphical text in English, in central Europe, and this includes all the above contradictory—but not necessarily mutually exclusive—elements, the embraced and unintended failures, the blind spots, and the (un)certainty. As Ahmed remarks, 'A willful politics might involve a refusal to cover over what is missing, a refusal to aspire to be whole'[107] and I, for one, am fine with that.

The Opacity of the Rainbow

The rainbow flag usually acts as the utmost signifier of being out and proud, of a cohesive community fighting for equality on all levels; a Western symbol that has permeated many places around the world. Jan Simon Hutta provides a parallel function of the flag that usually helms Pride Parades around the globe. He offers an image that points to the much more nuanced character of the symbol as a generator of a space of opacity and disobedience. In his essay 'Beyond the Politics of Inclusion: Securitization and Agential Formations in Brazilian LGBT Parades' he describes how the parade participants—one that is not limited by barriers and thus allows for a merging of participants and spectators and a blurring of the two ways of attending—take advantage of the space of limited visibility that is produced by the large flag. They use it to flirt, cruise, engage in touching and masturbating 'turning the space beneath the flag into a huge day-time and on-the-street cruising ground.' This is particularly significant for those individuals that are excluded by classist or racist behaviours at gay venues. It further points specifically to the manner in which, while pleasure is the common denominator, politics substantially rooted in capitalism and colonialism cause hierarchies and exclusions to those most in need of safer spaces. Hutta writes, 'Something of the proud claiming of visibility symbolized by the flag is being transposed into the secluded space underneath. The sense of a common cause, of parading *as* gays in close bodily contact, combined with the secluded shelter-ness, evokes a peculiar erotic sense of "geborgenheit"'.¹⁰⁸ Those partaking in the pleasurable activities veiled by the flag 'constitute', as Hutta poignantly puts it, 'the affective underside of the "respectable" flag, as it were.' He names the 'simultaneity of a sense of togetherness and transgression, of proud marching and hidden cruising, which emerge from the privacy-in-public underneath the flag'¹⁰⁹ as what makes this event so strong and telling of the diversity of the 'community', especially in light of a policing that consistently excludes people of colour, travestis, sex workers and other Others to the homonormative, white, well-off gays.¹¹⁰

LGBTQ+ people are often attacked for 'shoving' their deviance in people's face, for not performing 'proper' femininities and masculinities, for investing 'too much' in their gayness (meaning their preoccupation with the murder rates of LGBTQ+ folk, the homophobic agendas of politicians, the poor media representation etc.). I am not going to get into how or why these are homophobic and ignorant, I am not interested in justifying these with explanations, and I don't think it is necessary either. What I am interested in is seeing through the pretence of the rainbow flag, μισαλλοδοξία becoming transparent. It is the same people who accuse us of performance deviance who seem bent to see us perform these very things. Recently a case came to light in which Navid fleeing Iran and applying for asylum in Austria was rejected because he didn't know the significance of each of the colours of the rainbow flag.¹¹¹ This is another instance of the heterogeneity of the flag's symbolic significance, the implication of its West to East / South permeation and what that says about the mainstream LGBTQ+ community.

Another case saw an asylum seeker from Afghanistan rejected because he didn't act gay enough for the authorities to believe he was indeed gay.[112] The decision included such quotes as 'The way you walk, act or dress does not show even in the slightest that you could be homosexual', and the applicant's 'potential for aggression wouldn't be expected from a homosexual', because the man fought with others in the accommodation where he was being housed. He reportedly had few friends and liked spending time alone or in small groups, leading the official to question in his report: 'Aren't homosexuals rather social?' the Guardian reported.

The pretence of the flag in the hands of authorities and majoritarians unravels their deep (and painfully anti-subaltern) homophobia; no matter how one acts, how they socialise, what they know and how they frame their queerness, it is they who are the problem. It is their deviance that authorises violence against them whether it be deviance from normative performatives of femininities and masculinities or deviance from the expected deviance.

Opacity and I

Opacity is a mechanism that—beyond communication and protection—accommodates the need for privacy, especially when physical spaces fail to facilitate that. It is opacity, generated by language, silence, or detour that allows individuals the headspace necessary, away from neoliberal, consumerist, social-media-dictated ways of being connected continuously, having FOMO, or the compulsion to publicising one's every location, feeling, or meal. I have come to realise it is not only difficult to know how to activate opacity, especially when caught off guard, but it is particularly strenuous to maintain it. Deciding to work under an assumed name—or several for that matter, but here I am referring to 'Anna T.'—has been a constant source of questions and met with various attempts to uncover 'my real name'. I—in this case—decided to use a single letter and a punctuation symbol as a last name, thus making it clear that this is not—cannot be—a legal name and disclosing my negation in identifying with such a name. I did that to disassociate myself from any one nationality and of course the patriarchal nature of my given last name (being the genitive—possessive—of my father's last name) in an attempt to have agency over how I would be called and introduced to people. I furthermore did so to make online searches harder, and keep as much of my private life (and images of my body) as opaque as possible, in an age when the demand for voluntary documentation as well as state surveillance is unprecedented. Despite the efforts to make away with the 'pseudonym' and find out the 'real' name, and the work this demands on my behalf, I find this simple language-based tactic has indeed afforded me some comfort. 'Opacity turns out to be not only a category within the field of a critique of vision, but also as a category within the field of chronopolitics' writes Lorenz,[113] creating links to the function of opacity in the case of the closet, the different veils and linguistic tactics to the here and now, the temporality of the event of concealing and the tactics' ephemeral nature but also their relation to the social, both as a response to it, and as being conditioned by it.

Disenfranchised

While such cultural productions (language, music, dance, performances, etc.) are not created with the intent to take over or substitute normative or mainstream culture, as other 'active' modes of questioning would, I have argued that they are forms with the power of resistance. They refuse to be assimilated and 'normalised', choosing instead to produce an alternative performative universe that provides a safer space of expression and which, unwitting, also holds the potential to mock and subvert the norm. They use performative silence, performative passivity, detour, and opacity to escape clarity, linearity, and normative ways of gendered expression, as well as the political correctness of highbrow culture, mixing instead seemingly paradoxical sets of mores and social stances, activating the absurd, shattering the entitlement of full access and complete transparency. Overall, I understand the slangs as a refusal of silence while activating performative silence, as a resistance to being idle while employing passivity, and a direct subversion of the cultural products of the status quo through detouring. The slangs remain in a rather liminal space between inactivity and straightforward revolutionary action. They are a form of creative resistance, a way of producing a parallel social space of expression whose existence might, in some ways, indirectly affect the mainstream as well. These languages, when used in the vicinity of outsiders, are indeed audible but not transparent; they remain opaque, allowing the non-speakers to identify the speakers as belonging to a particular group, but not being able to pinpoint what group that is. They thus create a rift in the (supposedly) homogenous social fabric.[114]

Cage used silence as a means to not be silent / silenced, in a manner similar to the one queer subjects opt-out of mainstream modes of communication and produce separate sonic spaces with specific membership habitus. While art is made in order to be public and communicated (at least in most cases)—and Cage's art was very much so—these languages are intended to be communicated within certain limits, those of the social space they help to produce, operating in a circular fashion where the social space (closet) produces the language. The language then re-affirms said space. I think the way they operate in producing rifts in broader society is by the casual, perhaps accidental moments they engender. They do not need to be translated, and one does not need to be fully aware of the speakers' subjectivities, but the sheer fact that certain

. Non-conforming individuals speaking (and / or performing) an unfamiliar dialect might be all it takes to create the impression that there is a very much present, active, and creative community producing its own subculture. Arguably that might already be enough. These queer slangs might not produce new, politically informed, revolutionary terminology. Nevertheless, they are very much present, occupying a terrain between explicit action-oriented politics and compliance. They operate under the cover of opacity and empower the marginalised, giving them space for existence, expression, and safety. Queer slangs are anti-authoritative and as such, according to Katz 'they reveal the power of the individual to construct meaning unauthorized by dominant culture—and all the while, under its very nose.'[115]

It is not by accident that during the Greek military dictatorship of the late '60s and early '70s, popular satirical theatre used Kaliarnta as a way to avoid censorship. Actors substituted 'precarious' words for Kaliarnta terms, introducing these words to a general audience and letting this audience figure them out for themselves. In the UK a few years earlier, between 1965 and 1968, a BBC radio show aired on Sunday afternoons which addressed the 'entire family' and featured two out-of-work camp actors who used Polari. This was at a time when homosexuality was still illegal in the UK.[116] Through practices like these, and of course the lack of watertight spaces within the social, terms from these slangs made their way into the mainstream, further subverting it in unintentional ways, in a manner that I can only describe as the oppressor using the tools of the oppressed to dismantle their own house.

I think queer slangs could be one of the answers to De Villiers' questions in the preface of his book *Opacity and the Closet, Queer Tactics in Foucault, Barthes, and Warhol*: 'What if we were to look at speech as nonrevelatory, outside the parameters of confession and truth, the humanist desire for reflection, and the ideal of transparency? What if we were to attend to its opacity? What would such an opacity look or sound like, and what would be its function?'[117]

Queer slangs obtain such nonrevelatory qualities, they disrupt binaries and thus function outside ideas of truth and confession. They negate the ideal of transparency. They can sound like Romani, like Greek, like Yoruba, like silence. They take detours and sound confusing. They may be camp, extravagant, flamboyant. They can be quiet, fast, and effeminate. They might throw shade.

While first writing this text I tried to create some tables with examples of words and expressions, transliterated and translated from Kaliarnta, Polari, and Pajubá into English, but I realised it was not going to work, and then that it was okay that it did not. I was forcing a transparency that did not want to be there. Throughout this work, I have only included terms that already exist in documentations of the slangs and already existing bibliography. I have resisted the initial need to share things I know that are not (to my knowledge) yet documented. What I was trying to accomplish (and miserably failed at doing) was beautifully commented on by Celia Britton, who says that camouflaged language can only be understood in a way that respects its opacity and does not reduce it to transparency. She writes:

> For the reader, too, opacity means that the text can never be grasped as a whole, that is, as a wholly known and therefore circumscribed entity. Instead, the areas that remain opaque mean that its borders are left undefined and open. Reading thus becomes similar to 'errance' (see chapter 1), in the sense that 'the wanderer [l'errant] ... seeks to know the totality of the world and knows already that he [sic] will never accomplish this and that herein resides the endangered beauty of the world ... He dives into the opacities of that share of the world to which he has access.'[118]

'One of the researchers I contacted, Paul Baker, directed me to an archive of Julian and Sandy episodes. The popular sketch of the two flamboyant out-of-work actors in 1965 London. Their sketches were part of the Round the Horne comedy show airing on Sundays from BBC radio. The show broadcast in other commonwealth countries too, which created a bridging between Polari and Australian Gayspeak. The protagonists would use Polari and sexual innuendo, always aimed at the straight character (Mr. Horne). I chose an episode I found particularly funny and representative of what their show managed to do. They used enough Polari to create a disruption in the linear understanding of the dialogues by people who didn't know Polari, they teased the straight guy, and they were creatively taking linguistic malleability a step further offering their own translations of Shakespeare into up-to-date Polari, including 'Two Omees of Verona', 'All's Bona that ends Bona', and 'As they like it' ('Live and let live I say', adds Sandy). I projected it right here, it was a black video with white subtitles. Some words I didn't get so you have to imagine that there were blanks in their place. It lasted for two minutes and acted as a conversation starter for queer slangs and my overall research. Creating, or rather re-producing, these moments of exclusion and disruption made some slightly uncomfortable and had them asking questions that ranged from scholarly to very personal.

Writing the dissertation was another way to work with text and more directly address the conundrum of working with opacity yet in an academic setting which demands clarity and explicitness. Not wanting to let go of opacity or betray it, but still producing a text that would qualify as a doctoral dissertation, I used performative writing: writing that entails elements of first-person narratives and thus selfhood and subjectivity, but also bibliographic references. I developed a style that uses slang terms or sentences, omits words, and makes up words that do not operate in English while abiding by the Chicago Style. For the most part. This was a way for me to keep the boundaries between the two modes of work blurred and incorporate affective, performative, and non-scholarly elements in a body of work that deals with ideas of deconstructing normativity and Western academia's requirement for linearity. By so doing I refused to fully give in to the binary or theory/practice and instead offer them as intertwined creative modes which employ performativity, improvisation, embodiment, textuality, and visuality in different degrees, while allowing for thematic and aesthetic overlaps.'

Minority[1]

> *Deslenguadas. Somos los del español deficiente.* We are your linguistic nightmare, your linguistic aberration, your linguistic *mestizaje*, the subject of your *burla*. Because we speak with tongues of fire we are culturally crucified. Racially, culturally, and linguistically somos *huérfanos*—we speak an orphan tongue.
> Gloria Anzaldúa, *Borderlands / La Frontera: The New Mestiza*

In the previous chapters, I used the terms 'minority' and 'minoritarian' frequently. I would now like to focus on the Deleuzoguattarian perspective of these concepts and explore how they offer tools to unearth the background and qualities of the slangs. I explored earlier the function of the slangs through a number of tactics related to visual and audio politics. I traced them to different minoritarian groups and talked about the closet's relation to them. Now I shift my focal point to another characteristic of slangs: orality. Throughout this chapter, I will show how the tension of orality / literature is addressed in the slangs as counter-cultural products, and how that became an integral part of my work in particular. Relatedly, I will employ Deleuze and Guattari's idea of 'minor literature', to dig out some other characteristics of the slangs, and then present my experiment with working on a written version of them through street art. As an artistic means, street art has been described by O'Sullivan as a potential 'minor art practice' that incorporates illegality, ephemerality, and making do with what one has.

Throughout my preoccupation with slangs, metaphors, and the closet, I realised that orality and oral tradition are often positioned at odds with literature. Wanting to address this tension, I turned to Deleuze and Guattari's

Kafka: Toward a Minor Literature as it deals with elements of minority from a written perspective. In that book, they focus on Kafka's work (a Jewish Czech writing in Prague German) and locate three characteristics therein which they identify as the preconditions of 'minor literature'. The first precondition concerns the deterritorialisation of a major language, an undoing of it through a minoritarian perspective.[2] The second addresses the political potential of such literature, stating that 'everything in them is political'[3] and 'its cramped space forces each individual intrigue to connect immediately to politics'. And the third is that everything in it takes collective value, in that there are no authors, no ownership, it is a DIT project always in the making.[4]

Although not immediately classed as 'literature' in the same way Kafka's *Castle* is, or Beckett's or Joyce's writings, the slangs discussed in this project contain Deleuze and Guattari's three characterising elements of 'minor literature', a literature that perhaps eventually becomes revolutionary.[5] I see the slangs' performativity and their undoing and redoing[6] of language as a majorly subversive tactic, one that creates subcultural communities and affords agency to their members. I will now explore how the slangs can be seen as minor literature in this sense. The Deleuzoguattarian concept indicates that to qualify as 'minor' it needs to deterritorialise a major language and be written in the major language from a marginalised or minoritarian position. Although not written, queer slangs use the major language of the nation state, skew it, alter it semantically, and include lexemmes from other major (often colonial) languages, combining them with linguistic elements from minoritarian groups (such as Romani and Kurmanji), much like Kafka's language is skewed and reshaped to reflect his location, background, and social status. Kafka's literature manages to disguise revolutionism in a similar way Kaliarnta and the other slangs do: using words that the oppressor understands but whose newly-acquired meaning escapes him. 'Minor literature doesn't exist "elsewhere" or "apart from" a major literature (this is not a dialectic) but still operates from within, using the same elements as it were, but in a different manner' points out O'Sullivan.[7] In the case of Kaliarnta, Greek is not a major language in the same way as the languages of the primary colonial powers (English, German, Dutch, French, Portuguese, Spanish) are, but it is major in that it is the official language of a nation-state. Consider how the nation-state renders certain individuals as sick or illegal, and its bureaucratic apparatus will do anything to suppress such individuals, their desires, and their expressions. It is the language in which pathological diagnoses are made, the language that names certain behaviours as illegal and penalises them, the language in which sin is named. It is also a language that in some ways may be considered major, due to its history, influence on (Western) philosophy and sciences, and due to the fact that it is still taught around the world (both in its modern and ancient form). A similar argument stands in the case of Polari; Polari utilises English, and Mediterranean Lingua Franca (a composite which includes among others Spanish and Portuguese). The 'majority' of the language, its imperialism, and current international permeation is indisputable. In the case of Pajubá, the distinction between colonial language, the enslaved peoples' languages of origin, and the native ones becomes clear along the lines of syntax. The vocabulary might be based on Bantu, Yoruba, and other African language families, as well as terms borrowed from African religious/spiritual practices, but structure is linked with the language of the coloniser, and so syntax is based on Portuguese.[8] The slangs' position is consistently minor and coming from the margins, a position that is reflected in the professions, social standing (or lack thereof), and legal status of the interlocutors, as well as the minor languages they choose to import elements from (Romani, Yiddish, Thives' Cant etc.). Additionally, I find another layer of deterritorialisation in the slangs' way of messing up hierarchies, not by doing away with them, but by calling out their arbitrariness. This messing with hierarchies comes in a variety of forms; some mess with established hierarchies of gender, others with class issues, or social status in the form of professional titles or honorifics. Laurent Berlant points out that:

> Deleuze and Guattari exhort people to become minor and to deterritorialise from the normal by digging a hole in sense like a dog or a mole. Creating an impasse, a space of internal displacement, in this view, shatters the normal hierarchies, clarities, tyrannies, and confusions of compliance with autonomous individuality.[9]

Arguably, by connecting through the slangs the speakers dig this hole Berlant speaks of, and a new area suddenly opens up, swallowing a bunch of subjectivities in the process.

The second precondition is that of the political nature of a minor literature. The individuals creating, communicating with, and being protected by the slangs are—in a historically and culturally specific manner—politically persecuted, marginalized, and threatened as the political system's moral and ideological enemies. As these languages provide sociopolitical critique, their statements are telling of the social positioning of the speakers, the social barriers they come across, and the political context that forces them to create such communication codes to begin with. 'Rodgers maintains that these words "enrich … our language immensely", they promote group cohesion, and they constitute a form of "social protest."'[10] The slangs are spoken by those deemed immoral; those eroding the values of normativity. Γκέι και λεσβίες, ιέρειες του αίσχους, είμαστε περήφανα η ντροπή του έθνους. The slangs are political not only because of the critique their lexemes apply, but primarily, because of the positionality of the speakers and the very need behind their creation. The slangs might be the only tool some of the speakers have access to, the only way to actively be the ones to exclude others and attain a sense of momentary privilege, the only way to laugh at the oppressor's face and get away with it.

The third characteristic is that everything takes collective value. 'What each author says individually already constitutes a common action, and what he or she says or does is necessarily political, even if others aren't in agreement. The political domain has contaminated every statement'[11] write Deleuze and Guattari. Queer slangs being the products of individual creativity and communal maintenance seem to embody that collective value. Communication here is about collectivity, and slangs are furthermore about preserving that collectivity in the form of a community. O'Sullivan, as quoted earlier, addresses explicitly the affirmation of a new community.[12] Slangs form communities not only by the sharing of the neologisms, the mannerisms, and the accompanying performativity but additionally by excluding the non-speakers, by having identified them as non-members of the community. Knowledge of the slang awards membership and membership allows access to learning the slang. One is rewarded for knowing the slang, but there is no prize for authorship, as this individualistic practice would go against the very nature of those idioms. They are created to protect and extend social cohesion within the community and bring the members together through sharing a laugh in this mutual linguistic world.

In addition to these three characteristics, Deleuze and Guattari account for another feature of minor literature. They mention that at the beginning of Kafka's *Castle* the children speak so quickly that nobody understands what they're saying.[13] „Eben kamen die Kinder mit dem Lehrer heraus. In einem dichten Haufen umgaben sie den Lehrer, aller Augen blickten auf ihn, unaufhörlich schwatzten sie von allen Seiten, K. verstand ihr schnelles Sprechen gar nicht." Much like children's made-up language, to avoid the tyranny of adults, Kaliarnta is spoken very fast to add an extra layer of difficulty in deciphering the meaning, and excluding non-queers. Polari also contains children's backslang and Pig Latin, playful elements from childhood brought into the here and now under a different set of circumstances but for similar reasons. Meanwhile, these tactics—despite evoking childishness—are used to unite against linear understandings of age, heteronormative expectations around reproduction and family, and focus on paths that escape 'conjugality and the nuclear family.'[14] I am referring to familial terms, age-related terms, or gender terms used in those languages in ways contrary to the regular or 'official' ones. How can this be done, and what does it entail? I will further pursue this in the next chapter.

Orality - Literature

I want to suggest that despite the slangs being primarily—if not exclusively—oral, and having few 'works' produced in them (poems, proverbs, radio show skits, music videos, and songs), the minority in them satisfies the three preconditions and affords them the title of 'minor'. Initially, I had hesitations in associating the slangs with the term literature, which perhaps always has connotations of highbrow culture, education, and privilege. After insightful conversations with a friend, and reading the material he suggested, I will avoid my initial impulse to re-appropriate minor literature and adjust it to 'minor speech', 'minor speak', or 'minor parlare', and instead point to the 'literaturity' of the slangs. The Western gaze has considered oral traditions as a primitive, ungraspable, and an authority-lacking manner of communication. But as soon as something is fixed within a community, and repeated, it becomes a 'letter', it becomes 'writing', eventually it becomes literature. It is often a component of mainstream ideology to discredit alternative cultures as lacking culture, or better yet, as lacking 'cultivation', and seeing their cultural productions as inherently inferior. Gay slang has been called 'the street poetry of queens'[15] activating simultaneous elements of non-domesticity, lack of academicity, potential illegality, as well as literary stylisation.

As Ings germanely notes:

In accepting that not all histories are equally privileged, we need to ensure that obscurity does not become cultural absence, and that essentially oral languages describing marginalised cultures are not denied a position in the national landscape. Indeed, the absence of records serves to reinforce only the survival of sanctioned narratives of cultural diversity. On a more pernicious level, the absence of records means that the histories of marginalised cultures remain unknown.[16]

This project attempts to

,   ,

, employing methodological tools that allow for them to be honoured while allowing them to stay behind the bushes, at the port, στα βατικανά των πλατειών, in the ships, the brothels, and the prisons.

Thinking of orality in relation to queerness, a recent incident came to mind. Civil unions (cohabitation agreements) were legalised for same-sex couples in Greece at the end of 2015, leading to celebrations by civil rights' organisations and LGBTQ+ groups, and condemnation and hate speeches from the conservative/religious right (including inciting of violent crimes against 'homosexuals' on behalf of Greek Orthodox bishops). One such cleric argued that same-sex practices between males are abnormal and referred to 'recent studies' which have indicated that mouth and throat cancers are not the results of smoking but of oral sexual practices which, he stated, are common only among homosexuals.[17] As such, these practices (and their agents) are not only immoral, but indeed deadly. Beyond the scientific fallacy of this statement (no such studies), and as socially repugnant as it might be, the connection (distorted and not fact-based indeed) between queerness (or non-normative sexual practices) and the oral is something that seems to go much further back, than contemporary Greece. The term 'sodomy', a biblical term, refers to both anal and oral sex, assigning them both to practices between males.[18] Deleuze and Guattari's fascination with Kafka's food-mouth, tongue, teeth descriptions brings to mind—apart from the material component of the construction of language—instances of pleasure and indulgence. It also reminds me of Virginia Woolf's *A Room of One's Own*,[19] which talks about the need for a space that one can occupy alone, in order to be, and produce, and where food and culinary pleasures are found throughout. Could the use of queer languages be another bodily pleasure in itself? Could the materialising of speech, much like written language, be a corporeal instance of delight in which those placed in the margins are set to explore?

«Μην είσαι γλωσσού!» I remember my grandma reprimanding me. Funny how this term is always used in the feminine form. Come to think of it I have only ever heard it being used for women and πούστηδες. 'You become mouthy', writes Ahmed, '[p]erhaps we are called mouthy when we say what others do not want to hear; to become mouthy is to become mouth, reduced to the speaking part as being reduced to the wrong part.'[20] Fixation with the mouth, and what the mouth does, seems to be a constant preoccupation of oppressive regimes and forms of discipline. You open it too often and say things others do not want to hear. «Δεν είναι ωραίο να βρίζει η γυναίκα!»

You open it and insert body parts you are not supposed to. You open it and consume too much food. 'You should take care of your figure, that's not a summer body!' You open your mouth and speak in tongues, and others are immediately made uncomfortable, or even worse, they ask you to say something in 'your tongue' expecting a spectacle. It is supposedly one's first language—or mother tongue—that inscribes one's sociolinguistic identity, and yet for some, the first language they learn is not necessarily a mother language. 'Most isiNgqumo speakers', writes Rudwick, 'perceive the code as "their language", and see it as the medium which captures most adequately who they are and how they see themselves in the world.' In such cases, it is the language one gets to know later in life through navigating social realms that are indicated by desire that reflects how they see themselves and how they read the world. 'However', Rudwick remarks, 'the perspective presented must not erroneously be understood as essentialist. The "gay culture", "Zulu ethnicity", as well as "gay-Zuluness" associated with isiNgqumo, has many different facets and reference points for different individuals and involves many idiosyncrasies.'[21] This point is central to the slangs. On the one hand, they utilise essentialist language, while on the other they simultaneously foreground the fluidity of all categories either through neologisms or the recontextualisation / reterritorialisation of already existing ones. Upholding the perception of an accurate contouring of the speakers might be another thing the slangs offer.

Parallel to an open theorisation of genders, sexualities, and kinship, language is also affected by re-thinking those categories along chronopolitical terms. One's mother tongue is not necessarily spoken by one's mother(s), it might not be the first language one learns, and indeed social positioning might inform one's language, or create it, to begin with. Willfulness might be an additional reason behind the slangs' existence and their speakers' hesitation to identify the national languages as their own. Willfulness, according to Ahmed, can be deposited in our bodies, and when that happens 'our bodies become part of a willfulness archive.'[22] The oral tradition of the slangs is such an archive of embodied willfulness. Having discussed the slangs as anti-languages, idioms that deterritorialise the major and laugh at normativity, willfulness strikes me as another indication of their counter-cultural position and power. A refusal to let go of certain desires becomes the opportunity for many other pleasures to come within reach. Willfulness against obedience or 'normality' creates support systems and linguistic universes that in chronopolitical terms, constantly produce the subject.

In the slangs' engagement with deterritorialisation I see a dismantling of the master's tools, to speak in Lordian terms. Contrary to Lorde's view[23] however, they have the potential of eventually delivering blows so consistent and strong, they may damage or leave permanent marks on the master's house, all the while using his own tools against him. The way I see that happening is through reterritorialisation and contamination. The slangs do not simply use an entirely new vocabulary or syntax, they de- and re-territorialise those of existing languages. They use the language of the nation-state, the syntax of colonial bureaucracy, and they metamorphose them for their own interest, making them reflect their own values. Consequently, these slangs do not simply exist in a vacuum or a socially watertight space; they are audible in the public domain, they spread, they infect the mainstream, they find their way on the radio, on stage, on TV. They sneak into the tools of the system and manage small cracks in its homogeneity and illusion of normality.

I want to take a brief detour—to deviate, as it were—and mention an important intervention that bridges queerness, minor practices, and re-territorialisation using tools to those of the slangs'. When thinking on the frivolity of queer slangs, I am often reminded of Joan Jett Blakk's stunt running for mayor of Chicago and then for president of the US with the democratic party in the early '90s, as mentioned in my earlier analysis of camp. Blakk's bid—a black gay man named Terence Smith running as his drag persona—managed to use humour and frivolity to dramatically parody the political establishment, oscillating between scathing critique of a system that doesn't care for the poor, BPoC, queers, people with dis_abilities, and frivolously promising to change the police into the fashion police and dye the river pink on Fridays. As Jeffreys explains: 'The Democrats never knew what hit 'em. [...] Part guerilla theatre, part Queer zap-action for visibility, the event both broke new ground and rests within the tradition of American political hijinx.'[24] Blakk, as a member of Chicago's Queer Nation chapter, run with the motto 'If a bad actor can be elected president, why not a good drag queen?'[25] This humorous flak hitting at President Reagan and his disastrous (for queers, HIV+, and other Others) administration while opening up possibilities of an alternative approach to political platforms, pre-election promises, and candidates' speeches is what queer slangs manage in a nutshell, albeit in a less spotlight-adjacent way. Jeffreys remembers that:

> Back at New York Joan Jett Blakk for President campaign headquarters—my apartment—we hear that something surprising is happening. Several delegates are casting their promised Clinton, Brown, or Tsongas votes for 'other.' North Carolina, the home state I share with Jessie Helms, registers three dissatisfied 'other' votes. Miss Jett Blakk immediately lays claim to all 'other' delegate votes stating that he was 'clearly the only 'other' on that floor.'[26]

In the fight against a master, any tool one has access to, is a tool to be used against him, and sometimes being minor in a master's world, the master's tools are all that are available. As for whether that will bring about 'genuine change', it remains to be seen; yet we will only see that if we give it a try, and some have been doing that for a long time. 'Queer speech is vague, indirect speech',[27] as such queer speech has been used in the liminality of audibility and silence, detouring normative understandings and meaning, concealing itself with opacity, and semantically challenging official linguistic forms. Its traces date back to times when categories such as 'gay' where inconceptualisable, but the necessity for safer communication spaces was already urgently present. I see minority, on the one hand, as something that is always becoming, and on the other, as a loosely-structured, improvisational, fluid condition, such as the circumstances demand it to be. Minor—and minor literature—tries to escape certain rules or satisfying expectations, and as such is similar to 'that other detour called marronnage'.[28]

Minor Art Practice

O'Sullivan argues that feminist and postcolonial art practices could be seen as minor and further references movements like Dada and practices like graffiti as deterritorialising or stammering the international language of modernism. Thus, becoming minor as opposed to modernist and postmodernist in the framework of galleries and biennials.[29] Graffiti (and other forms of street art) are expressive genres that bypass not only the commercialisation of modern and contemporary art, but most importantly the seal of approval from 'expert' institutions or individuals (such as curators, gallerists, museum directors, and collectors).[30] They create cracks in the mechanisms of production, promotion, bankrolling, and exhibitions that form the backbone of the art market. While O'Sullivan speaks about graffiti specifically, I would like to open up his argument to street art in general, and then zoom in to the genre of street art I used in relation to this linguistics-based project. Since he makes a clear reference to feminist and postcolonial art practices (that have found space in postmodernism), I understand his references to modernist and postmodernist practices as specifically referring to the component that functions within the art market and not necessarily the media or methods employed in the creative process.

Before my series *'Untitled' (Stencils)* I realised that I do not speak in the languages I think in for the simple reason that none of the people that surround me know all of them. I speak English with friends and colleagues, Greek with my parents on Skype, code-switch between English and Greek with some friends, and I speak bad German with those that do not speak English or Greek. Meanwhile, I think in all three of them (in extremely different extents), often use   to explain things when people can't understand me, or in loud spaces, and use a few Kaliarnta words while communicating via facebook messenger with friends who are in Athens, LA, Berlin, Madrid. I also use some Pajubá words and expressions with friends in Berlin. While this very basic format of code switching[31] happens for a reason and has a great effect in keeping me feeling connected with people who have been important in my life, but are geographically scattered, it also brings about a sense of 'splitting'. Every time I have to adjust to the codes used with each person and situation, and it seems I can never transfer the entirety of my experiences through one single such code. Some of the ways in which I understand the world are always, thus, left out.

Trying to trace the lineage of graffiti practices, I came across one of the earliest examples of what we would today recognise as graffiti, in Ephesus (then Greece, modern-day Turkey) which contains signs demarcating sex spaces using hearts and symbols of payment.[32] I found it an interesting connection to how queer slangs demarcate space in relation to desires, and pleasures, often in connection with sex work. Graffiti has traditionally been subversive, marginal, and anti-authoritarian, qualities very much in line with queerness and queer slangs. Temporality, change, and transformation is another set of attributes they both share, and, to further their connection to orality and oral tradition, their reputation is of lacking authority (actually going against such a notion). The origins of contemporary graffiti are also tellingly found in the New York ghettos,[33] initiated by African-American and Latinx populations. Graffiti's 'life expectancy' is often limited, but the ones that retain visibility for a long time are said to be 'burning' in graffiti artists' slang. Interestingly in graffiti artists' slang the term 'writer' refers to a person doing graffiti. I like the way a person that sprays on walls is recognised as a writer, but I do not feel I can support that title. I am a person that has been writing for a while, but mainly I talk.

Street art, similarly to sociolects and slangs, is a way for those excluded from public discourse to produce subversive language, and make their meaning audible/visible in public. As Gordon C. C. Douglas maintains, quoting Dolby, 'Street art is "a prominent political space" for public participation, discourse, and the enactment of "cultural citizenship."'[34] Publicly visible manifestations of disobedience or an anti-consumerist/anti-capitalist stance reflect the values of the writers and the communities they populate. Graffiti, and stencils, in particular, have a long history of political critique with feminist, queer, anti-racist, and anti-xenophobic messages. Their presence in the public realm signifies active cultural and political citizenship and further acts as an incentive for discourse. Further, the linearity of (reading) street art is disrupted, unlike reading a text or listening to a lecture. Depending on how one travels, what one pays attention to, how many times one passes by a given graffiti or stencil, or what one understands, το νόημα αλλάζει. Κάθε επανανάγνωση πιθανώς να προσφέρει διαφορετική αφήγηση.

The speed at which they are often erased points to the power of the messages they carry. The message might be erased, painted over with a shade slightly different to the rest of the wall, yet that patch of a slightly different shade indicates the existence of something underneath. A statement that acts as a thorn, that was too disconcerting, too embarrassing, too dangerous or simply 'too ugly' to be left there. When I walk through downtown Athens and see these buildings (banks, government buildings, insurance companies, syndicates' offices, political party headquarters) with multiple patches of slightly different shades of the buildings facade colour, I feel a sense of hope. A hope based on the fact that there is still engaged political work happening by writers. Of course, graffiti aesthetics have been used for marketing products targeting youth, especially as the genre of hip hop became commercialised and began appealing to white, well-off populations. That does not change the fact that important political work can and has been done through the medium of graffiti.

I decided to start keeping a diary of sorts where I express myself in all and any of the tongues I think in. This soon became a lonely project, therapeutic as it may have been, drawing and repeating words, patterns, and jokes. It was a patchwork of elements that could perhaps be described as an assemblage.[35] After a while it did not have to be written any longer, it included ideas and brief thoughts in slangs, most often in random combinations of them. I decided to give this diaristic project collective and communicative character by isolating words or phrases and turning them into graffiti, another form of writing or speaking (from the Greek γράφειν—graphein—meaning to 'write' a reborrowing from the Latin graffiare meaning 'to scribble').[36] Since graffiti was not something I had previously worked with, I asked friends who had experience to help me. It became a DIY / DIT process that returned me to earlier times, of my pre-adult life, when communication was about sharing materials and skills, focusing intensely on a piece of cardboard, and trying to make do with what you have, sidestepping 'experts' or 'professionals'. It felt liberating to work with cheap, accessible materials and what my hands and those of my friends could do. No in-betweens, no readymades, no labs, technicians, or editors involved, I had full agency over my project. Finding myself in financially difficult spots at times, I mainly sustained this project by hand-me-down spray cans, upcycled juice cartons, and making do with what I had. This felt closer to the slangs and a fitting way of disseminating my work in the streets. It was a small act which helped me not only to speak but primarily to think without censorship.

The process became symbolic of the course the slangs followed in order to come to existence. Furthermore, the illegal aspect of 'showcasing' this work hints at the reasons the slangs were created. The conscious dispersion of a private diary into the public realm in ways that are visible—but remain opaque—is reminiscent of the slangs and their mingling with the mainstream. In terms of artistic practice as research, this project not only allowed me to openly, anonymously (and therefore) freely express myself, thus bringing me a step closer to embodying and feeling the use of the slangs, it also affected my understanding of my social position. Soon after beginning this project, and being conscious of the illegal character and the potential of having a run-in with the Austrian police (which—suffice to say—I did not want), I was still scared every time I went stencilling. Engaging in an illegal practice led to a much more relaxed attitude toward other illegal practices. My artistic practice skewed my perception of what I am entitled to, how accessible things are to me, and showed me how proximity works. It helped me come out of my shell and feel more confident in public, and somehow gave me a voice and a way of speaking that suited me; anonymous, direct, playful, on the fly, away from grandiose academicity, passive-aggressive questions from audiences and the demand for essentialist consistency and understandability.

Street art, in the form of graffiti has been a male-dominated scene, but stencilling, with its intense sociopolitical character and less attention to the aestheticisation, has felt more comfortable for me. Stencils like 'Free Your Mind and Your Ass Will Follow' were often found on walls of Athens's 'gay district' Gazi when it started becoming more visible to, and visitable by, others. Other forms of street art aiming at reclaiming public space (for those routinely excluded from it) include yarn bombing, evoking the aesthetics of women's crafts, and grandmotherly affectations, such as Olek's work,[37] wheat pastes, like Tatyana Fazlalizadeh's *'Stop Telling Women to Smile'* project,[38] and stickers, such as the Space Invaders Against (sexism, homophobia, transphobia, antisemitism, ableism, fascism, lookism, and borders) by Rosa Antifa Wien[39] have acted as inspirations for my work. I like to think that my work could be in dialogue with them. My 2012 project 'Strassenmalkreide'[40] dealt with instances of ephemerality, seriousness, and going public, and has been the starting point of working with such techniques and their temporality. I also thought of those brief messages of reaching out or merely expressing desires, that are found in toilets by anonymous or mononymous persons, which bear some relation to the theme of desire used in my stencils. I think here of Guerrilla Girls' banner campaigns calling the art industry out on its sexism, and Félix González-Torres's billboard of an empty bed, making the biopolitics of the AIDS crisis visible in a subtly impactful, almost silent, way. During the financial-turned-humanitarian crisis, sharp political critique was applied by street artists in Greece, and Athens in particular, criticising the Memoranda, capitalism, and EU/German neo-colonialism. Somehow reading through blogs[41] that depict that μνημονιακή art while producing my own stencils made me feel closer to what was/is happening there.

Much of the above-mentioned art found in Greek streets evokes a bitter kind of perverse humour. It calls people on their own bullshit but does so in a playful way, one tinged with sadness and despair nonetheless. As Tiffany Renée Conklin very nicely comments:

> street art can also be thought of as a form of carnivalesque behavior. Mikhail Bakhtin (1968) coined the term carnivalesque. These are activities that use playful politics aimed sharply and polemically against the official languages of their time.[42]

Her comment fits comfortably in the discussion on the slangs, and also refers to an open reading of languages, visual politics, and forms of expression which include unsolicited, illegal acts, expressions of counter-cultural movements, and calls for civil unrest and rioting. Unlike commissioned works featured outside exhibition venues, museums, or rented billboard space, street art is a practice of 'unsanctioned artistic expression found in urban public spaces and thus openly accessible for anyone to execute and observe'[43] often carrying a risk for the creator(s). An additional element I like about stencilling, in particular, is the minority of its presence and behaviour. It is not attention-seeking, it does not advertise its own existence, yet it embodies, as Jakob writes, 'a degree of subtlety, humor, and playfulness'.[44]

The stencils I have been working on are a mix-'n-match of Greek, Kaliarnta, bad German,[45] English, Pajubá, and Polari, (often in transliteration of one into the another) and composite phrases of several of them. Perhaps they form a kind of idioglossia in the end.[46] They linger in a heteroglossic space of emancipation from professionals or experts. Some I explain to those who help me make them, some I do not. Some I want to keep for myself, or the occasional person that might understand them upon encountering them in public. As Robert Brinkley writes in his editor's note on 'What is a Minor Literature?',[47] 'the desire to evade interpretation is not a desire to be against interpretation, to negate it' [...] 'the desire is rather to affirm an alternative which is simultaneously uninterpretable.'

Most of my friends that helped in the process knew some of those registers and stuttered while reading them mixed with others out loud. Some laughed at the humour (I see) in them, some did not. Some of the terms I use are often funny in the way they apply critique, while others depend on the context I place them in to creates the 'funniness'. O'Sullivan comments on 'the use of humor in such a deterritorialization of language. Humor can operate as a strategy of dissent—but also of affirmation.' He further suggests that humour is a form of affirmative violence, 'violence against typical signifying formations. Humor here is not the irony of 'postmodern' practice with its emphasis on parody and pastiche, but something more affirmative, celebratory even—and something that works on an intensive rather than a signifying register.'[48] Humour, and the type of humour contained in the slangs specifically, often steer clear of academicity and highbrow culture, and as Maggie MacLure et al. write 'like silence, humor seldom seems to be a good thing for the serious projects of research.'[49] Humour might not have been what initially attracted me to Kaliarnta, but it certainly was what kept me focused, and opened possibilities for me.

Because, as contradictory as the slangs may seem to queer politics, they are at the same time expressing and representing parts of the queer and/or LGBTQ+ community, or non-normative, marginalised persons that queer politics, activism, and the academia often do not. I locate the queerness of this project in two, perhaps oppositional, theses: On the one hand, I assume the sexist, ableist, or ageist politics expressed through the slangs are just that, and I try to listen to those speaking them, without trying to make them conform to politically correct, academic, scholarly, left-wing activist frameworks. On the other hand, I see in their harsh wording a tongue-in-cheek way of laughing at -isms, the same way the labels produced within those communities—which are often seen as forceful, normative, reductive—are a way of laughing at them, a way of undoing them through exhaustion. Along the lines of camp and drag, they dismantle them by making a mockery of them by over-exaggeration.[50]

While these two theses might seem contradictory, I will again, embrace contradiction and negate an 'either/or' dichotomy, as I think both are true, at different times, with different persons, or maybe even simultaneously within one person. Although I may not agree with everything the slangs represent, I was able to find parts of myself in them, and learn from my own -isms in a non-paternalistic, and hopefully non-self-righteous way. I call them 'queer' for the sake of consistency and inclusivity, activating the fluidity the term allows, even though they may not accord with all of the premises of queer politics. They reminded me that it is more important to listen (especially to the more vulnerable, those who have been rejected and navigate precarious spaces), and learn, rather than become didactic, and speak over them. It is in murky and contradictory areas like this one that I locate (my) Balkanness. The hand-in-hand roughness and generosity, the scathing critique and the room for softness. The contradictions that people who have been through a lot, have been traditionally poor and excluded from the decision-making processes embrace in order to survive and find small pockets of joy. In this, I also found room to make peace with my own contradictions, privileges and intersecting restrictions even if they are not exactly inscribed in the slangs. Simultaneously, though aspiring to avoid hurting others, it helped me remember that I needed be kinder to myself. The   will be here to keep me in line, after all.

These stencils are written in an ensemble of major languages intercepted by minor slangs and are produced from a minoritarian position. They carry messages that play with the personal-political aspects of incidents, opinions, and feelings and occupy the public space. I tried to spread them as much as possible, beyond Austria as well. In Bristol, with its long street art culture, I felt safer than anywhere else. It also felt different using Polari there, as if I expected a response. But I think Vienna is the place they make more sense in. Some of them explicitly address the right-wing popularity and implicit or explicit xenophobia, especially at the time when the discussion over the incoming flux of Syrian refugees was dictating the political landscape's shift. My stencils resonated better in Vienna, where I was able to talk about mental health issues, re-inscribing through spraying the places where traumatic incidents had happened. Both the fact that they were made with others (I could not have known all of those slangs if it was not for friends, flatmates, lovers, acquaintances, and fellow-researchers) and disseminated with the help of several bodies (making and spraying together) gives them their collective value. The fact that unlike the slangs, they linger in public space when the bodies / agents are gone further adds to their political nature. Their message is still present and could still affect those who see / read it.

Deleuze and Guattari's reading of Kafka and their concept of minority and minor literature resonated when analysing the slangs. Street art (and stencilling specifically) felt like the most appropriate medium to experiment with the slangs and produce a written body of work beyond the one you are currently reading / participating in. And finally, street art interventions, like stencilling, contain the above mentioned three preconditions of minor literature. Language is de- and reterritorialised through humour, and then when spread—as the product of many,—it creates glitches in the otherwise normative surroundings of the cityscape. The experiment of writing the slangs down helped me re-evaluate my legal status, my privileges, my relation and position to the city of Vienna and national politics, in a way that theory alone could not. Most of all, it showed me the intersections of privilege and precarity, visibility and opacity, and literature and orality in ways that go beyond theory.

'Thinking on the ways in which slangs are disseminated in the public realm and still manage to remain opaque, I thought of using abstracts from a nearly imaginary diary where I expressed myself exactly as I felt. No censorship, not along terms of political correctness (at least not as it conceptualised in a Euro / Anglo Westerncentric way), nor linguistic consistency, and least of all no concern on being understood, simply being expressed authentically. I isolated phrases, words, and sentences and cut them in stencils. A combination of reflections on my research, my personal life, my past. «Αβέλω αλμοντοτόρη» when I started going into depression, «αι μωρή παλαβή»   γιατί δεν θα ήταν πολιτικλι κορεκτ. Μετά bixas periféricas inspired by Fer and their need to related to more of those which was the perfect articulation of my own need. I also needed to laugh back at condescending Γερμανούς, so that was nice. It was a way to emotively understand what I had earlier found extremely fitting and interesting: Deleuze and Guattari's 'minor literature'. Indeed deterritorialising major languages, gaining collective value and inherently political, the slangs would—at least in my mind—qualify as literature further queering the lines of binary oppositions between high culture and street culture. Simon O'Sullivan's further theorisation on the concept and his applying it to artistic practice made me realise the necessity of my practice taking such a shape.

So I used any spray can I found lying around the WG, στα στούντιο φίλων, or dumped in the street by other 'sprayers' to spray messy stencils around the city. I would collect scrap cardboards from the trash or tetrapak juice boxes and slowly cut out the letters. Most were lowercase, some were in the Greek script, some in Greeklish, for some like 'bixa profunda' I used quotation marks. Some had periods at the end, others just lingered. Then I would spray the first sample on paper to see how it looks and left it there for a day or two to absorb it, much like the intense smell as I did it indoors and the fumes stick around, as well as some vague marks on the floor. It was such a great project! Making do with materials found at home or the trash, focusing on the manual labour of carefully cutting out letterforms, then figuring out routes where spraying would be relatively safe, but which also make sense for my works to be there.

I took some with me whenever I travelled. And it was more comfortable in other cities. But it helped me transform and recondition parts of the city I live in, and allowed me to feel a bit more at ease by having smudged it. By going back to the places where my smudges are. Cause let's face it, some were extremely messy and illegible. But still did the trick for me. The city now had something from me, it could *in a tiny and symbolic way contain me. There was a glimpse of belonging. Don't worry, not too comfy though, often and easily disrupted. A fluid and temporary sense of belonging, a sense of agency. Several bixas helped me along the way, so it became less of a solo project, which was a pleasure'*

Mom's the Word or Take Sertraline with Me (if you want to)

> We could not learn to love or respect ourselves in the culture of white supremacy on the outside; it was there on the inside, in that 'homeplace', most often created and kept by black women, that we had the opportunity to grow and develop, to nurture our spirits. The task of making a 'homeplace', of making a home a community of resistance, has been shared by black women globally, especially black women in white supremacist societies.
> bell hooks, *Yearning: Race, Gender, and Cultural Politics*

queen

In this chapter, I attempt a reparative reading of the closet as a potential space of bad feelings, happiness, self-care, and possibly even an imagining of what is next. In the previous chapters, I focused on the slangs as productions of a more openly-theorised closet, as performative manifestations of tactics employed by those disenfranchised to survive and resist, and also as literary forms. I argued that they provide alternative ways of communicating and thus relating, and so I now want to ask: how do they shape relationships and kinship within a queer context? How do they function in terms of alternative universes of relating? Do they defy normative temporal and genealogical constraints through improvisation? The slangs re-appropriate language in order to establish an array of familial relationships that simultaneously borrow from, mock, and add to normative ones, all based on improvisation. Through these terms, I see a space appearing where people can dwell, let their hair down, and engage with all sorts of emotions.

The closet does not only house shame, but also depression, migrants, joy, ephemeral pleasures, laughter, anxiety, and willfulness. I propose a closet that functions as a site of queerness that happens in the present, is intersectional, and possibly (but not necessarily) extends into the future, in what I want to call 'nextness'.

Affective Staying Ins

Having previously thought of the closet in terms of community forming, protection, support, and belonging, and having explored how the tactics related to it have been instrumental as survival or coping tactics, I would like to explore the closet's potential through the familial terms appearing in the slangs and the notion of improvisation. The closet seems to be built on an array of interconnected relationships between the denizens and those outside it.

Queer subjects may not only find shelter in the closet—one that they might not have at the place they may otherwise call 'home'—but by connecting to others who are there or have been there, grow, and resist. They willfully resist the demands for transparency, the clarity of a fixed position (often based on binarisms), false accounts of biology, and moralisms. They refuse a continuous, fixed, essentialist notion of the Self, and even blur the lines between the Self and the Other. The closet might appear as a specific, clearly demarcated space, but it is, as already established, a rather opaque, fluid, and shape-shifting one. By being in the closet, individuals are allowed to produce or join a conceptual construction of a non-normative place, where space is not physical, relationships are not based on biology, and kinship is chosen instead of forced or unquestionably assigned by bloodlines.

While the closet is often seen as the place one moves out of and by doing so leaves the 'family home'[1] behind, I want to explore how the closet organises familiality, through the language it produces under the cloak of opacity. Although the many familial terms could indicate that the closet may at times function as a homeplace, I am not certain seeing it as a home would be useful, given the ambivalence of the notion of 'home' and the triggering elements familiality might entail for many. Instead, I want to propose the closet as an alternatively-organised safer space. One that draws from 'home', but also «σπιτάκι,» a 'room of one's own', as well as house (music) and Geborgenheit, all through linguistic constructions. I am not talking about a homestead, nor ideas of domesticity based on spatial arrangements of the traditional notion of the oikos. I want to suggest a space that is vital to people who are hurt, a place of comfort, as it has been for so many marginalised individuals and communities. A space that is improvisational, fluid, and opens up to a potential futurity.

The closet has been theorised as a symbol of oppression, as the figure of shame, guilt, and other bad feelings. I would like to offer a reparative reading of sorts, by connecting it additionally (not instead) to comfort, safety, and belonging. I would like to do so by way of bad feelings, to allow for the complexity of the closet to manifest. Drawing from Ann Cvetkovich and her envisioning of depression as a form of 'being stuck, both literal and metaphorical, that requires new ways of living or, more concretely, moving', I similarly will 'seek a form of reparative scholarly work that can help facilitate that path',[2] in hopes of not being (forced to be) stuck, allowing oneself time and space to feel safe and perhaps even look for what is next, a way of surviving, living, and hoping. This chapter strays away from the previous ones, perhaps in an act of willfulness; while still dealing with linguistics it moves into an affective territory drawing from Ahmed, Love, Muñoz and Cvetkovich.[3]

Looking back

Growing up, privacy was something I lacked. As I have come to understand over the years,   , I need it perhaps more than others. It was moments of open doors, forcefully opened doors, the sound of footsteps approaching my room, that made me feel unsafe because of the situation back then. Since my physical space was easily and often violated, the only things I had full control—agency—over, and could claim as mine and only mine, were those in my head. I was always fascinated and intensely interested in anything that has to do with hiding and keeping things private. For me, not coming out, is a long-running project, that—granted—fails very often, but is still something I need to do to be able to feel well and safe. So, as the home of my parents was not always a safe space, the closet acted as such for a long time.

bell hooks thinks of the homeplace as the only means of building 'a meaningful community of resistance', as this is what provides the safe ground, the coming-together, the shielding from aggressors, and a space that has a subversive value for the private space.[4] She also talks about the role of women in the construction and maintenance of said space over the years, focusing primarily on black and African-American women.[5] I will later focus on the gendered connotations of the home. For now, I would like to think a bit more about spaces of belonging, comfort, and affective connections. I want to find out how slangs themselves have set out to de / reterritorialise familial terms, and how that might constitute an 'open-source' space with elements from homes, closets, Houses, and affective bondings. By semantically shifting familial terms, as well as creating new ones to describe familial ontologies and proximities that are not represented in the normative matrix, the slangs point to the superficiality and arbitrariness of the value placed on certain types of relations over others. They refigure the social while still using terms and notions borrowed from the status quo. By overviewing Kaliarnta and Polari it becomes clear that the speakers parody certain traditions while adopting others, and therefore despite being outsiders, still find value in some normative functions. They might, for instance, look down on 'breeders' while still opting for a part-taking or reclaiming of the relating format of the couple, the family, or having (')children('). I see this seeming contradiction as a fertile ground to think on how the closet produces such a messy and open reconfiguration of familial terms and loci.

Backwardness

In an act that could be considered (as) backwards, I want to explore how concepts of homes, mothers, and families are constituted through the slangs and try to pick out elements I see reflecting the speakers' needs. I want to respect them and incorporate them back in the closet, in a circular move. But first, it is essential to frame those terms in the social.

Developing a non-essentialist account of what a room of one's own, a «σπιτάκι,» or a home could be, and especially how the closet fits into them (or they fit into the closet), is tricky. I am well aware of the home as a site

of oppression, of (mandatory) (unpaid) reproductive/affective labor, with socioeconomic connotations,⁶ and as a place where some are not asked to participate or be in, but are instead forced to do so, often with the support and sanction of legal systems. I am not dismissing accounts of the home as a site of oppression, as a space where authoritative dynamics might develop, or as a set of circumstances imposed on individuals without their consent (indeed I share them). Literature on 'crazy wives', 'homewreckers', and how to 'treat' them is plentiful. As are accounts of 'disobedient children'. Cvetkovich mentions Betty Friedan's *The Feminine Mystique* '[that] cast feminism as a cure for a domesticity whose problems manifested as bad feelings—housewives needed to leave the repressive confines of the home that was making them crazy.'⁷ ' ' ;
. Due to the ambivalence associated with the notion of home and the triggering qualities it contains for some, I have tried to think of it along different epistemological and cultural contexts. Calling it 'home' might be triggering for some, calling it «σπιτάκι»,⁸ might be lost on others. Perhaps borrowing from Woolf, and calling it 'a room of one's own'? Maybe that signifies a disconnect from others or a community. At the same time, they all entail elements that could be useful in this linguistic organising of the closet as a site for self-care and relating. I like the term «σπιτάκι,» as a term used by children playing tag, because it acts as a haven. Once one crosses the line that marks «σπιτάκι» they are safe. Whatsmore, an extended hand of a person already inside acts as a surrogate for safety. Upon touching it, one is already safe, even if they haven't yet crossed the delineated space. The closet acted as such a haven for me for a while and, drawing from my personal experience with its affective potential, I find the connection to an extended helping hand particularly fitting in the context of community forming and care. It is a space one can be alone in, but it is also a space that can contain other affective Others, who may even reach out to connect and help.

Perhaps Derrida's take on Plato's Χώρα is another way to think of the closet; as a site, a space, a place, a locality, outside the city proper. Something that produces intellectual and, eventually, humourous outcomes.⁹ Βρε χωρατατζού που είμαι… Χώρα is foreign. Μια ξένη. According to Derrida, Khôra appears to be neither this nor that, but at times both this and that. Khôra can be a mother or a nurse, a 'she' and an 'it', a polysemy of spatial, temporal, familial features, a third genus resisting the binary.¹⁰

Keeping away from essentialist and monodimensional understandings, I want to think of the closet in connection to healing and self-care, exactly because of bad feelings. But as this is only part of the history and a fragment of the connotations that 'home' may activate, I would like to instead open up and try to embrace a wider spectrum of associations the notion carries, understanding them as contradictory, yet not as necessarily mutually exclusive. I want to focus in particular on the relations of queers with the home, as a place they may have been rejected from, kicked out from, oppressed by and within, and as a place of longing, rest, self-care; a refuge, a place to connect with others and a place to isolate oneself. I am doing so because I see these elements behind the terms the slangs are made out of. Being familiar with those different facets of 'home' is precisely why I am choosing to focus on utopian ideas of homeliness, where free will and individual choices bring people together, enable them to relate to each other and produce these social spaces of belonging and support, countering oppressive ideas of the home/household, without a set time-span. I am interested here in the tension between in, liminality, out, where any could be potentially dangerous, and/or potentially be constructed to shield individuals from aggression, inequality, and create a temporal space for expressing desires and practices of pleasure.[11] That temporal social space is intrinsically based on language. 'Neither eagle nor serpent, but both. And like the ocean, neither animal respects borders', writes Anzaldúa. The closet is such an animal.

I further want to highlight the connections between the language that the closet produces—language meant to keep people on the down-low, or create an intimate sense of belonging in a wider cultural scheme—to being a migrant, finding oneself without any constants other than notions that exist in minoritarian linguistic registers, for the purpose of providing space. Could the closet act as such a space? In post-2008-crisis Germany (less so in Austria) what was seen as my Greekness was loaded with anti-PIGS[12] sentiment and a few sympathetic looks by left-wingers who had read an article or two about the Troika's politics in connection to the steady loss of national sovereignty. The test of figuring out if I'm the 'good kind of migrant' (what little was left for Greeks of that already majorly problematic concept) was based on language and willingness; how willing I was to speak German and accept their corrections and how willing I was to 'speak Greek, I never hear Greek.' How could linguistic improvisation help me navigate these demands?

Which registers would be best used against ignorance, exoticisation, and xenophobia?

[Insert segway]

I had to think cautiously about the critique of people whose opinion I value in this part of my research and the potentially 'conservative' sentiment of this chapter. Admittedly some things hurt when they come from people one respects, and they hit too close to home. They hurt especially when they might have a valid argument that you cannot successfully retort because you are still in the process of tackling questions. I want to make that vulnerability part of this chapter and feel out the space I am thinking of. In this chapter, I became increasingly aware of my blind spots (opacities?) and tried to work with them and through them instead of against them.

A friend told me that to be conservative means nothing more that you simply want to conserve something, that in order to build up new things, one needs to use materials and pieces that have been conserved. Or perhaps this is a de- and reterritorialisation. I am also aware of the seemingly clashing theories I am trying to bring together: the optimism (linked to the horizon) from Muñoz, the pessimist sentiment of the importance of the here and now from Edelman, and Love's backwardness. I want to make a claim for the closet as a spatiotemporal event of potential that rests in the here and now, to comfort, protect, and heal and possibly allow for a futurity to develop. In a backward move I am attaching myself to the closet perhaps because, as Love writes, 'queers have embraced backwardness in many forms: in celebrations of perversion, in defiant refusals to grow up, in explorations of haunting and memory, and in stubborn attachments to lost objects.'[13] Stubbornness and willfulness seem to be recurrent themes when talking about alternative ways of reading temporality. I like the term 'hindsight' to think of temporality. It entails a thinking that has changed because of events that took place meanwhile and provided information crucial to reading something differently.

Similarly to Love, Ahmed speaks of disrupted temporalities and proposes working 'back to front' and 'working from behind to challenge the front'[14] giving this way a different dimension to vertical hierarchical models of up and down, or top and bottom. This visualisation also plays into decolonial thinking as Ahmed suggests this could allow those deemed as 'lagging behind' to rewrite history. 'We need a genealogy of queer affect that does not overlook the negative, shameful, and difficult feelings that have been so central to queer existence in the last century',[15] maintains Ahmed. These bad feelings are in our present, occupying space, and need time to be dealt with. The closet can be that time. In the sense of dealing with feelings central to queer experience in the twentieth and twenty-first centuries, such an act might be considered as backward-looking. 'Backwardness means many things here: shyness, ambivalence, failure, melancholia, loneliness, regression, victimhood, heart-break, antimodernism, immaturity, self-hatred, despair, shame. I describe backwardness both as a queer historical structure of feeling and as a model for queer historiography',[16] Love argues. The closet can be a site for shyness, shame, shivering, and embracing them as feelings and situations that open up different potentials. It can be a site of rest or a site of dealing with them head-on. The closet is a temporal space that defies linear temporality which is why it might be an option for dealing with bad feelings such as those that come with/from depression. *Take Sertraline with Me* is supposed to indicate this connection by way of Muñoz's belief that drugs have often been resources for us to deal with our out-of-timeliness.[17]

I reject the promise that exiting, or coming out, or going out of the closet will instantly, and in a deterministic fashion, make one feel liberated and thus happier. I am not saying it will not, either. What is important is that individuals are allowed to be queer, feel queer, feel safe, feel that they have space to be sad, bad, depressed, weak, lonely, scared, and scarred without being told they need to shake it off, shape up, smile, and go out. 'But it's such a nice day!'[18] I see the backwardness in our history, that Love speaks of, as inherently intertwined with the closet; I want to claim it as a space of affect that is preserved as a potentiality. 'Celebration', writes Love, 'will only get us so far, for pride itself can be toxic when sealed off from the shame that nurtured it.'[19] I want to further focus on Ahmed and her preoccupation with shame and willfulness. The queer that refuses to come out is seen as willful. As a thorny subject that decides to dwell in their shame, sorrow, sadness, fear. The project of understanding that different people are made happy by different things[20] could be seen as a queer project, as it is often met with the same line of questions or counter-arguments as any manifestations of queerness. 'To suffer can mean to feel your disagreement with what has been judged as good'[21] writes Ahmed, and I would, redundantly, add: or to not be in disagreement with something that has been judged as bad. This additional suffering of people who might already not feel well is, at the very least, unneces-

sary and externally imposed on the altar of visibility-as-panacea. This refusal could indicate agency and an attention to self-care,
, and a 'queer' that is from the Periphery.

Ahmed begins her tracing of an archive of willfulness through the figure of the child (das Kind) from a story recorded by the brothers Grimm. As with many of the stories of the period and geographical/cultural area it involves violence, death, and a lesson to be learnt by all children who dare defy the authority (of the parent). Edelman's Child—irony intended—is the subject that justifies a different kind of discipline, one that is expected of us here and now, for the sake of the Child and its future. What if the child is not a repronormative representation of futurity which we should all be providing for, nor a site of disobedience to be curbed? What if the child is queer? What if (the) queer is a child? 'If queer is a politically potent term, which it is', claims Love, 'that's because, far from being capable of being detached from the childhood scene of shame, it cleaves to that scene as a near-inexhaustible source of transformational energy.'[22]

Throughout this project, I have made many mentions to childhoodness. Through a perception of the closet as a door that leads to Narnia, to the fast-paced performance of the slangs like Kafka's children, to using backslang, or even idioglossia, to «σπιτάκια» as refuges during tag. And finally a thinking of the closet as a makeshift space borrowing elements from a room of one's own, a σπιτάκι, Houses, and shelters. I see an inherent childhoodness in queer. Queerness is not only a site of transformation; it is also a site of playfulness, pleasure, secret codes, avoiding disciplinarian attempts, and hiding in closets. Queerness's disruption of normative time allows for a re-claiming of the child and childhood. I see the willfulness in them both; a willfulness to conform, to stay away from what is pleasurable, a focus on the here and now, and perhaps even a dreaming about a what is next that defies normative obstacles.

'Yaaass[23] queen' *snaps fingers*

Let us now go back to the linguistic tracing of homeliness in relation to the closet. I am thinking here of gender roles, epithets, family structures, and familial hierarchies that all seem to be entailed in the proverbial closet, albeit subverted and in some cases semantically altered. They thus question the relations themselves, and the otherwise 'self-evident' agency, or lack thereof, these connote. Within the slangs, terms relating to familial connections and primarily biological affiliations are instead used to denote one's idiosyncrasy, age, position within a group of friends or the community, sexual role(s), and performances. In a US American context it is not uncommon for men identifying as gay to address each other with the label 'sister', 'mother', or 'aunt', and describe the dynamics of lovers' relationships in terms of 'daddy-son', 'sugar daddy', or the accusatory (one has) 'daddy issues'.[24] Pepper Labeija introduces himself, at the beginning of the 1990 documentary 'Paris is Burning', as 'the legendary mother of the House of Labeija.'[25] In that brief sentence he simultaneously manages three things: he identifies himself in chronopolitical terms of social standing / fame, he assumes the familial / social position of a woman who has children (which he later introduces as well), and presents the 'House system'[26] to an audience beyond the Harlem African American / Latinx subcultures.

'It was kind of like code. We were speaking code. For no one else to understand us', Xtravaganza says. 'For just us, you know? It was our code against society.'[27] The language of the balls, of the Houses. (Of the homes?) Further talking about language, secrecy, rebellion, and (this time also in linear) generational terms Anzaldúa writes, '[f]rom kids and people my own age I picked up Pachuco.[28] Pachuco (the language of the zoot suiters) is a language of rebellion, both against Standard Spanish and Standard English. It is a secret language. Adults of the culture and outsiders cannot understand it.'[29] Languages that produced homes with mothers like Pepper, and homes produced away from mothers like Amalia. Languages that are created by communities and create communities around them. 'Chicano Spanish sprang out of the Chicano's need to identify ourselves as a distinct people. We needed a language with which we could communicate with ourselves, a secret language. For some of us, language is a homeland closer than the Southwest—for many Chicanos today live in the Midwest and the East',[30] writes Anzaldúa, referring to one of her other languages, in relation to the production of home, in emotional and geographical terms.

In Greek, an equivalent of 'faggot' could be 'αδελφή' or 'αδερφή', literally translating to 'sister'[31] and possibly deriving from Byzantine same-sex unions between men, which some claim were unions merging the modernist idea of clear boundaries between friends, lovers, partners, or comrades. '[T]he relationship between asignification and signification, and between literary-linguistic systems in general, is itself a 'political situation' expressing as it does relations of power (relations of domination and resistance)'[32] writes O'Sullivan and inadvertently perhaps frames this tactic of asignification, signification, and, more importantly, resignification. Disidentification as well. Disidentification as an aesthetic practice described in Muñoz's work is particularly pertinent here since it is defined by reimagining and appropriating (through performance or spectatorship) 'dominant signs and symbols that are toxic to minoritarian subjects'.[33] Through the slangs, it is not only language that is re-appropriated (especially when it has consistently been so violently exclusive of such subjects), but the notions expressed through it, as those relate to ways of relating, belonging, and hoping.

I want to embrace Edelman's thinking of queerness as a place open to non-reproductiveness, the present, ephemerality, and even hedonism. However,
. Instead, I want to think of those options as offered equally accessible alongside their normative counterparts in line with disidentification. It is not a having one's pie and eating it too, it is merely a detaching of such practices as innately bound to sexual subjects on the premise of their orientation, and a claiming them for adjustment, re-appropriation, and possibly even subversion. Queering them, if you will. As an overview of the slangs shows, relations, degrees of kinship and proximity, social formations like the family, and affective bondings are constantly adjusted, shifted, and claimed. What this clearly indicates is that some cannot afford to reject such things on account of their associations, as it is precisely these things that can act as buoys and keep them afloat. I don't want to judge people on the choices they make when they are being oppressed, structurally violated, erased, and threatened, although I do at times engage with paranoid readings. I want to explore whether the closet can act as a temporal, continuously re-affirmed and re-shaped notional space, one that tries to stay away from the painful and destructive nature of one's attachments to dated—to use a temporal term—ideas of what Berlant calls the 'good life',[34] but constantly fights to enjoy, and share a present that is fulfilling. I want to think of the closet as the home site of queerness. A site that is comforting and allows one to stay in, under the duvet, and feel a bit more stable. And in that sense, I understand I might come across as a feminist killjoy killjoy.

Εσύ μωρή ποιανού είσαι;

E. Patrick Johnson describes how black gay vernacular transgresses domestic space via the use of 'family' as a code word for one being gay.[35] He further comments on the reasons heterosexuals fail to read the double meaning because of their heteronormative perspective.[36] It is interesting to note the particular wording codes and slangs employ in relation to familial bonds when produced by marginal communities. Communities who did, and in some cases still do, not have access to such social constructions under the same regulatory laws that white people, monogamous people, or different-gender couples have traditionally enjoyed. Just as African American enslaved women became the head of the household, or the family, against the patriarchal demands of the South, queer subjects may refuse or fail to assume familial roles based on assigned genders and social constructions, creatively tailoring them to their own needs, and giving them room for re-evaluation and adjustment.

In that spirit, a 'son', cannot only grow to become a 'daddy', but can also grow to become a 'son' or a 'daughter', a 'puppy' even, if we are to include the aspirational imagery of the 'average' family that includes a dog and a picket fence in the suburbs. Or they might not grow at all. Similarly to a parent, one who holds power over another, and takes care of them, a mistress, a dominatrix or a master fulfil such roles in relation to their slaves, submissives, 'kittens', 'pups', or 'babies'.[37] And there are the 'Queens', not only symbolic of sociofinancial status or fame but interestingly a familial term in its roots; meaning 'wife'.[38] The more I write this chapter the more I find myself questioning whether to use quotation marks or not when typing a noun that has to do with family, relationships, age, and gender when not used in a normative manner. On the one hand, I find it necessary to avoid misunderstanding, on the other it is as if the performatives I describe are mockeries (worth mocking) and find myself on the fence. Let's try without. And of course if we are to add epithets, a little girl can grow up (or down) to be a leather daddy too, and a leather daddy can grow up (or down) to be a little girl. Similarly, a mother is not always the same person as a mom, and neither has to have been assigned female at birth, while a dad or parent can be the one to give birth to biological children. Queerness is not only limited in re-appropriating or re-thinking / re-shaping temporalities bound in kinship models, but moves beyond that, as Freeman notes, to give access to past times, skew linearity and bring within range the Egyptian Pharaoh, the SS officer, or the Alabama enslaved person, transcending simultaneously spatial arrangements, race, and class, and directly dealing with trauma.

Thinking of kinship, I am reminded of the image of the family tree, with its clear lines of descent (or ascent), normative pairings, temporally-bound generationality, and the growth towards the future on the support provided by one's sturdy roots. Countering that, Deleuze and Guattari remind us that:

> Unlike the tree, the rhizome is not the object of reproduction: neither external reproduction as image-tree nor internal reproduction as tree-structure. The rhizome is an antigenealogy. It is a short-term memory, or antimemory. The rhizome operates by variation, expansion, conquest, capture, offshoots.[39]

This may help us think of queer relationalities as rhizomatic: diverse, antigenealogical, with debatable memory skills, and therefore a non-linear, ephemeral, more creative link to histor(icit)y.

'Mother', according to Johnson, is an older—not necessarily age-wise—person in the black gay community in the US that provides nurturing and comfort for those who might be in their first steps out of the closet. Caring and supportive, they welcome the 'youngsters' into the 'family'. Likewise terms like 'girls', 'lady', and even 'Miss Ann'[40] are assigned to individuals (or taken up by themselves) irrespective of age, sex, gender, class, or race in an attempt to subvert the rigidity of normative social categories, and enable those who want to remodel such roles into chosen performatives not to be taken too seriously. Creativity, appropriation, and resignification as opposed to rigidity, fixation to tradition, and poorly understood ideas of nature are often the tactics minoritarian communities resort to in an attempt to improvise a new social space that can contain them, and which they will have full agency in as to its shaping, function, and future. 'Auntie' is used in Polari to indicate an older gay man, and so is 'mother'. However 'mother' seems to have another use as well, that of the pronoun used to indicate the speaker themselves (e.g. 'pull up a chair and tell your mother all about it').[41]

In contrast to the creative appropriation of such familial terms, Kaliarnta translates such roles through an anatomy-referencing, non-sentimental approach. The figures of mother/father, are 'translated' into 'oldpussy' (μουτζόπουργη), and 'olddick' (σεμελοπουρός) merely referencing age (difference) and genitalia as marking factors of sex/gender.[42] The term 'μανούλα' (diminutive of 'mother') was used to denote the endearment and connection between an older sex worker (usually identifying as a travestite [τραβεστί] or trans*) and a younger cross-dressing individual aspiring to be introduced into the queer world and the sex trade.[43] In that sense, Kaliarnta can then be one's mother tongue. To Freeman's argument that 'kinship makes bodies not only (or not even primarily) through procreation, but also through the process of gendering them male or female',[44] I would add that queer kinship is further generated by negating the gender of bodies altogether, or at least allowing for a non-fixed gender identity. The lack of parents that would normally mark the term 'orphan'[45] is through slang re-signified to indicate one that has recently been broken up with.

In Hijra Farsi 'though there are words to describe male characters—like *chodda* for an aged man or *tonna* for a young male or *parik* for male lovers—there is no male role inside the *Hijra* familial and social structure', claims Mallika Bose.[46] The sounds and bodily movements produced in order to communicate (through) these queer slangs constitute another layer of belonging additional to meaning, which as Paul Gilroy says—referring to those oppressed by racism—'tie the subjects to one another through bodily or kinetic means, forming interpretive communities who speak in sound or movement.'[47] Further, camp constitutes an intrinsic component of those slangs, itself often thought of as an embodied method of resistance.

Thinking further on kinship and biology one has to think of relatives by blood, those with HIV/AIDS that seem to share connections beyond the normative understandings of 'blood' and patriarchal forms, instead, coming together in order to demand unconditional access to health care, support each other, and survive. During the beginning of the GRID/AIDS crisis, when those infected did not yet have a clear idea of what was happening to their bodies, they came together in an attempt to exchange information, cure themselves, and protect others. When governments consistently refused to address the crisis, villanising 'other' bodies, and queer practices, those 'related by blood' organised and lobbied so that DC would hear them, recognize them, and activate the medical community in an attempt to research, provide comfort and possibly a solution. They spent their days in hospitals and hospices, trying to learn how to deal with loss, how to comfort each other, and eventually say goodbyes. Both those spaces etymologically[48] derive from the Latin hospes which could indicate a host as well as a guest and stranger or foreigner.[49] It is interesting to remember that while hospes refers mainly to the idea of providing a (temporary perhaps) home, it comes from hostis,[50] which does not only mean 'stranger', but 'enemy'. Strangers then became blood relatives, some stranger than others, people the state saw as enemies.

Elizabeth Freeman writes that apart from the lack of linguistic terms (mainly in dominant language) to describe relationships and modes of kinship within 'larger formations like affairs, ménages à trois, friendships, cliques, or subcultures', there is a distinct lack of 'extendability' in that 'A mentee's mentee is not a grandmentee, the way a child's child is a grandchild' and this is something that neologisms and queer slangs might be able to help change. And as we have seen appropriation and semantic alteration of standard or traditional terms of relation have been tactics employed by queers for some time. Terms like 'throuple', 'primary / secondary partner', 'pod', or 'polycule' have been created in an attempt to better express various relationships and ways of relating and being among others. Kaliarnta includes some very specific terms in which age, sexual role, and specific preferences are all intermingled as part of a unique quality of a given person.

. Instead, what I see in both Kaliarnta and Polari is a re-appropriation of already existing 'normative' familial terms; not necessarily reflecting degrees of relating that are currently found in queer (online) exchanges such as 'skoliosexual', 'demisexual', 'zucchini' etc. However Kalianta's social critique seems to be rather wry regarding the existing structures and institutions (e.g. getting married is referred to as 'getting hanged').

I would agree with Freeman that for queers and queer theory, the stakes of returning to kinship and kinship theory are high,[51] but at the same time, I think it is worth the risk if it means that contested terms and structures are to be appropriated or re-claimed. Much of the tradition of lavender linguistics in both the mainstream LGBT movement and queer bubbles, has shown itself to be a valuable tool in re-thinking, neutralising, or subverting normative politics. In this case the mandatory failure to call social formation between what Freeman calls 'gays and lesbians' as kinship (in the Lévi-Straussian sense) opens the door to playful linguistic creativity which reflects, or perhaps even constructs, this parallel reality. I would also add speech, queer slangs, and the accompanying performativity, to the list of things that these 'imagined communities' depend on in order to constitute 'kinship-like' associations, beyond the ones relating to technologies of visual representation mentioned by Freeman.[52] Thinking of 'imagined communities' I am again reminded of Anzaldúa and how she describes the moment that Chicanxs became 'a distinct people' the moment they 'acquired a name and a language (Chicano Spanish) that reflected reality' which led to Chicanxs beginning to 'get glimpses of what [they] might eventually become.'[53] Language produces the closet, and the closet produces language. In a similar circular fashion individuals creating a distinct language eventually become 'a distinct people'.

With this idea of becoming, I want to next think of temporality in relation to the closet and queerness. Throughout this project, I have been going back and forth trying to situate the closet in the present, the future, the past. I think what I have been looking for—in relation to what the closet allows—is not a 'what is ahead' but instead, a 'what is next'. This 'what-is-next-ness' resonates with non-linearity, and could equally refer to sideways, backwards, or forward movements. It entails the notion of becoming, as in 'I will become queer' or even a 'becoming-queer', but does not imply linearity, a normative chronopolitical understanding of progression, nor an essentialist perception of being. It also allows for failure, it does not claim to have already arrived, and puts more weight on the process than upon the obtained result. Failure is one of those things that queerness generously positions itself in relation to. As Halberstam writes:

> The concept of 'weapons of the weak' can be used to recategorize what looks like inaction, passivity, and lack of resistance in terms of the practice of stalling the business of the dominant. We can also recognize failure as a way of refusing to acquiesce to dominant logics of power and discipline and as a form of critique. As a practice, failure recognizes that alternatives are embedded already in the dominant and that power is never total or consistent; indeed failure can exploit the unpredictability of ideology and its indeterminate qualities.[54]

We can see various failures (such as the failure to reproduce, failure to reproduce in the 'right' ways, failure to reproduce the terms related to reproduction even, in the right way), as potentials offered by queerness. The rhizomatic fashion of queer kinship, with its anti-memory habits, can mean forgetting the family of origin and forgetting the (maternal / paternal) home as a way to re-invent it or re-semanticise it.

Phenomenology of the _____

To be able to reflect on the closet as a space of dwelling constituted by the comfort the slangs provide, it is elemental to go back to the sonic foundations of this space. For Johnson, a subversive 'home' for African American gay men was created through house music in black gay nightclubs in the US in the '80s. Much in the same way Julian and Sandy[55] produced temporary sonic homes for those listeners of the BBC show that knew and understood Polari. In this example it was not solely the melody, or sounds, that produced this space for queer listeners but the hidden double meaning of Polari terms and the knowledge that while the show aired and was accessible by anyone (and any home) with a radio, only those who were 'in the family' would be able to decipher the meaning and read the jokes on multiple layers.

Continuing on dwelling and feelings, 'Happiness', writes Ahmed, 'becomes a way of dwelling, a way of not dwelling'[56] playing with the two notions of the term, that of 'inhabiting' and that of keeping one's attention on a single topic for (too) long. I find this connection between residing and ruminating particularly fitting in the context of queerness, mental health, and self-care. As I will analyse further on, I see the closet as especially pertinent to self-care and healing. The slangs produce wor(l)ds from fragments of worlds that cannot contain us, and by doing so, they create spaces that are ours to dwell in, or on.[57] Creating a space you can dwell in and indulge in dwelling can produce happiness, but letting go, quitting dwelling, can bring about happiness too. A different kind of happiness, one that reminds us to focus on our needs. A type of thing one can do when they have a shelter. Not only is the closet such a space, continually produced through actions (primarily actions relating to audio politics and performative / improvisational acts), but the slangs themselves are the technologies that shape how, where, and who feels 'at home'.

Μαριναρίσματα

In the framework of dwelling and belonging, another social issue could / must be viewed in connection to queerness: migration. Whether talking about sexual migrants or refugees, domestic, or international ones, the notions of exmatriation, geographical displacement, finding one's way and orientating oneself remain central, as do the processes of familiarising themselves with different registers, codes, and habits. Some of us may have experienced coming out, or going in, as a migratory process or as a process of finding or going back to a home that had not existed before. In the process, I lost homes, ruined some, created several, entered deep existential crises over the very notion, thought in new tongues, and code-switched. These made me feel more connected than before when sharing cultural references. I was also able to reassess my feelings and connections to places, and see them change dramatically, rendering places that were once to be avoided at any cost havens, and vice versa. I can't say that I have managed to heal childhood traumas, but the process has been therapeutic nevertheless. Relating to others became a conscious process and a survival tactic. Feeling at home without families or anything familiar became a new way of being. What came with those geographical and cultural displacements was also a new relationship to language; not simply national languages and dialects but in terms of identifiers, in lack of a better term. Migrant, dyke, native, student, privileged, local, queer, bi, expat, gay, κουμμουνόσκελη, lesbian, poor, Greek, Balkan, unemployed, straight, British, researcher, εγχώρια εγώ μωρή;! *μεσολαβή*. Identifications and interpellations. These very different identifiers, in turn, changed the way I positioned myself in each space and situation.

Reflecting on this prompts me to wonder, who understands me, in which language and which cultural setting. In which language is my thinking produced, and how do I switch between different ones? In which language(s) do I relate to others and what language is my sense of humour? Especially when it comes to answering the last question, the broad topic of belonging, and socialising, entertaining, and creating or partaking in joyful moments arises. While mainly mixed, there are clear indications that   is my preferred language for intellectual and professional matters,   is my 'good migrant'/bureaucracy language, and   is my cussing language. It is also the language I use to talk to non-human animals, and the language I express feelings in. The   and   of the above are for conversations with friends, and brief reaction DMs. There are still plenty of moments I feel a word is not adequately translated or expressed in whatever language I speak at that point, and if I do not give myself enough time to process it, find an equivalent, or phrase it differently, I spurt it out in what—judging by the looks I receive—is a completely incomprehensible language to my interlocutors. Sometimes I get embarrassed and rush to 'fix' it, others I just keep going thinking or hoping that others will not notice or bother. Some of these times, the word I am substituting for an   one is   ; others,   , sometimes   , and less often a word from   . And while I get embarrassed thinking these are indications of my poor skills in   or   —or fear that this will be the conclusion my conversation partners will soon arrive upon—the truth is that in most of these cases, code-switching happens simply because there are no translations that encompass the cultural connotations of what I want to express. This awkward code-switching has become my constant and a shelter of sorts. 'Travelling under the queer sign becomes a way of occupying political space and of claiming territory as one's own residence or home' writes Ahmed[58] and I will appropriate and re-contextualise it for this text. It is interesting when others who share some of those languages are in proximity, and operate under a similar code-switching pattern, the speed of which sometimes does not even allow others to understand that a 'slip' like that happened. But what I have found important is the way in which this has given me the chance to reinvent what mother tongue means for, and to, me and how clearly unrelated that is to any national ideas of a mother land, or a mother (quotation marks at your discretion). In contrast, it is closely associated to ideas of mothers (quotation marks at your discretion), and tongues, and lands.

I have positioned the closet as a space for dwelling, and as dwelling allows for rhizomatic ways of relating, healing and dreaming, it is interesting to examine the possibilities this creates in terms of hope and nextness. This is an important component of what the closet can facilitate. I am thinking in particular here of those who cannot afford to dream of a future, often because of the precarity in which they live. Polemics that demand queerness to be exclusively situated in the here and now often come from privileged positions. I think of *Paris is Burning* as an example where those who have been refused things do not have the luxury to refuse them, they simply cannot afford not participating in those performances and those counter-cultural celebrations, and definitely cannot afford to not participate in narratives of hope and utopia. Relatedly, I think of John Coney and Sun Ra's *Space is the Place*[59] where a narrative that bridges past, present, and future offers hope for the latter, and does so by transcending space.[60] And by the same account, some would argue that Sun Ra's preoccupation with power, authority, and narratives of 'the good life', is giving in to an assimilationist sentiment, but it well could be a disidentificatory process. Writing on temporalities in connection to otherness I often thought of Janelle Monáe, a musician whose work often defies forms and genres or simply blurs the lines between them, whose 2018 album is proposed as an 'emotion picture'. In it, Monáe introduces audiences to dirty computers. Dirty computers (queers and BPoC but also other Others like poor and working-class people and migrants) go through different stages in their fight against oppressive regimes in a dystopian future (?) where they are being robbed off of their memories and history. Monáe, a queer person, proposes in this emotion picture three stances / phases: reckoning, celebrating, and reclaiming.[61] Monáe creates visual or audio references to some of Monáe's idols (Baldwin, Prince, Haring, Brown) and displays an (afro)futuristic universe filled with cyborgs. Channelling Muñoz's out-of-timelines Monáe often mentions how some people live in the future or transcend time and move between future, past, and present at will.[62]

To go back to *Paris is Burning*, I think of Venus Xtravaganza's claim (before she got strangled by a client trying to raise funds to, as she put it, 'become who [she] wanted') that she merely wanted to be 'a spoiled, rich, white girl living in the suburbs.'[63] Xtravaganza wanted to partake in a number of otherwise 'normative' rituals, institutions, and lifestyle options that would affirm her 'realness' which she so desperately competed for in the Balls.[64] An actual house in the suburbs, or orienting herself towards it, may have been Xtravaganza's idea of a home, or it could have additionally been next to the House of Xtravaganza. Along similar lines, I think of the final scene from 'Strella'[65] where former convict Yiorgos spends the holidays with Strella, a trans* sex worker he fell in love with, and who—as we learn during the film, and Strella knew all along—is his biological child. In a small working-class apartment in Athens, surrounded by others, they decorate the space and try to create a new life for themselves, one based on hope, fighting, or coming to peace with their past. Panos H. Koutras and Panayiotis Evaggelidis created a utopian space for a family that allows both elements of a family of origin and a family of choice to exist. This family includes persons from all walks of life, ages, status, and most importantly manages to transform the figure of the child from a figure that is, as Edelman writes, the fantasmatic beneficiary of a future, to a queer person that skews past and future to create their own home from scraps, repaired trash, and genuine love going against the all too familiar 'bury your gays' trope.

I first wrote the following in the aftermath of the Pulse massacre in Orlando. I have to think of how the space of the lesbian / gay / queer club can feel like a safer space and evoke themes of familiality that go beyond immediate kinship, often activated by affective responses to sonic stimuli. As Ann Cvetkovich reminds us, quoting cartoonist Lynda Barry 'We don't create a fantasy world to escape reality, we create it to be able to stay.'[66] The plastic nature of the slangs is such a fantasy world being performed, materialised even. Embodied improvised practices, be they speech, gestures, camp, drag, or dance, have been joy-activating ways of keeping on. Muñoz calls dance 'an especially valuable site for ruminations on queerness and gesture'[67] and quotes Merlau-Ponty writing that 'the dance floor increases our tolerance for embodied practices.'[68] I think of the economy of the closet, and how it formed the gay bar / club, as a space which comes alive mainly when others sleep and functions as a place for desires to be expressed, communities to be formed, and time to be queered. I think of Pulse, the gay club in Orlando, Florida, where people got together to dance to Latin music, only to experience a massacre. I think of Babylon from *Queer As Folk*, the fictional club that was the premise of much of the show's action and how it was bombed in the show's final season. Muñoz, prompted by McCarthy's images of gay clubs, remembers his own youth in sexually ambiguous places and writes, 'the mosh pit was not simply a closet; it was a utopian subcultural rehearsal space.'[69] Working on closets, desires, embodied practices of pleasure and liberation, with a particular focus on people from the Periphery, people of colour, migrant bodies, and class, I want to share Justin Torres' piece which he wrote στον απόηχο του Ορλάντο. An emotional piece on safer spaces, marginalised subjects, belonging, and familiality, Torres writes:

> Maybe your Ma blessed you on the way out the door. Maybe she wrapped a plate for you in the fridge so you don't come home and mess up her kitchen with your hunger. Maybe your Tia dropped you off, gave you cab money home. Maybe you had to get a sitter. Maybe you've yet to come out to your family at all, or maybe your family kicked you out years ago. Forget it, you survived. Maybe your boo stayed home, wasn't feeling it, but is blowing up your phone with sweet texts, trying to make sure you don't stray. Maybe you're allowed to stray. Maybe you're flush, maybe you're broke as nothing, and angling your pretty face barside, hoping someone might buy you a drink.

Maybe your half-Latin-ass doesn't even speak Spanish; maybe you barely speak English. Maybe you're undocumented.[70]

The finale of *Queer As Folk* (S5 E13) is set in an undone Babylon (after a bombing attack, discussions of homophobic violence and how to overcome it) with Brian and Michael dancing to no music. As they dance, we get glimpses of a packed club, replete of music, laser beams, and confetti. All their friends are there, happy. Michael's closing monologue before the music completely takes over is 'So the thumpathumpa continues. It always will, no matter what happens, no matter who's president. As our lady of disco, the divine miss Gloria Gaynor, has always sung to us: "We will survive."'[71]

The cheesiness and stereotypical banality of this scene is an aesthetics inextricably linked to futurity and hope. In a place of dance, sex, and drugs, destroyed by homophobia and bigotry, these queers overcome violence and guided by a gay anthem keep on dancing. In the face of hardship, pleasure and the ability to project into a future is what keeps these characters going. This cliché finale is a message of hope, perseverance, and of the importance of safer spaces that develop in relation to the closet and materialise ephemerally in clubs, bars, saunas, parks, bedrooms, streets, back alleys, TV shows, literature, parlare, tunes, and screens.

I had to think / feel further on loss and closets, and our spaces when this happened. Ήμουν στη Σύρο όταν διάβασα τα νέα στο facebook. Μούδιασα. Δεν ξέρω πια παρα μόνο λίγα άτομα στην Αθήνα. Έστειλα μηνύματα. Ήταν κι αυτ@ μουδιασμέν@, εξαγριωμέν@ κι έτοιμ@ για δράση. Θα πήγαινα Αθήνα για μία μόνο μέρα, αλλά θα ερχόταν ένας κυκλώνας που ενδεχομένως θα μας απέκλειε στο νησί και πιθανώς να έχανα την πτήση μου, οπότε βρέθηκα Αθήνα κάπως άξαφνα, με τα πράγματα βιαστικά πεταμένα στη βαλίτσα. Τα κλειδιά τα ξέχασα στο συρτάρι μου. Τώρα είχα άλλη εγγύτητα με το γεγονός. Ήμουν στην πόλη που έγινε η δολοφονία, που τραβήχτηκαν τα βίντεο του λιντσαρίσματος, που πέθανε ο/η Ζακ/Zackie Oh!, που θα ακολουθούσε ο μιντιακός διασυρμός, οι πορείες, οι παρεμβάσεις, τα σιχαμερά σχόλια. Συνειδητοποίησα για μία ακόμη φορά ότι οι καουμπόιδες, οι νοικοκυραίοι, και οι Έλληνες έχουν κυριεύσει τα πάντα στη μεταμνημονιακή Ελλάδα. Ένιωσα φριχτά μόνη, ασύνδετη με την κοινότητα, σαν τουρίστρια της οποίας η όποια υποστήριξη πιθανώς να μην ήταν ευπρόσδεκτη. Αφού έφυγα, μάλλον είμαι a deserter, a quitter, προδότρια. Φυσικά κανένα άτομο από την κοινότητα δεν μου είπε κάτι τέτοιο, όλα ήταν στο κεφάλι μου, δικοί μου φόβοι. Αποφάσισα να πάω βόλτα στο κέντρο να νιώσω connected, να αφήσω και μερικά λουλούδια στου Ζακ. Έκανα κύκλους γύρω απ' τη Γλαδστώνος σχεδόν ανήμπορη να πάω στο σημείο. Τελικά πήρα ένα ροζ τριαντάφυλλο από τον κύριο με το καροτσάκι με τα μικροπράγματα που βρίσκεται πάντα εκεί και κατευθύνθηκα προς τα κει. Δεν ήταν δύσκολο να το βρω. Λουλούδια, μπόλικη χρυσόσκονη, και ρέινμποου πραγματάκια. Μπροστά στο κλειστό ρολό 'ΔΟΛΟΦΟΝΕ' και πάνω γράμματα προς τον Ζακ/Zackie Oh! Δεν τον γνώριζα προσωπικά, μόνο ιντερνετικά, νομίζω κατέβηκε Αθήνα την εποχή που εγώ έφευγα. Δεν έχει σημασία όμως. Πάλεψε για να σπάσει το στίγμα για τ@ οροθετικ@, τ@ σεξεργάτ@ς, ήταν εθελοντής σε HIV/AIDS οργανώσεις και στην ΟΛΚΕ, έκανε drag shows όπου ξεμπρόστιαζε την ελληνική κοινωνία. Η ατάκα 'μωρή he died for you' που τραγούδησε σε ένα νούμερό της η Zackie Oh![72]—και την οποία πολλά ελληνικά μίντια βρήκαν προφητική—είναι τόσο βαθιά περιγραφική της ελληνικής πραγματικότητας. Ένα συνοθύλευμα αισθητικών και αναφορών (ελληνοχριστιανικότητα, τουρμπο ποπ, ευρωσκεπτικισμός και 'μένουμε Ευρώπη') ενοχικότητα, και κατηγορίες, και φυσικά αναπραγωγικομαλότητα by way of Παναγίτσα's immaculate conception. Η Zackie Oh! φοράει μακριά φούστα, έχει καρέ μαλλί, και από το αμάνικο μπλουζί της φαίνεται το biohazard tattoo της στο μπράτσο.

Στις πορείες μαζί με τα συνθήματα για τη βρώμα της ετεροπατριαρχίας το πλήθος τραγούδησε Madonna's 'Like a Prayer' αντί για προσευχές. Στην κηδεία πέταξαν glitter. Το κουίρ πένθος παίρνει άλλες μορφές, μορφές που ταιριάζουν στις άλλες μορφές συγγένειας και εγγύτητας που αναπτύσσονται· λόγω ανάγκης, λόγω συνθηκών. Το πένθος—στο οποίο η κουιρ κοινότητα έχει μακρά θήτευση— εκφράζεται μέσα από κλάμα και συνθήματα, τρικάκια και graffiti, χορό και τραγούδι. Και κυρίως την υπόσχεση ότι τα αδέλφια μας, οι αδελφές, οι μανούλες, our mamas and our abuelas, our daddies, άφησαν πίσω τους δημιουργίες που μας συντροφεύουν και μας βοηθάνε στις μάχες που έρχονται. Στις θανατοπολιτικές απαντάμε με τσαμπουκά «Ήτανε και Ζακ, ήτανε και Zackie, στους νοικοκυραίους εμείς βάζουμε γκαζάκι», τρυφερότητα, και χιούμορ (όταν μπορούμε). Οργή και θλίψη η Zackie θα μας λείψει! *glitter bomb* #Justice4ZakZackie

Nextness

Synthesising Munoz's disidentification—where the minoritarian subject cannot afford the luxury to think about the future or the pleasure of having a history—and Edelman's polemic towards any aspirations of futurity because we have historically been excluded from it, I want to propose a fragile closet. A space, time, and event that allows for manifestations of history, past, memory, anti-memory, hope, and future all encapsulated by nextness. Nextness—a tenant of the closet—that does not move linearly, and works with trauma, through pain, via pleasures, brings into proximity moments of 'past' events, future projections, and being in the 'here and now'.

If the closet allows for an imagining or dreaming of what might come next, one that refuses to abide by simplistic binaries such as 'conservative' vs. 'progressive', how would that function? How would that imagining—one based in all sorts of feelings—work? Maybe Edelman's view is a depressive one, and now I can see it differently. I feel it more. I do not think of it so much as an ideology, but as a need he expresses, and, in that way, I can relate to it. The future can feel stressful, normative, ambitious. Sometimes you just

and forget   future   . Sometimes high theory does not help, and the repetitive strokes of crafts are the only thing therapeutic. Allowing for nowness to happen. Maybe a what-is-next feeling will come up, maybe not. Maybe an opening up to what-is-nextness is vital for some to keep being in the present, while for others not so much, but in either case, a safer space of comfort produced culturally (by language, visuals, or gestures) can perhaps manifest.

Muñoz argues that 'heteronormative culture makes queers think that both the past and the future do not belong to them. All we are allowed to imagine is barely surviving the present.'[73] I would argue that we are not even allowed a place at the table of the present as state laws, the AIDS epidemic, institutionalised homophobia, bathroom laws, sterilisation prerequisites, openly homo/transphobic parliamentarians, lack of visibility/representation, and homo/transphobic violence indicate. It is precisely for these reasons that a closet that causes a rift in linear time is crucial with its ability to locate itself in the past, future and present employing tools that transcend age and normative understandings of growing up. I want to choose to be able to play hide and seek, and hide in closets, speak Pig Latin, and see them as 'sites of embodied and performed queer politics and describe them as outposts of actually existing queer worlds'[74] as Muñoz writes referring to public sex sites, dance floors, festivals, and stages. I think these embodied and performed politics are the politics of the slangs, of opacity, and of concealment that the closet provides. Through those, queer spaces materialise, some of which might take place in the future. To Edelman's Child as 'the fantasmatic beneficiary of every political intervention' I want to counter the child as queer. While the legitimisation of oppressive politics often happens in the name of the (white, upper-class, native) children, let us be realistic and call out the use of the child in such situations as what it is; another offering in the altar of profit and bigotry. To Edelman's assertion of 'fighting for the children'[75] as a confirmation of the absolute value of reproductive futurism, I see a 'fighting *the* children'. Normativity is continually fighting to discipline and assimilate figures that are not (re)productive, who perform flamboyant performatives, who speak gibberish, and activate opacity to create and sustain counter-cultures.[76] What if it is a disruption of normative linear temporalities that leads children to become adults and bear children that instead allows for children of all biological ages to play, and learn, and grow into not becoming adults? Or become. And then undo it. Or bear children, or not, or raise children, or adults, or not.

Queers (are the children that) confuse 'mama' and 'dada', mispronounce, and make words up. They play dress-up. They hide in closets, and make up worlds that fit them, they develop affinities beyond race, class, age, ability, or gender. They are those who do not have reproduction as their (sole) purpose in life.[77] By using (typically) children's tactics to evade being understood, trying to get away with deviation without being punished or straightened up, queers exhibit a willfulness, which for Ahmed, already includes them in the kinship of willfulness's archives. I want to think here of the child as willful, as queer, as full of possibilities, ever-changing, ready for adventure, vulnerable, chasing knowledge, learning and connecting through playing, expressing emotions openly, and even throwing tantrums. Straight time demands that everyone grow up; and in a linear fashion at that, leaving playfulness behind, with non-reproductive bodies appearing as willful children, as Ahmed suggests, or rejecting linearity by growing sideways, as she writes inspired by Kathryn Bond Stockton.[78]

I see this willfulness to grow linearly as resonating with the right to refuse what does not fit you, a right that is ingrained in feminist and queer traditions. I further understand the rejection of the mandatory call to come out as connected to the rejection of the call to grow up straight. No, I won't come out. I won't go into the streets. At least not today. Not now. But on my own time. (We could ask whose time is it that demands the outing anyway?) I can stay in. Conceived thus, going back into the closet might be a form of willfulness and migration. To not be happy where you are expected to be happy and instead perform a displacement.

To return to the visual politics of my project, I would like to go back to visions, or imaginaries of the future, that seem to be so clear, specific, and within reach in normative narratives, and so out of reach when it comes to derailing (from) normative lines. I see (for lack of a better term) the future in queer terms as inherently opaque. I feel it being abstract, elusive, and ever-changing. I do not see it as excluding specific dreams, but merely challenging their harmful structures, and oppressive forms. Opacity allows for shape-shifting or abandoning original goals for the sake of others that are more fit. It allows for mistakes, failure, going back, and down, and going forth, and moving sideways, and going upwards. Opacity allows not having to tell anyone 'what your (ten-year) plan is'. It can mean having a plan, several plans, or no plan at all, but it means not having to report to anyone, and keeping things for yourself and those the plans actually include / affect.

As contradictory as it may (seemingly) be to argue in favour of a politics of concealment or the possibility of a closetedness, especially in relation to those queers with disabilities while having previously presented languages that while affirming concealment and closetedness are strongly lookist and ableist, I'm not sure this discrepancy necessarily leads to an 'either / or' situation. Instead, I see it as part of the innate amalgamation of queerness, the inscribed messiness, allowance for contradictions, not looking for a Western, 'scientific', clear, and consistent answer.

'Queer and feminist histories are the histories of those who are willing to risk the consequences of deviation',[79] writes Ahmed. We can understand these deviations as from straight time, linear temporalities, essentialist ideas of kinship, and prefab notions of futurity and hope. 'A willfulness archive is premised on hope: the hope that those who wander away from the paths they are supposed to follow leave their footprints behind'[80] she wrote recently. An embracing of the closet and a willfulness to give it up might not only allow feelings to be felt, but also a reflection of, or on, different tenses to happen. And through this focus on traces, and backward feelings of clinging onto objects, backwardness comes into the foreground again, through archives, objects we will not let go of, and a lack of straight lines.

"gets up, moves closer to the cupboards"
'-Ayuda me please
"She shakes spray can.
She puts on a black latex glove, gives one to Naomi. They spray a Bixa Bitte! stencil on the inside of the cupboard.
They take the gloves off."

Some of the decisions, as with all artistic production, come to be due to financial, spatial, or other restrictions. But in any case, it is important for me, especially when looking back, to see the works anew, and thus examine the elements, not as the products of pragmatic decisions that had to be made, but their aesthetic value, emotional impact, and overall contribution to the project. I find it essential to situate them in the context in and for which they were developed and acknowledge the temporal aspect and the lessened proximity this might imply.

Λοιπόν για να μην τα πολυλογούμε γιατί έχετε κι εσείς δουλίτσες ... While this project embodied almost all important elements of my project, periphery, minority, opacity, failure, the issue of what or who is illegal and of course the invisible community or need for belonging and not being disciplined for it, it was still lacking my actual voice. The sound of how I speak those languages and dialects, my accents, my mistakes. I wanted to finish with something that directly communicates feelings and doesn't shy away from vulnerability. And this is what this right now attempts to do.'

Tô passada!

> Inga tinga kare. Nanti palaryee ... nanti omee.
>
> *Unknown*

As I am writing this, individuals suspected of being non-binary, trans*, gay, 'homosexual', or practising same-sex sexual acts are discriminated against, abused, tortured, imprisoned, and murdered, acts often sanctioned by the state. To claim that the closet is exclusively a space of oppression and shame is to neglect those situations and the precarity some people live in. To say that the closet is a thing of the past in the Global North / West where admittedly the legal system (for the time being) does not include such harsh punishments, is to turn a blind eye to situations where people are discriminated against in the workplace, housing, health care or other services and social situations. To claim that the closet is no longer relevant is to embrace binarisms that ignore the nuanced ways in which opacity functions.

This project began with a focus on the proverbial closet and the mechanisms of metaphors in the production of social space. I presented an overview of the international permeation of the expression 'come out of the closet' one that showed the extent to which the expression was adopted and the implied relevance of its existence. I still wanted to find out if the claim that Steven Seidman made in the late '90s—that the closet is no longer relevant in the experience of US individuals—stood true. Next, I proposed a theorisation of the closet that defies dichotomies and goes beyond the binaries of in / out and bad / good. A paranoidly reparative theorisation that, in line with queerness, is fluid, embraces liminalities, and understands the closet as an event that happens constantly. I went on to think not only of how language constructs the closet but also how the closet constructs language. I presented eleven registers (which for the sake of simplicity and   I called 'queer slangs') from several different geographical and cultural settings which were created for under-the-radar communication, constructing temporal loci of safety, belonging, and (oral) pleasure. To better situate these slangs, I gave an outline of lavender linguistics in terms of linguistic creations, speech patterns, and lexicography. This first chapter closed with a thinking-through of these slangs as performances, focused on their aesthetics and particular characteristics and crossed over to how I used the closet and its creations in my thinking and work in the format of a performance.

In the second chapter, I focused on tactics of survival and resistance and employed visual and audio politics and their performative aesthetics to do so. I introduced the notion of opacity, as generated within postcolonial theory in connection to creolised languages in a Martinican context, and argued that opacity is both what generates the closet and what the closet, and by extent the slangs, create / s. Opacity, passivity, silence, and detour were each presented as tactics that are not intended to bring the master's house down; they are primarily concerned with the safety and well-being of Others. While focusing on safety and well-being, they inadvertently deliver some serious blows to the master's house by corrupting one of the master's most valuable tools: language. I traced opacity beyond the operation of the slangs in the aesthetics of concealment that clothing and my own name stand for. I located opacity's ephemeral nature and significance to moments of pleasure underneath the rainbow flag in public space. I attempted to answer the question of what would a non-revelatory, queer speech sound like by using the slangs throughout my work activating opacity as I went.

Next, I delved further into the aesthetics of the slangs and their oral qualities. I brought out the tension between orality and literature and activated queerness to read them beyond dichotomies and either / or structures. I made the claim that the slangs are a form of literature, and a 'minor literature' at that, and drew upon Deleuze and Guattari's conceptualisation of this literature. They thought of a literature that deterritorialises a major language, that is political, and collective. I read the slangs as a minor literature, one that does many things including; de- and re-territorialising major national languages, making a political statement on the social position and values of the speakers, and spreading to form communities, finding its way in social strata that the status quo presents as watertight from deviation. I discussed how I have applied these in my practice and prompted by O'Sullivan's ideas on what could constitute 'minor art practice' I developed a series of stencils written in the slangs which I then sprayed as public interventions around European cities. By looking at the slangs as minor literature I saw better how they are rooted in other struggles, which makes them less specific and creates a broader transhistorical framework through which to view them. Through this lens, I could also see how the slangs may contribute to bigger conversations on margins, creativity, survival, and cultural production as a necessity.

Finally, I combined affect theory with postcolonial and queer theory. Through exploring the familial/relational terms of the slangs, I proposed reading the slangs and the closet as an ephemeral setting gleaned from childhood in which to dwell, and by allowing bad feelings, to connect, comfort oneself and heal. A space connected not only to queerness in terms of sexualities and gender identities but disability and migration as well. I thus attempted a reparative reading of the closet that *can* contain shame yet shame is not the defining characteristic of it. Instead, the social spaces that the slangs and the closet produce are safer spaces of rest, ones that allow for a thinking of what is next, if one wants to. A what-is-next that can be seen as a response to a need for hope and futurity that is queer. 'Queer' as in 'fluid', 'ever-shifting', and 'open'. Open and safe enough to include reterritorialised visions of what could be next.

Σ' αυτό το πρότζεκτ η κουιρ θεωρία συναντήθηκε με την μετααποικιακή, τη ντικολόνιαλ και τις γνώσεις της Περιφέρειας/ των Περιφερειακών/ Περιθωριακών μέσω της γλωσσολογίας και των εικαστικών. Πρότεινα εδώ ένα μοντέλο έρευνας βασισμένο στην αδιαφάνεια και τις εικαστικές μεθόδους, και αντίθετα με την επικρατούσα άποψη περί ανωτερότητας της λογοτεχνίας έναντι της προφορικής παράδοσης, πρότεινα τον προφορικό πολιτισμό σαν ένα είδος λογοτεχνίας χρησιμοποιώντας την Deleuzoguattarian έννοια της ελάσσωνος λογοτεχνίας. Είκασα ότι η ντουλάπα δεν είναι μια μεταφορά του παρελθόντος αλλά υπερβαίνει τον χώρο και το χρόνο και ως εκ τούτου είναι ένα σύστημα του μέλλοντος και του παρόντος, και του παρελθόντος (κάποι@ δεν έχουν την πολυτέλεια να ξεγράψουν το παρελθόν, άλλ@ δεν έχουν την πολυτέλεια να ξεγράψουν το μέλλον, και οι ιστορίες μας είναι πολύτιμες). Ενέπλεξα μανούλες and Mothers, and aunties όπως προκύπτουν και σκιαγραφούνται από τις αργκώ και θεώρησα ότι οι αργκώ αυτές κατασκευάζουν σπιτάκια, χώρους εφήμερης προστασίας, στοργής, και κεφιού μέσω παιχνιδιάρικων εργαλείων (υπερβολή, σαρκασμός, επανεννοιολόγηση). Ασχολήθηκα τέλος με την κριπ θεωρία και κυρίως τα κακά συναισθήματα σαν κομμάτι ενός λεξιλογίου των γνώσεων της Περιφέρειας/των Περιφερειακών (όχι, δεν είμαστε όλ@

καλά!) και σαν άλλον ένα λόγο που η ντουλάπα είναι ένας χώρος με πολλές δυνατότητες και χρήσεις.

Throughout this project, I used words and phrases that reflect my way of thinking. This might make the text inaccessible in its entirety by some. It was a simultaneously liberating experience and a scary one, as I was for the first time allowing access to ways of constructing my thought. As Bhabha says 'I use[ed] the language I need[ed] for my work.'¹ The moments of inclusion and exclusion activated by opacity, are here to remind the reader / participant of the omnipresence and fleeting nature of such tactics, and the recurring need for safer spaces, especially in a project as exposing and personal as this. The theme of childhoodness, via activations of fairy-tales and magic closets, of pig Latin or craft-making as an expression of feelings one has a hard time articulating otherwise, is also present throughout this work. I see an innate connection between 'queer' and the Child, oral histories of children's mischief and its aftermath, but also an open and ever-changing envisioning of what-is-next. Another element I wanted to use was personal writing that defies academic tradition, that may be silly, attempt bad jokes, and remind myself and the reader / participant not to take ourselves too seriously. That is something risky in the context of a formal publication, and so I have to state that I do take this very seriously, and consequently reduced the jokes, though normally I am very funny.

Unresolved tensions encircled my work; the primary one being between attempting a research project to shed light on minoritarian tactics while one of those tactics was opacity. I had a lot of back and forth, deleting things I thought may have shed 'too much light' or would have been 'too Western', then acknowledging myself being the product of a crossroads of (the overlapping) West, Periphery, and the Balkans. I am also the product of a lower-middle-class normative family, yet have occupied different social milieux. I am also an artist by training but have pursued an academic path which is very often contradictory in methods and, of course, in how it is perceived by other artists and academics. I am not a linguist, and my interest was never in exposing or documenting the slangs, I drew from such experts and compiled the slangs in a novel way that highlighted intersectionality, humour, survival, and ultimately offered a philosophical reading of them via postcoloniality. I connected lavender linguistics with poststructuralism, and literature with orality employing philosophy, aesthetics, archives, and popular culture to do so. Maybe what I have done is not philosophy. As Sara Ahmed writes, 'Not philosophy also attends to "the not," making "the not" an object of thought. Not philosophy is also a philosophy of the not.'[2] (emphasis in original) I activated conventional methods of research and gradually discovered that failure, 'low theory', and admitting to having failed, forgetting,[3] repeating, and undoing, felt better. And so I embraced discrepancies as they reflect my social make-up; primarily, I embraced them as willful children's hands poking through the ground. Against the demand for clarity, consistency, and answers as the only result of a good research project. Instead, what I share with the reader/participant is my journey on a topic so close to my heart. That journey includes academic formalisation, footnotes, and bibliography, but also poems, contracted forms, diary entries, memories, and fears. I share a body of work that through publication, spraying, and uploading becomes more visible and more accessible than before, but itself retains a degree of opacity and refuses to give straightforward answers.

What I have managed to do here is offer an alternative reading of the closet that allows it to be a creative space. So is the closet a space, a time, an event, a locus, a Χώρα, a σπιτάκι, an apparatus, a room of one's own, a mother, a nurse, an animal, a liminality, a shelter, a House, or a metaphor? Ναι, γιατί όχι; Furthermore, I showed how this creativity manifests through tactics of survival and resistance of immense political value. I presented the linguistic registers produced within this alternatively and more openly theorised closet, and tried to contour the speakers respecting the cultural and temporal specificity of each slang. Given the whiteness and Westernness of the discourse around the closet and the term 'queer', my aim to shake it and connect it with non-white, non-European, non-academic, and non-privileged contexts was attempted through a reading of queer theory through postcolonial theory. Through employing Glissant's opacity and detour, Anzaldúa's mestizas, and Muñoz's view of futurity, combined with analyses of the slangs (primarily Kaliarnta), I pursued a 'queer' that is critical of its roots and opens up to new messy interpretations from the Periphery. By exploring the permeation of the closet through an expanded view of linguistics, I brought the slangs—as a creation activated by several of queerness' tactics—into an epistemological terrain that is not exclusively located within a Western and academic context. Through autobiographical elements and an affective reading of the closet, I offered a re-imagined closet; one that could contain all kinds of feelings, and all affective Others.

Further, drawing from my mother language, and the language of (my) childhood, I thought of the site of the closet that constitutes a safer space along terms of a room of one's own, a σπιτάκι. The reparative reading of the closet offered in this project, of a closet as a shelter, where Geborgenheit happens, could only be possible by situating myself and my research amongst postcolonial thinkers and their work, focusing on my relation to Balkanness, to the island where I spent the first seventeen years of my life, and a firsthand knowledge of Kaliarnta. It could only come to be through a focus on intersectionality and precarity, as σπιτάκι is there for those most vulnerable.

If some things still seem opaque to me, I try not to take it as necessarily meaning I have not understood them, but instead feel I should allow them to be near me for the time it takes until we connect; if we ever do. Opacity as a research method (as contradictory as those terms might be) has shown me the importance of time and generosity, two things that are not usually considered valid factors while trying to find or prove something. Time is always the here and now, the 'I want it yesterday', the 'it should have happened already', and generosity is almost incompatible with 'professionalism'. I am thankful for and to this process, which for me started very much in terms of 'I should have already done it a long time ago', and strict time-plans for the next several years of my life, but ended up being a lesson in patience, understanding of ununderstandingness, and generosity of space and time for oneself, for others, and for notions and feelings to set in and find their own space in whichever proximity they choose to you. Opacity further helped me appreciate confusion, and I hope this project also created moments when this was possible for the reader / participant. The confusion I speak of is not only the one produced in public when disenfranchised people take over a language and produce an aural strangeness; but my own confusion when parts of my research were opaque to me. This frustrating process pointed out my privileges as much as it did my disadvantages, and I hope that through creating a body of work premised on opacities, codes, and semantic alterations I have managed to do something similar with the reader / participant.

I chose to use parts of the codes mentioned, often without translating them to the main language of this project, as well as to activate opacities, and some silences. I opted for a structure that started out linear but became more like a rhizome. A rhizome of lines that go on and on, and others where derailed trains lay. I spread thoughts and feelings expressed in those codes throughout several cities. This has been an integral part of the project in order not simply to research and talk about something, but activate it, create moments of disruption, frustration, perhaps even an awareness of moments of exoticisation of scripts to certain readers. And through those moments, where their inner voice stumbles as they try to read through the text, embody and affectively absorb the outcome of such tactics of resistance.

Another theme I explored in this project was the temporal element and that of temporal displacement, not only by narrating my own life, or referring to slangs that were created a long time ago as willfulness archives, but that of going back in order to attempt a different approach at futurity. Throughout this project, elements of geographical, temporal, and cultural displacements appear as often as those of linguistic shifts. I understand the closet as an event that materialises ephemerally, that is not necessarily of a certain era, and is certainly not obsolete or irrelevant. I see the slangs, whether in their archival format of lexicography or in their audible nature, as chronopolitical indications of resistance and survival that refuse to be limited to specific realms, and further, refuse to die.

Throughout this project, I engaged with feelings of all sorts and decided to end the last chapter on a note of hope, a stance that allows people to have something to hold on to and keep on keeping on for when all else fails. I know it's sometimes a taboo in some circles, or as Love put it 'It is also the case that bad feelings have a certain prestige within academic discourse both because of their seriousness and also because of their relation to long philosophical traditions of negativity ("lack" becomes "loss").'[4] However, as health difficulties throughout this project have not always allowed me to find it easy to stay focused on the things I enjoy, things I want to create, or others I want to connect with, it became more and more important to create a space that allows for something positive.

This project has been a labour of joy, worry, and depression, a safe space, and a haunted place. I have derived immense pleasure from it, I understood a lot, got confused, learnt new things, and got to meet great people. Through it, the past seven years of my life are somehow documented. And now I will move on to either carrying or teaching, whichever comes first.

IMPASSE.

Endnotes

Introduction

1   Édouard Glissant, Betsy Wing trans. *Poetics of Relation* (Ann Arbor: University of Michigan Press, 1997).
2   Celia Britton, *Édouard Glissant and Postcolonial Theory: Strategies of Language and Resistance* (Charlottesville, Va: University Press of Virginia, 1999), 25.
3   I do not wish to romanticise precarity, especially given that there are colleagues, friends, and many many others in far more precarious situations than mine. I believe it is important to mention the term as it is being discussed among peers side by side with what Joois writes: 'as a critical concept and rallying cry, "precarity" has perhaps not shaken off this ambiguity (and this is something to reflect on). In contemporary political theory as well as "political art" "precarity" is both rejected as the perverted result of neo-liberal, global capitalism and in a way glamourized: the precarious individual is, as the British sociologist Guy Standing calls it, celebrated as a modern hero: always moving, always connected, devoid of a stable identity etc.' Joost de Bloois, 'Making Ends Meet: Precarity, Art and Political Activism' (public lecture/exhibition, Stedelijk Museum Bureau Amsterdam, NL, August 13, 2011), 6.
4   Poem by Guillermo Gómez-Peña performed at Pigott Theater, Stanford University, as part of Performance Studies International, June 19-28, 2013. https://www.youtube.com/watch?v=ooEQFDOXHrc (accessed December 3, 2018).
5   Stuart Hall, *Representation: Cultural Representations and Signifying Practices* (London: Sage, 1997), 5.
6   'A more detailed juxtaposition of "strategies" with "tactics" can be found in the work of Michel de Certeau, who argues that strategies always imply a spatial position of power or property (thus calculation from a safe position), whereas tactics are dependent on time and seizing the right moment, "on the wing" as it were.' Nicholas de Villiers, *Opacity and the Closet: Queer Tactics in Foucault, Bar-*

thes, and Warhol (Minneapolis: University Of Minnesota Press, 2012), 19. Michel de Certeau, *The Practice of Everyday Life*, trans. Steven Rendall (Berkeley: University of California Press, 1984), xix.

7   José Esteban Muñoz, *Cruising Utopia: The Then and There of Queer Futurity* (New York: New York University Press, 2009), 56.

8   'Using notions of emic (insider's point of view) and etic (outsider's point of view) theory, Boellstroff argues that one element of a queer methodology might be to upset this distinction and allow for the emergence of theory from both "within" and "without".' Kath Browne and Catherine J. Nash, introduction to *Queer Methods and Methodologies: Intersecting Queer Theories and Social Science Research*, eds. Kath Browne and Catherine J. Nash (London: Ashgate, 2010), 21; Tom Boellstorff, 'Queer Techne: Two Theses on Methodology and Queer Studies' in *Queer Methods and Methodologies*, eds. Kath Browne and Catherine J. Nash 217.

9   Browne and Nash, *Queer Methods and Methodologies*, 7.

10 Lynda Barry, 'What It Is' in Ann Cvetkovich, *Depression: A Public Feeling* (Durham & London: Duke University Press, 2012), 203.

11 Paul Baker, *Polari: The Lost Language of Gay Men* (London: Routledge, 2002), 86-105; Paul Baker, *Fantabulosa: A Dictionary of Polari and Gay Slang* (London: Bloomsbury Academic, 2004), 4-5.

12 Elspeth Probyn, 'Writing Shame' in *The Affect Theory Reader*, eds. Melissa Gregg and Gregory J. Seigworth, (Durham and London: Duke University Press, 2010), 76.

13 Stacy Holman Jones and Tony E. Adams, 'Autoethnography is a Queer Method' in *Queer Methods and Methodologies*, 197.

14 Ibid., 199.

15 Ibid., 196.

16 Ibid.

17 Ibid., 207.

18 This is an endnote to remind you that you too participate in this book with constant back-and-forths.

19 Gloria Anzaldúa, *Borderlands/La Frontera: The New Mestiza* (San Francisco: Aunt Lute Books, 2012).

The Chronicles of the Closet

1. 'Fairy tales have always occupied the ambiguous territory between childhood and adulthood, home and away, harm and safety.' Judith Halberstam, *The Queer Art of Failure* (Durham and London: Duke University Press, 2011), 44.
2. George Chauncey, *Gay New York: Gender, Urban Culture, and the Making of the Gay Male World, 1890–1940* (New York: Basic Books, 1995); Michael P. Brown, *Closet Space: Geographies of Metaphor from the Body to the Globe* (London: Routledge, 2000). Steven Seidman, *Beyond the Closet: The Transformation of Gay and Lesbian Life* (New York: Routledge, 2002).
3. *Online Etymology Dictionary*, s.v. 'closet', http://www.etymonline.com/index.php?term=closet (accessed December 3, 2018).
4. Ibid.
5. 'The timing of the metaphor can be linked to the rising popularity of its material signifier in domestic space.' Brown, *Closet Space*, 5.
6. *Google Ngram Viewer*, s.v. 'closet', https://books.google.com/ngrams/graph?content=closet&year_start=1800&year_end=2008&corpus=15&smoothing=3&share=&direct_url=t1%3B%2Ccloset%3B%2Cco (accessed November 4, 2016).
7. I will come to that later, in my analysis of the figure of the child and childhood/childishness/childhoodness in the next chapters and chapter four in particular.
8. A simultaneity that speaks perhaps to the relation between the economy of the closet and the market it created within capitalist structures and the rising popularity of the actual furnishing item in need of more storage space as consumerism was becoming an integral part of the economy.
9. 'Like much of campy gay terminology, "coming out" was an arch play on the language of women's culture—in this case the expression used to refer to the ritual of a debutante's being formally introduced to, or "coming out" into, the society of her cultural peers.' Chauncey, *Gay New York*, 7.
10. I use the term 'women' here as it is the term that was used back then given the strict binary that upheld this social institution.
11. While the expression is primarily associated with the English upper-class, Chauncey says that '[t]his is often remembered as exclusively a ritual of WASP high society, but it was also common in the social worlds of African-Americans and other groups.' Chauncey, *Gay New York*, 7.
12. Brown, *Closet Space*, 5.
13. Chauncey, *Gay New York*, 7.

14 There are some very interesting expressions from the time prior to the '60s to denote the different personas LGBTQ+ people assumed based on the space they were navigating and its safety or lack thereof. Being openly queer or closeted were expressed through metaphors such as 'let one's hair down /putting one's hair up' respectively, additionally another hair-styling-related metaphor 'dropping hairpins' was used to indicate dropping hints that would allow fellow queers to recognise each other. Ibid., 7-8.

15 'A gay man's coming out originally referred to his being formally presented to the largest collective manifestation of prewar gay society, the enormous drag balls that were patterned on the debutante and masquerade balls of the dominant culture and were regularly held in New York, Chicago, New Orleans, Baltimore, and other cities.' Ibid., 7.

16 I do realise that certain sexualities that don't necessarily fall under the LGBTQ+ umbrella may not be properly represented by this simplification, but I would like to clarify that I use the term with the plus symbol in the end to connote precisely those who don't identify as any of the social categories described by the initialism and may be anywhere in the sexualities/genders matrix as well as beyond (BDSM, asexual, poly, diverse fetish communities etc.).

17 *Online Etymology Dictionary*, s.v. 'metaphor', http://www.etymonline.com/index.php?term=metaphor (accessed November 4, 2016).

18 Eve Kosofsky Sedgwick, *Tendencies* (London: Routledge, 1994), xii.

19 I am not only referring to the phenomenon of repeated coming outs, but also the ephemeral nature of the closet with its materialisation and dematerialisation at any given moment.

20 Ivan Lupi, Email conversation with the author, October 20, 2012.

21 Nika Autor, Maria Hera, Email conversations with the author, April 13, 2012.

22 Nastja Goloskokova, Email conversation with the author, November 6, 2013.

23 Müco, Email conversation with the author, February 23, 2016.

24 The sources of the above information vary and include my own knowledge from social contexts I have lived in, interviewing individuals (who identify as LGBTQ+ and as straight/hetero) from linguistic backgrounds otherwise inaccessible to me.

25 Here I refer to such ontologies as LGBT and not so much 'queer' subjectivities.

26 Pardis Mahdavi, 'Passionate Uprisings: Young People, Sexuality and Politics in Post-Revolutionary Iran' *Culture, Health & Sexuality*, September-October 2007; 9 (5): 445-457.

27 Ali Ahmadi, 'Is 'Coming Out' a Western Construct?, *The Huffington Post*, November 29, 2014, http://www.huffingtonpost.com/ali-ahmadi/is-coming-out-a-western-construct_b_6226434.html.
28 Oaxaca's Third Gender, Video, directed by Bernando Loyola. New York City: VICE Media Inc., 2013 http://www.vice.com/video/oaxacas-third-gender.
29 Lynn Stephen, 'Sexualities and Genders in Zapotec Oaxaca', in *Latin American Perspectives*, Issue 123, Vol.29 No.2, Sage Publications, March 2002, 41-59.
30 Lukas Avendaño. *No soy Persona soy Mariposa*. Video. Mario Patiño. Pachuca, Mèxico. 2015. https://vimeo.com/144735012.
31 Johanna Schmidt, 'Redefining Fa'afafine: Western Discourses and the Construction of Transgenderism in Samoa' in *Intersections: Gender, History and Culture in the Asian Context*, Issue 6, August 2001, http://intersections.anu.edu.au:80/issue6/schmidt.html; Roberta Perkins 'Like a Lady in Polynesia The Māū of Tahiti, the Fa'a Fafine in Samoa, the Fakaleiti' in *Tonga and More' Polare* magazine: March 1994 Last Update: September 2013, http://www.gendercentre.org.au/resources/polare-archive/archived-articles/like-a-lady-in-polynesia.htm.
32 Sharyn Graham, 'It's Like One of Those Puzzles: Conceptualising Gender Among Bugis', *Journal of Gender Studies*, 13:2 (2014): 107-116, DOI: 10.1080/0958923042000217800
33 Michel Foucault, 'Technologies of the Self', in *Technologies of the Self: A Seminar with Michel Foucault*, eds. Luther H. Martin, Huck Gutman, Patrick H. Hutton, (Massachusetts: Tavistock Publications, 1988), 16.
34 'Casarino therefore acknowledges the political continuity and centrality of the closet as outlined by Sedgwick yet allows for the simultaneous pursuit of "other types" of (nondialectical) solutions to the problem than the always already foreseen "coming out." This is also where I situate my own attempt to examine queer strategies and processes that might overcome the vicious circularity of the dialectic of the closet.' De Villiers, *Opacity and the Closet*, 17.
35 I use the term 'ghetto' here in the sense it is often used in reference to the LGBTQ community, or LGBTQ-related businesses and services in Greece. It is frequently seen in personal ads where individuals ask to meet others who are exclusively 'outside the ghetto' meaning people who do not have LGBTQ-identifying friends, and do not frequent LGBTQ establishments. These ads often further indicate fatphobia, femmephobia, and queerphobia.
36 Judith Butler, introduction to *Of Grammatology* by Jacques Derrida (Baltimore: Johns Hopkins University Press, 2016), xi.

37 'Abya Yala, which in the Kuna language means "land in its full maturity" or "land of vital blood", is the name used by the Panamanian Kuna people to refer to the American continent since before the Columbus arrival.' https://en.wikipedia.org/wiki/Abya_Yala (accessed December 3, 2018). Sandra Monterroso, Email conversation with the author, February 1, 2016.

38 Anzaldúa, *Borderlands/La Frontera*, 44.

39 Eve Kosofsky Sedgwick, *Epistemology of the Closet* (Berkeley and Los Angeles: University of California Press, 1990), 71.

40 Someone who does not experience sexual attraction until they establish a better understanding, a connection, or relationship with the other person. 'For Queers By Queers' http://forqueersbyqueers.tumblr.com/terminology (accessed December 5, 2018).

41 'Someone who can feel a romantic attraction towards others and also enjoy romantic relationships in theory, but not needing that affection to be reciprocated or be in a relationship with the one the feelings are directed towards. Either that, or they may stop feeling the attraction once in a relationship or stop enjoying it.' 'Asexuality: List of Romantic Orientations', http://www.asexuality.org/en/topic/119238-a-list-of-romantic-orientations/ (accessed December 5, 2018).

42 'The romantic attraction to gender non-binary individuals.' 'For Queers By Queers', http://forqueersbyqueers.tumblr.com/terminology (accessed December 5, 2018).

43 Someone who is attracted to both males and females but considers the attractions toward both distinct. 'For Queers By Queers', http://forqueersbyqueers.tumblr.com/terminology (accessed December 5, 2018).

44 'The sexual attraction towards female-identified people regardless of one's gender. Gyne-Skolioromantic: The sexual attraction towards female-identified people as well as gender variant individuals. 'For Queers By Queers', http://forqueersbyqueers.tumblr.com/terminology (accessed December 5, 2018).

45 'A zucchini is a partner in a queerplatonic relationship. The commitment level between partners is often considered to be similar to that of a romantic relationship, but with platonic love. Zucchinis may be of any romantic or sexual orientation.' 'Asexuality: Zucchini', http://www.asexuality.org/wiki/index.php?title=Zucchini (accessed December 5, 2018).

46 Lavender linguistics is a branch of linguistics that focuses on communication patterns, lingos, slangs, argots, cants, neologisms, as well as mannerisms, phonetic expressions, and delivery of LGBTQ individuals. It has been particu-

larly developed by William Leap. William Leap and Tom Boellstorff, *Speaking in Queer Tongues: Globalization and Gay Language*, eds. William Leap and Tom Boellstorff, (Urbana: University of Illinois Press, 2004).

47 Slang is defined here as '1. a kind of language occurring chiefly in casual and playful speech, made up typically of short-lived coinages and figures of speech that are deliberately used in place of standard terms for added raciness, humor, irreverence, or other effect; 2. language peculiar to a group; argot or jargon: thieves slang.' *The Free Dictionary*, s.v. 'slang', http://www.thefreedictionary.com/slang (accessed December 5, 2018); Argot is defined here 'as a specialized vocabulary or set of idioms used by a particular group: thieves' argot.' *The Free Dictionary*, s.v. 'argot', http://www.thefreedictionary.com/argot (accessed December 5, 2018).

48 Ildikó Gy. Zoltán, 'The Nature of Slang: Spoken, Creative and Transient', in *Studia Universitatis Petru Maior –Philologia*, Petru Maior University of Târgu-Mures, (2009) 228-234., 228.

49 'Further expanding the already large class of Foucauldian apparatuses, I shall call an apparatus literally anything that has in some way the capacity to capture, orient, determine, intercept, model, control, or secure the gestures, behaviors, opinions, or discourses of living beings. Not only, therefore, prisons, mad houses, the panopticon, schools, confession, factories, disciplines, juridical measures, and so forth (whose connection with power is in a certain sense evident), but also the pen, writing, literature, philosophy. Agriculture, cigarettes, navigation, computers, cellular telephones and-why not-language itself, which is perhaps the most ancient of apparatuses-one in which thousands and thousands of years ago a primate inadvertently let himself be captured, probably without realizing the consequences that he was about to face.' Giorgio Agamben, *What is an Apparatus? and Other Essays*, trans. David Kishik and Stefan Pedatella (Stanford: Stanford University Press, 2009), 14. I have stated above that I want to suggest a reparative reading of the closet that perhaps sees the closet as the antithesis of the panopticon, and as an apparatus that disrupts surveillance and the discipline that follows it. Agamben's description above brings out these elements of the closet and language that orient, intercept, and communicate opinions and discourses of living beings through a position where the connection to power is equally clear. Although in this case what is clear is which end of the power spectrum the speakers are situated.

50 Stephanie Rudwick, '"Gay and Zulu, we speak isiNgqumo": Ethnolinguistic Identity Constructions', *Transformation: Critical Perspectives on Southern Africa*, Number 74 (2010): 123.

51 Elias Petropoulos described himself as an 'amateur researcher' and 'folklorist' and is the only one to have conducted research and documented Kaliarnta to such an extent. Elias Petropoulos, *Kaliarnta* (Athens: Nefeli, 1971), 3.

52 Πεταχτό Κόρτε, Αρνουβώ Σατυρικόν Φύλλον, 25 Νοεμβρίου 1904 (Fleeting Flirt, Art Nouveau Satirical Periodical, 25 November 1904) Nikos Sarantakos, 'Καλιαρντά από το 1904!', *Sarantakos* (blog), published December 27, 2017, https://sarantakos.wordpress.com/2017/12/27/kaliarnta/; Nick Nicholas, 'Kaliarda XXVII: Sarantakos', *Hellenisteukontos* (blog), published December 30, 2017, http://hellenisteukontos.opoudjis.net/kaliarda-xxviii-sarantakos/; Nick Nicholas, 'Kaliarda XXIX: 1904, addendum' *Hellenisteukontos* (blog), published January 4, 2018, http://hellenisteukontos.opoudjis.net/kaliarda-xxix/.

53 Petropoulos, *Kaliarnta*, 12; Leonicos, 'Καλιαρντά από το 1904!', *Sarantakos* (blog), December 27, 2017, https://sarantakos.wordpress.com/2017/12/27/kaliarnta/.

54 Petropoulos, *Kaliarnta*, 3.

55 Ibid., 11.

56 Τραβεστί (transvestite) was/is a term used in a Greek-speaking context to refer to a transfeminine person. The term is now considered by many outdated and pejorative but for the cultural context of Petropoulos' project (and even after it) it would have been relevant.

57 [Camp is] 'a form of cultural resistance that is entirely predicated on a shared consciousness of being inescapably situated within a powerful system of social and sexual meaning that resists the power of that system from within.' David Halperin quoted in De Villiers, *Opacity and the Closet*, 20.

58 Moe Meyer, 'Reclaiming the Discourse on Camp' ed. Moe Meyer, *The Politics and Poetics of Camp* (New York and London: Routledge, 1994), 2.

59 Baker, *Polari*, i.

60 Welby Ings, 'Trade Talk: the Historical Metamorphosis of the Language of the New Zealand Male Prostitute Between 1900-1981', in *Women's History Review* (2012) 21:5, 773-791. 778.

61 *Wikipedia* s.v. 'Pajuba', https://pt.wikipedia.org/wiki/Pajub%C3%A1 (accessed December 5, 2018).

62 Pêdra Costa, Email conversation with the author, April 5, 2014.

63 'Many travestis themselves speak a Yoruba-based dialect, pajubá, as a sociolect that is particular to their population and also allows them to communicate

among themselves and avoid both civil and police surveillance (Wolfe 2006).' Vek Lewis, *Crossing Sex and Gender in Latin America* (New York: Palgrave Macmillan, 2010), 103.

64   Ibid.

65   Emy Ruth De Quiros Gianan, 'The Evolution and Expansion of Gay Language in the Philippines', (BA in Political Science, University of Santo Tomas, Philippines, 2008); 3. Alba, A. Reinerio, 'In Focus: The Filipino Gayspeak (Filipino Gay Lingo)' *National Commission For Culture and The Arts* Website, 2006, http://ncca.gov.ph/about-culture-and-arts/in-focus/the-filipino-gayspeak-filipino-gay-lingo/ (accessed November 5, 2016).

66   Ibid.

67   Cynthia Grace B. Suguitan, 'A Semantic Look at Feminine Sex and Gender Terms in Philippine Gay Lingo.' (Presentation, Sexualities, Genders and Rights in Asia: 1st International Conference of Asian Queer Studies. Bangkok, Thailand: AsiaPacifiQueer Network, Mahidol University; Australian National University, July 2005). https://openresearch-repository.anu.edu.au/handle/1885/8681?mode=full; Alba, A. Reinerio, 'In Focus: The Filipino Gayspeak.'

68   Michael L. Tan, 'Survival through Pluralism: Emerging Gay Communities in the Philippines', in *Journal of Homosexuality* 40 (February 2001): 117-142, DOI: 10.1300/J082v40n03_07.

69   Sonny Atencia Catacutan, 'Swardspeak: A Queer Perspective' (Presentation, Multimedia and Popular Culture Class, Los Baños: University of the Philippines Open University, 2013). https://prezi.com/hoog_fqpyosx/swardspeak-a-queer-perspective/.

70   Ibid.

71   Ibid.

72   Tom Boellstorff, 'Bahasa Gay is Bahasa Gaul', *Indonesian Language Online Resource* (2009) http://www.bahasakita.com/blog/bahasa-gay-is-bahasa-gaul/ (accessed December 5, 2018).

73   Zdenek Salzmann, James Stanlaw, Nobuko Adachi, *Language, Culture, and Society: An Introduction to Linguistic Anthropology* (Boulder: Westview Press, 1998).

74   Leap and Boellstorff, *Speaking in Queer Tongues*, 187.

75   Ibid., 198.

76   Ibid., 197.

77   *Λεξικό Τριανταφυλλίδη* s.v. «ξενομανία», «Ξενομανία, η [ksenomania] υπερβολική και άκριτη προτίμηση για καθετί το ξενικό, με ταυτόχρονη περιφρόνηση για καθετί το εγχώριο και το εθνικό». http://www.greek-language.gr/greekLang/

modern_greek/tools/lexica/search.html?lq=%CE%BE%CE%B5%CE%B-D%CE%BF%CE%BC%CE%B1%CE%BD%CE%AF%CE%B1&dq= (accessed November 10, 2016).

78 Hugh McLean and Linda Ngcobo, 'abangibhamayo bathi ngimnandi', in *Defiant Desire: Gay and Lesbian Lives in South Africa*, eds. Mark Gevisser and Edwin Cameron (New York and London: Routledge, 1995), 180.
79 Ibid., 164.
80 Ibid., 165.
81 Ibid.
82 Ibid., 167.
83 Ibid., 184.
84 Ronald Louw, 'Mkhumbane and New Traditions of (un)African Same-sex Weddings', in *Changing Men in Southern Africa*, ed. Robert Morrell, (Pietermaritzburg: University of Natal Press, 2001) as quoted in 'Gay and Zulu, we speak isiNgqumo' Ethnolinguistic Identity Constructions, Stephanie Rudwick, *Transformation: Critical Perspectives on Southern Africa*, Number 74 (2010): 114.
85 Ibid.
86 Ibid.
87 Ibid., 127.
88 Ken Cage, *Gayle: The Language of Kinks and Queens: a History and Dictionary of Gay Language in South Africa* (Johannesburg: Jacana Media, 2003), 19.
89 Ibid.
90 Ibid., 11.
91 Ibid., 9.
92 Ibid., 11.
93 Ibid., 12.
94 Shiba Mazaza, *Design Indaba*, March 13, 2015 http://www.designindaba.com/articles/creative-work/keep-touch-dope-saint-jude-featuring-angel-ho.
95 Ings, 'Trade Talk', 784.
96 Ibid., 785.
97 Ibid., 776.
98 Ibid., 784.
99 Ibid., 785.
100 Muhammad Safeer Awan and Muhammad Sheeraz, 'Queer but Language: A Sociolinguistic Study of Farsi' *International Journal of Humanities and Social Science* Vol. 1 No. 10. (2011): 128. http://www.ijhssnet.com/journals/Vol_1_No_10_August_2011/17.pdf.

101 Kira Hall, 'Intertextual Sexuality: Parodies of Class, Identity, and Desire in Liminal Delhi' University of Colorado, *Journal of Linguistic Anthropology*, Vol. 15, Issue 1, 125–44, (2005). Kira Hall, '"Go Suck Your Husband's Sugarcane!" Hijras and the Use of Sexual Insult', in *Queerly Phrased: Language, Gender, and Sexuality*, eds. Anna Livia and Kira Hall, (New York: Oxford University Press, 1997), 430–460.

102 Kira Hall, 'Hijra/Hijrin: Language and Gender Identity' (PhD Dissertation, University of California, Berkeley, 1995) 166.

103 Hall, '"Go Suck Your Husband's Sugarcane!"', 452.

104 Mark McBeth, review of *Queerly Phrased: Language, Gender, and Sexuality*, by eds. Anna Livia and Kira Hall, JAC Vol. 20, No. 4 (Fall 2000), pp. 983-988. http://www.jstor.org/stable/20866382. 987.

105 Hall, "Go Suck Your Husband's Sugarcane!", 436.

106 'By employing Bell's seven point criteria for language analysis, data for the present study has been analysed. Linguistically, Farsi contains its own vocabulary and shows various syntactical and morphological differences from the other 'mainstream' languages. Sociolinguistic analysis shows that Farsi is as good a language as any other. However, the number of its lexical items is small which is perhaps because of its limited and private usage.' Safeer Awan and Sheeraz, 'Queer but Language', 127.

107 Nidhi Dugar Kundalia, 'Queer language' *The Hindu Magazine*, November 30, 2013, http://www.thehindu.com/features/magazine/queer-language/article5407840.ece.

108 Ibid.

109 Safeer Awan and Sheeraz, 'Queer but Language', 127.

110 Kundalia, 'Queer language'.

111 Nicholas Kontovas, 'Lubunca: The Historical Development of Istanbul's Queer Slang and a Social-Functional Approach to Diachronic Processes in Language' (MA thesis, Indiana University, December 2012), 35.

112 'Turkish Argot | Labunya. Labunyaca', *Mavi Boncuk: Cornucopia of Ottomania and Turcomania* (blog), February 14, 2006, http://maviboncuk.blogspot.co.at/2006/02/turkish-argot-labunya-labunyaca.html.

113 Kontovas, 'Lubunca', 1.

114 Mavi Boncuk,'Turkish Argot | Labunya. Labunyaca'.

115 Kontovas, 'Lubunca', 10.

116 Ibid., 20.

117 Ya'ar Hever, Skype conversation with the author, February 15, 2015.

118 Wikipedia, s.v. סלנג להט"בי (LGBT Slang) https://he.wikipedia.org/wiki/%D7%A1%D7%9C%D7%A0%D7%92_%D7%9C%D7%94%D7%98%22%D7%91%D7%99 (accessed October 27, 2019).

119 Liat Granierer, Email conversation with the author November 27, 2019.

120 'Ibn Shoshana Dictionary: The Illustrated Version', LGBTQ magazine WDG, February 10, 2019, https://www.wdg.co.il/%D7%9E%D7%99%D7%9C%D7%95%D7%9F-%D7%90%D7%91%D7%9F-%D7%A9%D7%95%D7%A9%D7%A0%D7%94-%D7%94%D7%92%D7%A8%D7%A1%D7%94-%D7%94%D7%9E%D7%90%D7%95%D7%99%D7%99%D7%A8%D7%AA/#&gid=1&pid=1 (accessed October 27, 2019).

121 'What to collectively call people whose sexual and gendered practices and/or identities fall beyond the bounds of normative heterosexuality is an unavoidable and ultimately unresolvable problem.' Don Kulick, 'Gay and Lesbian Language', *Annual Review of Anthropology* 29:243–5 (2000): 243.

122 Ibid., 259.

123 'While supporters argue that it provides a way for gay people to find and connect to one another, critics argue that there cannot be a "homosexual language" because there is no monolithic gay experience.' Shannon Weber, [Review of the book Language and Gender Research from a Queer Linguistic Perspective: A Critical Evaluation by Michaela Koch] *G&L* VOL 5.1 (2011): 153–57, doi: 10.1558/genl.v5i1.153

124 'In defining "queer linguistics" Koch outlines a few definitions before ultimately championing the approach that Wong et al. define "as the socio-linguistic study of language use without recourse to identity categories"'. Shannon Weber, Review of Language and Gender Research from a Queer Linguistic Perspective: A Critical Evaluation by Michaela Koch (2008)

125 'Middle English (used in falconry in the sense "recall"): from Old French reclamer, from Latin reclamare "cry out against", from re- "back" + clamare "to shout".' Lexico, s.v. 'reclaim', https://www.lexico.com/en/definition/reclaim (accessed October 29, 2019).

126 Kulick, 'Gay and Lesbian Language', 246.

127 Ibid.

128 Ibid., 247.

129 Penelope Eckert, 'Three Waves of Variation Study: The Emergence of Meaning in the Study of Sociolinguistic Variation', *Annual Review of Anthropology* 41:87–00 (2012): 97.

130 Benjamin Munson, *Do I Sound Gay?*, DVD, Directed by David Thorpe (San Francisco: Spectrum, 2014).
131 Michael Schulman, 'Is There a "Gay Voice"?' *The New Yorker*, July 10, 2015.
132 Munson, *Do I Sound Gay?*.
133 Kulick, 'Gay and Lesbian Language', 264.
134 In 2011, Lister's journals were recognised by Unesco as a 'pivotal document' in British history and added to the Memory of the World register. The diaries were 'a comprehensive and painfully honest account of lesbian life', said the UN cultural body.
135 Anna Livia, 'Disloyal to Masculinity: Linguistic Gender and Liminal Identity in French', in *Queerly Phrased*, eds. Anna Livia and Kira Hall, 359.
136 Nick Nicholas, 'Kaliarda XII: Attestation from 1904, 1934, and 1938', *Hellenisteukontos blog*, published November 29, 2017, http://hellenisteukontos.opoudjis.net/kaliarda-xii-attestation-from-1904-1934-and-1938/.
137 'Deleuze and Guattari offer a detailed and complex "open system" which is extraordinarily rich and complex. A useful way into it is to follow the concepts of coding, stratification and territorialization. They are related in the following manner. Coding is the process of ordering matter as it is drawn into a body; by contrast, stratification is the process of creating hierarchal bodies, while territorialization is the ordering of those bodies in "assemblages", that is to say, an emergent unity joining together heterogeneous bodies in a "consistency."' Edward N. Zalta, *The Stanford Encyclopedia of Philosophy*, s.v. 'Gilles Deleuze' (Stanford University, Stanford, Published online Sep 24, 2012) http://plato.stanford.edu/entries/deleuze/.
138 'Assemblage theory is an approach to systems analysis that emphasizes fluidity, exchangeability, and multiple functionalities. Assemblages appear to be functioning as a whole, but are actually coherent bits of a system whose components can be "yanked" out of one system, "plugged" into another, and still work. As such, assemblages characteristically have functional capacities but do not have a function—that is, they are not designed to only do one thing.' Thom Swiss, 'I'm Melvin, a 4G Hot Spot' in *Theories of the Mobile Internet: Materialities and Imaginaries*, eds. Andrew Herman, Jan Hadlaw, Thom Swiss, (London and New York: Routledge, 2015), 210.
139 Ahmed, *Willful Subjects*, 204.
140 I am referring here to publications that circulated under publishers either as books or journal articles and I am not including the unofficial dictionaries that

circulated among the communities themselves such as the Ibn Shoshana dictionary mentioned earlier.
141 Kulick, 'Gay and Lesbian Language', 248.
142 Ibid., 249.
143 Ibid.
144 Ibid., 251.
145 Leap and Boellstorff, *Speaking in Queer Tongues*, 193.
146 Kulick, 'Gay and Lesbian Language', 258.
147 Dan Savage, 'Savage Love: Bill, Ashton, Rick', *The Stranger*, May 15, 2003 http://www.thestranger.com/seattle/SavageLove?oid=14267.
148 Dan Savage, 'Savage Love: Gas Huffer', *The Stranger*, June 12, 2003 http://www.thestranger.com/seattle/SavageLove?oid=14566.
149 Judith Butler, *Bodies that Matter: On the Discursive Limits of 'Sex'* (New York; London: Routledge, 1993), 228.
150 Kulick opines that 'They [i.e. Rudes & Healy] do not entertain the idea that the uses of "she" they analyze might be a parodic strategy of distancing speakers from stereotypes, or that calling males "she" might be a commentary, not on women but on gender—precisely its lack of naturalness, lack of control, and nastiness.' Kulick, 'Gay and Lesbian Language', 254; And earlier he quotes Penelope & Wolfe who according to him also missed the mocking factor of gender and not women, and he writes 'In a later paper, Penelope & Wolfe (1979) use examples from *The Queen's Vernacular* to illustrate their argument that "what is usually regarded as 'gay' slang consists of quite ordinary (and derogatory) terms for women.... [G]ay males use these terms among themselves for the same reasons straight males coined them, as a way of verbally trivializing and abusing women" (Penelope & Wolfe 1979:10).' Ibid., 253.
151 Mathias Danbolt, 'Dismantling the Serious Machine: An Interview with Gavin Butt', *Trikster* #3, 2009, http://trikster.net/3/butt/1.html.
152 Susan Sontag, *Against Interpretation, and Other Essays* (New York: Farrar, Straus & Giroux, 1966); 291.
153 Ibid.
154 I draw in particular from Susan Sontag's *Notes on Camp* and Moe Meyer's 'Reclaiming the Discourse on Camp'. I agree with Meyer that Sontag 'sanitised' camp and perhaps 'softened' its connection to deviant sexualities (in this case 'homosexuality'), but I do appreciate the openness Sontag allows in her theorisation of camp, which is not anchored to sexualities, and is therefore a more

'open-source' technology. Susan Sontag, *Against Interpretation*; Moe Meyer, 'Reclaiming the Discourse on Camp', 1-19.

155 Sontag, *Against Interpretation*, 275.

156 Justin Torres, 'In praise of Latin Night at the Queer Club', *The Washington Post*, June 13, 2016, https://www.washingtonpost.com/opinions/in-praise-of-latin-night-at-the-queer-club/2016/06/13/e841867e-317b-11e6-95c0-2a6873031302_story.html.

157 Tracy Baim, *Out and Proud in Chicago: An Overview of the City's Gay Community*, ed. Tracy Baim (Chicago: Agate, 2008), 186; Kali Holloway, '10 Best Satirical Campaigns for President of the United States', Alternet, September 23, 2015, https://www.alternet.org/2015/09/10-best-satirical-campaigns-president-united-states/ (accessed November 17, 2016); Owen Keehnen, 'Kisses For My President: An Interview With Queer Nation Presidential Candidate Joan Jett Blakk', *Queer Cultural Center*, http://www.queerculturalcenter.org/Pages/Keehnen/Blakk.html (accessed November 17, 2016).

158 Drag'in for Votes, YouTube, directed by Elspeth Kydd and Gabriel Gomez, Chicago, 1990, https://www.youtube.com/watch?v=vxUxgiFbRJs and https://www.youtube.com/watch?v=BIIBRIOIPZ4 (accessed November 17, 2016).

159 'Myer (1994a) has also called attention to the ways in which camp "has become an activist strategy for organizations such as ACT UP and Queer Nation" (p. 1; see also Bergman 1993b, Román 1993).' Kulick, 'Gay and Lesbian Language', 255.

160 Rusty Barrett, 'Supermodels of the World Unite! Political Economy and the Language of Performance Among African-American Drag Queens' in *Beyond the Lavender Lexicon: Authenticity, Imagination and Appropriation in Lesbian and Gay Languages*, ed. William Leap (Buffalo and NY: Gordon & Breach, 1995), 207-226.

161 Sara Ahmed, 'Happy Objects' in *The Affect Theory Reader*, eds. Melissa Gregg and Gregory J. Seigworth, (Durham and London: Duke University Press, 2010), 31.

162 Jonathan Katz, 'John Cage's Queer Silence or How to Avoid Making Matters Worse', *Queer Cultural Center*, http://www.queerculturalcenter.org/Pages/KatzPages/KatzWorse.html (accessed November 17, 2016).

163 Jonathan Katz, 'Passive Resistance: on the Success of Queer Artists in Cold War American Art', *Queer Cultural Center*, http://www.queerculturalcenter.org/Pages/KatzPages/KatzLimage.html (accessed November 17, 2016); and Jonathan D. Katz, 'The Silent Camp: Queer Resistance and the Rise of Pop Art', *Queer Cultural Center*, http://www.queerculturalcenter.org/Pages/KatzPages/KatzCamp.html (accessed November 17, 2016).

164 Katz references how 'Caroline Jones does a remarkable analysis of Cage's silence as a means of opposition to the Abstract Expressionist ego in Caroline A. Jones, "Finishing School: John Cage and the Abstract Expressionist Ego", Critical Inquiry (Summer 1993), 643-647.' Jonathan Katz, 'John Cage's Queer Silence'.

165 'The most significant historical account of Cage's gay life, based on two remarkably candid interviews with Cage, is to be found in Thomas Hines, 'Then Not Yet "Cage"': The Los Angeles Years, 1912-1938" in *John Cage: Composed in America*, eds. Marjorie Perloff and Charles Junkerman (Chicago: The University of Chicago Press, 1994), 65-99.' Jonathan Katz, 'John Cage's Queer Silence'.

Opacity

1 'Thus opacity is a category within the visible that works against hierarchy, wounding, and domination' writes Lorenz reminding us both the field from which opacity is borrowed (the visual), and the fields in which it is applied (the social) as it undoes it. Renate Lorenz, *Not Now! Now! Chronopolitics, Art, and Research* (Berlin: Sternberg Press, 2014), 11.

2 De Villiers, *Opacity and the Closet*, 21.

3 Beyond the slang or cant varieties which have lent lemmata to the queer slangs mentioned in the previous chapter, and the slangs of hobos, actors, sex workers, thieves, merchant navy officers, spivs, magkes, and others, I would like to mention the slangs developed primarily by youth incorporating elements from various migrant languages and native ones. One example is Rinkebysvenska in Sweden and Kebabnorsk in Norway, which comprise Turkish, Arabic, Bosnian/Croatian/Serbian, Kurdish, Spanish, Greek, and Romany in the case of the former and Turkish, Kurdish, Arabic, Urdu, Pashto, Persian, and Punjabi in the case of the latter. Marie-Noëlle Godin, 'Urban Youth Language in Multicultural Sweden', Scandinavian-Canadian Studies/Études Scandinaves *Aucanada* Vol. 16 (2006): 126-141. http://scancan.net/article.htm?id=godin_1_16 (accessed November 18, 2016); *Wikipedia* s.v. 'Kebabnorsk', https://en.wikipedia.org/wiki/Kebabnorsk (accessed November 18, 2016).

4 Orie Endo (遠藤織枝), 'Nushu', (Paper presented at the Association of Asian Studies Annual Conference, March, 1999), http://nushu.world.coocan.jp/aas99.htm (accessed November 18, 2016); *Omniglot: The Online Encyclopedia of Writing Systems and Languages* s.v. 'Nüshu (女书)', http://www.omniglot.com/writing/nushu.htm (accessed November 18, 2016); Christie K K Leung, 'Women Who

Found A Way Creating a Women's Language', *Off Our Backs* 33, no. 11/12 (2003): 40-43; Lawrence Lo, 'Nushu', *Ancient Scripts*. http://www.ancientscripts.com/nushu.html (accessed November 18, 2016).

5 Judith Butler, *Gender Trouble: Feminism and the Subversion of Identity* (New York: Routledge, 1990), 13.

6 Melanie Kaye, 'Sign' in *We Speak in Code: Poems and Other Writings* (Pittsburgh: Motheroot Publications, 1980), 85.

7 'Tell your immediate family', he would say. 'Tell friends, neighbors, people in the stores you shop in, cab drivers, everyone.' And he urged heterosexual people to be our allies, to interrupt derogatory remarks and jokes, to support us and offer aid when needed. If we all did this, he said, we could change the world. Warren J. Blumenfeld, 'Everyone's Issue: Coming Out isn't Just for LGBT People any Longer', *LGBTQ Nation*, October 11, 2016. http://www.lgbtqnation.com/2016/10/everyones-issue-coming-isnt-just-lgbt-people-longer.

8 Heidi Minning, 'Qwir-English Code-Mixing in Germany: Constructing a Rainbow of Identities', in *Speaking in Queer Tongues*, 624.

9 Simon O'Sullivan, 'Notes Towards a Minor Art Practice', *Drain: Journal of Contemporary Art and Culture*, 2005, http://www.drainmag.com/contentNOVEMBER/RELATED_ESSAYS/Notes_Towards_Minor_Practice.htm (accessed November 18, 2016).

10 Petropoulos, *Kaliarnta*; Kontovas, *Lubunca*; Paul Baker, *Polari*.

11 Baker, *Polari*.

12 Costas Canakis, *Kaliarnta*, DVD, directed by Paola Revenioti (Athens, 2014).

13 As a native Greek speaker with a certain proficiency in English and a significant degree of immersion in those cultures (as ambiguous as a comment like that may be) after having lived in Greece and England, I believe I am capable of understanding the cultural context and the role this plays in understanding the specific references, the humor, and the 'tone' of those slangs. I don't think I would be able to fully appreciate these slangs had I only known the official languages without having been immersed in the culture. The other slangs remain inaccessible to me, leaving me in the position of a mere researcher/observer, drawing from what the users tell me.

14 Nicholas Kontovas, a researcher who is the only one so far (December 2018) to have published in English a thorough study of Lubunca, claims the same to be true of it.

15 Petropoulos, *Kaliarnta*.

16   James W. Chesebro, *Gayspeak: Gay Male & Lesbian Communication* (New York: Pilgrim Press, 1981), 45-47.
17   Butler, Introduction, xxv.
18   Πετρόπουλος, *Καλιαρντά*, 9.
19   Costas Canakis in *Kaliarnta*.
20   Sara Ahmed, *The Promise of Happiness*, (Durham and London: Duke University Press, 2010), 151.
21   Ibid.
22   Petropoulos, *Kaliarnta*.
23   Revenioti, *Kaliarda*.
24   Elizabeth Freeman, 'Queer Belongings Kinship Theory and Queer Theory' in *A Companion to Lesbian, Gay, Bisexual, Transgender, and Queer Studies*, eds. George E. Haggerty and Molly McGarry, (MA: Blackwell, 2007), 309.
25   Σοφία Τατίδου, '5 Καθημερινές Λέξεις με Ενδιαφέρουσα Ετυμολογία' Φιλολογική Θεώρηση, June 28, 2016. https://philologikitheorisi.blogspot.com/2016/07/lekseis-me-endiaferousa-etymologia-kai-simasia-idiotis-skiouros-sarkazo-sxoleio-kollyva.html.
26   Baker, *Polari*, 2.
27   Ibid., 190.
28   Ibid., 13.
29   Kontovas, *Lubunca*.
30   Glissant, *Poetics of Relation*, 95.
31   Though I transfer Glissant's call for the right to opacity, and a breaking of transparency—both of which I stand for—I must say that I don't find this dualism compatible with the larger framework of thought in which my work is situated. In particular using queer theory, queerness, and liminalities as integral elements of my thinking process, it becomes a bit limiting—problematic some would say—to refer to those two qualities as inherently oppositional and on a strict binary. Thinking of the terms in plural form, or making clear they are not by default two sides of the same coin, but rather multiplicitous, combinable, and activatable in diverse settings and in various ways, also allowing for an overlapping, I think might provide some solution.
32   Lorenz, *Not Now! Now!*, 18.
33   Glissant, *Poetics of Relation*, 189-194.
34   Judith Halberstam, *The Queer Art of Failure*, (Durham: Duke University Press, 2011), 129.

35 'A different, anarchistic type of struggle requires a new grammar, possibly a new voice, potentially the passive voice.' Ibid.
36 'Passive /pæs v/adjective: a homosexual man who takes the insertee role in anal intercourse, and may also be quiet and effeminate.' Paul Baker, *Polari*, 185.
37 Hugh McLean and Linda Ngcobo, 'Abangibhamayo bathi ngimnandi', 164.
38 Ann Cvetkovich & Karin Michalski, transcript of the film in *Impasse*, eds. Käthe von Bose, Ulrike Klöppel, Katrin Köppert, Karin Michalski & Pat Treusch, (Berlin: B_books Verlag 2015), 18.
39 Associated Press, 'Russia Passes Anti-Gay-Law', *The Guardian*, June 30 2013, https://www.theguardian.com/world/2013/jun/30/russia-passes-anti-gay-law; Colin Stewart, 'Proposals for New "Gay Propaganda" Laws; Europe Worries', *76 Crimes*, April 19 2016, https://76crimes.com/2016/04/19/proposals-for-new-gay-propaganda-laws-europe-worries/; Michael K. Lavers, 'Indonesian Lawmakers Considering LGBT Propaganda Bill', *Washington Blade*, March 8 2016, http://www.washingtonblade.com/2016/03/08/indonesian-lawmakers-considering-lgbt-propaganda-bill/.
40 TNYT Staff, 'Robertson Letter Attacks Feminists', *The New York Times*, August 26 1992, https://www.nytimes.com/1992/08/26/us/robertson-letter-attacks-feminists.html.
41 Britton, *Édouard Glissant and Postcolonial Theory*, 26.
42 Ahmed, *The Promise of Happiness*, 38.
43 Mariella Mosthof, 'Can Hannah Gadsby's Nanette Bring Queer Storytelling the Attention It's Due?' *Slate*, July 20, 2018, https://slate.com/human-interest/2018/07/hannah-gadsbys-nanette-isnt-comedy-but-its-a-fine-example-of-queer-storytelling.html.
44 Glissant, *Poetics of Relation*, 190.
45 I would like to mention here the etymological roots of the word barbarism deriving from the Greek 'βάρβαρος' (meaning barbarian) as a reference to all other nations based on what the Greeks perceived to be the sounds they made when talking 'bar bar bar' which for them did not constitute language and thus the echomimetic 'barbar' (Eng. barbarian) meant an uncivilised savage. The Greek Wikipedia entry writes: βάρβαρος < αρχαία ελληνική βάρβαρος < ηχομιμητική λέξη (από την ηχομιμητική λέξη βαρβαρ, έτσι όπως ηχούσε η ομιλία των άλλων γλωσσών στους αρχαίους Έλληνες) *Wikipedia* s.v. 'βάρβαρος', https://el.wikipedia.org/wiki/%CE%92%CE%AC%CF%81%CE%B2%CE%B1%CF%81%CE%BF%CE%B9.
46 Glissant, *Poetics of Relation*, 189.

47 Ibid., 120.
48 'The most crucial dimension of this cultural hinterland is language. In colonies where there were indigenous languages that the colonizers could not understand, these provided a "naturally" opaque protection for the colonized. In the Caribbean, however, the only available language was Creole, and it was equally available to both master and slave. It therefore became a question, for the slaves, of developing within the common language strategies for nevertheless eluding the master's comprehension. They gradually formed a particular usage of Creole, which the master did not understand but did not realize that he did not understand. Camouflage is inherent in the basic structure of the language. An emphasis on loudness and a jerky, accelerated delivery that appears to be meaningless or even nonsensical in fact serves to communicate, secretly, the real meaning: "Creole is originally a kind of conspiracy that concealed itself by its public and open expression.... this form of nonsense... could conceal and reveal at the same time a hidden meaning" (Caribbean Discourse, 124-25).' Britton, Édouard Glissant and Postcolonial Theory, 25.
49 Frantz Fanon, *Black Skin, White Masks*, trans. Charles Lam Markmann (London: Pluto Press, 1986), 25.
50 Ibid., 17.
51 Ibid., 8.
52 Britton, *Édouard Glissant and Postcolonial Theory*, 20.
53 In both his works *Poetics of Relation* and *Caribbean Discourse* he outlines the economic and literary production processes that go hand in hand and showcases how the manipulation of linguistic elements (primarily oral) shrouded in opacity was a mode of resistance against the colonial regime. Glissant, *Poetics of Relation*; Édouard Glissant, *Caribbean Discourse: Selected Essays*, trans. Michael J. Dash (Charlottesville: Univ. Press of Virginia, 1999)
54 As bell hooks writes: 'When I realize how long it has taken for white Americans to acknowledge diverse languages of Native Americans, to accept that the speech their ancestral colonizers declared was merely grunts or gibberish was indeed language, it is difficult not to hear in standard English always the sound of slaughter and conquest.' bell hooks, *Teaching to Transgress: Education As the Practice of Freedom* (New York: Routledge, 1994), 169.
55 Glissant, *Poetics of Relation*, 194.
56 Jeannine Murray-Román, *Performance and Personhood in Caribbean Literature: From Alexis to the Digital Age* (Virginia: University of Virginia Press, 2016), 96.
57 Ibid.

58 Ibid.
59 Celia Britton, *The Sense of Community in French Caribbean Fiction* (Liverpool: Liverpool University Press, 2008), 37.
60 Ibid., 36.
61 hooks, *Teaching to Transgress*, 170.
62 Ibid., 171.
63 Ibid., 167.
64 Britton, *Édouard Glissant and Postcolonial Theory*, 19.
65 Anzaldúa, *Borderlands/La Frontera*, 59.
66 Britton, *Édouard Glissant and Postcolonial Theory*, 22.
67 Ibid., 25.
68 Britton, *The Sense of Community in French Caribbean Fiction*, 191.
69 Halberstam, *The Queer Art of Failure*, 98.
70 'In his 1964 Playboy interview with Madelein Gobeil, when asked, "What did you feel while reading the book he devoted to you?" Genet responds: A kind of disgust—because I saw myself naked and stripped by someone other than myself. In all my books I strip myself but at the same time I disguise myself with words, choices, attitudes, magic. I take pains not to damage myself too much. Sartre stripped me without mercy. He wrote about me in the present tense. My first impulse was to burn the book. Sartre had handed me the manuscript. I finally allowed him to publish it because I've always felt compelled to be responsible for what I evoke.' De Villiers, *Opacity and the Closet*, 14.
71 Katz, 'The Silent Camp'.
72 Kulick, 'Gay and Lesbian Language', 274.
73 Jonathan D. Katz, 'Performative Silence and the Politics of Passivity' in *Making A Scene* eds. Henry Rodgers and David Burrows (Birmingham: Article Press, 2000), 97-103, 99.
74 'The kind of silence I'm referring to is a specularized, performative and highly ironized silence—a form of political engagement now so distinctly undervalued in a post-Stonewall gay political context as to render it all but invisible as political gesture. But, to put it, blandly, the times were different under a savagely policed, McCarthyite America and silence could and did prove effective as a strategy of dissent.' Katz, 'The Silent Camp'.
75 Katz, 'Performative Silence and the Politics of Passivity', 101.
76 'Foucault has already noted, silences are as much a necessary part of a particular discourse as the things that are said within it. He also includes "misunderstanding" as something that always involves "a fundamental relation to

truth"(55/74).' Mark G. E. Kelly, *Foucault's History of Sexuality Volume I, The Will to Knowledge* (Edinburgh: Edinburgh University Press, 2013), 45.

77 'This experimental and open process is one Sedgwick explicitly links to epistemology and representation, to meaning, but I would also like to allow for the possibility of nonmeaning and nonknowledge as "queer" strategies (as she alludes to when she speaks of gaps and lapses of meaning). This is what I am calling queer opacity. Against the hermeneutics of sex as a field of meaning to be deciphered and interpreted, the oeuvre is not decrypted for the secret truth of sexuality or seen as simply a result of sexuality.' De Villiers, *Opacity and the Closet*, 16.

78 'The word Foucault uses here, which Hurley translates as "misunderstanding" is méconnaissance, literally "misknowledge". This is a word that lacks an entirely adequate translation into English. For this reason Hurley takes the unusual step of retaining the French word in brackets on the next page, p. 56. Elsewhere Foucault explains the relationship of méconnaissance to truth more straight forwardly, saying "la connaissance est toujours une méconnaissance" "knowledge is always a misknowledge".' Kelly, *Foucault's History of Sexuality*, 45.

79 *The Free Dictionary*, s.v. 'mis-', http://www.thefreedictionary.com/mis- (accessed May 25, 2016).

80 Ibid.

81 *Online Etymology Dictionary*, s.v. 'queer', http://www.etymonline.com/index.php?term=queer&allowed_in_frame=0 (accessed November 4, 2016).

82 Adrienne Rich, 'Cartographies of Silence' in *Poems* (The World's Poetry Archive, 2012), 10.

83 Κωνσταντίνος Π. Καβάφης, *Καβάφης: Ατελή Ποιήματα, 1918-1932*, επιμ. Renata Lavagnini (Αθήνα: Ίκαρος, 1994).

84 'In contrast, gay artists did what they had always done—because it was all they could do—constructing distinctions through the recontextualization of the extant codes of culture, reworking those codes to their own benefit. These gay artists made an art, as they had made every other aspect of their lives, that appeared to function within the terms of the national consensus. Anything else was simply too dangerous.' Katz, 'The Silent Camp'.

85 De Villiers, *Opacity and the Closet*, 136.

86 Katz, 'Performative Silence and the Politics of Passivity', 103.

87 Ibid.

88 Ibid., 102.

89 Katz, 'Passive Resistance'.

90 Michel Foucault, *The History of Sexuality Vol 1*, trans. Robert Hurley (New York: Pantheon Books, 1978), 27.
91 Katz, 'Performative Silence and the Politics of Passivity', 102.
92 Britton, *Édouard Glissant and Postcolonial Theory*, 25.
93 Glissant, *Caribbean Discourse: Selected Essays*, 163-165.
94 Ahmed, *Willful Subjects*, 175.
95 Ibid., 176.
96 Aaminah Khan, 'Muslim, Queer, Feminist: It's as Complicated as it Sounds' Blog Post on *jaythenerdkid* (blog), February 23, 2014, https://jaythenerdkid.wordpress.com/2014/02/23/muslim-queer-feminist-its-as-complicated-as-it-sounds/; Amber Rehman, 'My Hijab Doesn't Oppress Me, It Empowers Me', *The Huffington Post*, May 5, 2013, http://www.huffingtonpost.ca/amber-rehman/feminism-hijab-canada_b_2808850.html.
97 I am bringing the hijab and the niqab into the conversation because of their opaque potential. Similarly to my analysis of the closet, the hijab and the niqab are thought of here as potentially emancipatory deliberate practices.
98 Hanna Yusuf, Maya Wolfe-Robinson, Leah Green, Caterina Monzani and Bruno Rinvolucri, 'My Hijab Has Nothing to Do With Oppression. It's a Feminist Statement' *The Guardian*, June 24, 2015, http://www.theguardian.com/commentisfree/video/2015/jun/24/hijab-not-oppression-feminist-statement-video.
99 Suzana Milevska, 'Veils/Folds/Events' in *Not Now! Now!*, 104-5.
100 Δημητρης Αναστασοπουλος, «Οι Κουκούλες και ο Νόμος τους», Ελευθεροτυπία, July 12, 2009, http://www.enet.gr/?i=news.el.article&id=62456; Βαγγέλης Μπάδας, '«Περί κουκούλας»: Μια Διεπιστημονική Ματιά στα Διεκδικητικά Βεστιάρια', Blog Post at *badas1*, http://badas1.blogspot.co.at/(accessed May 25, 2016).
101 Jacques Derrida, 'How to Avoid Speaking: Denials', in *Derrida and Negative Theology*, eds. Harold Coward and Toby Foshay (Albany: SUNY Press, 1989), 86.
102 Nathalie Malinarich, 'Profile: The Zapatistas' Mysterious Leader', *BBC News*, March 11, 2001, http://news.bbc.co.uk/2/hi/americas/1214676.stm; He further shares his relationship to language during his upbringing, 'one way or another, we became conscious of language—not as a way of communicating, but of constructing something. As if it were a pleasure more than a duty.' In connection to the previously mentioned difference between academic/artivist linguistic creativity he further states: 'In the underground, unlike the world of bourgeois intellectuals, the word is not what is most valued. It is relegated to a secondary position. It was when we got to the indigenous communities

that language hit us, like a catapult. Then you realize that you lack the words to express many things, and that obliges you to work on language. To return time and again to words, to put them together and take them apart.' García Márquez and Roberto Pombo, Interview with Subcomandante Marcos, 'The Punch Card And The Hourglass' trans. in *New Left Review* 9, London, (2001): 77. https://newleftreview.org/II/9/subcomandante-marcos-the-punch-card-and-the-hourglass (accessed May 25, 2016).

103 Homi K. Bhabha, foreword to the 1986 edition of *Black Skin, White Masks* by Frantz Fanon, Charles Lam Markmann trans., (London: Pluto Press, 1986); xxxiv.

104 Ahmed, *Willful Subjects*, 150.

105 Ibid., 152.

106 Giorgio Agamben, *The Coming Community*, trans. Michael Hardt (Minneapolis and London: University of Minnesota, 1993), 86.

107 Ahmed, *Willful Subjects*, 184.

108 Hutta further explains the term as such: 'an analytical term I have developed in my research, making use of the untranslatable German notion of "Geborgenheit" (roughly: security, comfort, sheltered-ness, see Hutta 2009: 256-65, 2010b: 84-169).' Jan Simon Hutta, 'Beyond the Politics of Inclusion: Securitization and Agential Formations in Brazilian LGBT Parades', in *Queer Futures: Reconsidering Ethics, Activism, and the Political*, eds. Elahe Haschemi Yekani, Eveline Kilian, Beatrice Michaelis (London and New York: Routledge, 2016), 77.

109 Ibid., 77-78.

110 Hutta makes clear in his text that there is a strict separation of the 'dignified' members of the community, who are allowed visibility, and those who are not. This separation happens along class lines, which in Brazil coincide with racial lines. The parades are organised by and demonstrate the presence of white, cis, middle-class gay men, while the more vulnerable members of the community (poor, POC, sex workers, trans* folk) are kept off the floats and therefore out of the public eye. It is they that claim spaces of opacity to indulge in pleasures, and by so doing mock the organisers as well as on-lookers that want to attend a 'dignified' event.

111 Eventually, a court overruled the decision and Navid was given asylum Shannon Power, 'Gay Asylum Seeker Denied Visa for not Knowing what the Pride Flag Colors Meant' *Gay Star News*, August 14, 2018 https://www.gaystarnews.com/article/gay-asylum-seeker-denied-visa-for-not-knowing-what-the-pride-flag-colors-meant/#gs.hvmUHaM

112 AFP, 'Austria Rejects Afghan's Asylum Bid Because he "Did not Act or Dress, Gay"' *The Guardian*, August 15, 2018 https://www.theguardian.com/world/2018/aug/15/austria-accuses-afghan-asylum-seeker-of-pretending-to-be-gay
113 Lorenz, *Not Now! Now!*, 20.
114 Of course, many slang words have made it into the mainstream, and the mainstream world doesn't even know it has been 'pervaded' by queer slang terms. Such cases have been well documented in both Kaliarnta and Polari, with terms like «τζους», «ντάνα», «κωλομπαράς», and «μπάρα» entering everyday Greek parlance and similarly, mainstream English now includes such terms as 'butch' and 'naff' (which, according to which source one picks, is either an acronym for Not Available For Fucking, indicating someone straight, or an acronym for Normal As Fuck indicating something drab and unfashionable), which now refers to something tasteless.
115 Katz, 'John Cage's Queer Silence or How to Avoid Making Matters Worse'.
116 It was decriminalised in 1967 in England and Wales. Sexual Offences Act 1967, Chapter 60, http://www.legislation.gov.uk/ukpga/1967/60/pdfs/ukpga_19670060_en.pdf (accessed November 24, 2016).
117 De Villiers, *Opacity and the Closet*, 5.
118 Britton, *Édouard Glissant and Postcolonial Theory*, 153, 156.

Minority

1 I am using the term minority not only to refer to the idea of the Deleuzoguattarian minority, becoming-minor, and minor literature, but also as a politically charged term in reference to ethnic, sexual, religious, ideological, political, gendered, dis_abled, neurodiverse/neurodivergent categories who have been consistently misunderstood and marginalised, and still have to fight for civil equality and rights despite their numbers or percentage in relation to the overall population. I decided to use it as a loan from Muñoz and also a reminder of the problematics of democracy when it comes to the rights of minorities, of how things gain value in numbers alone, how things that are not graspable become comparable and measurable, and how this almost always means losing track of the affective impact on individual experiences.
2 'A minor literature is not the literature of a minor language but the literature a minority makes in a major language. But the primary characteristic of a minor literature involves all the ways in which the language is effected by a strong

co-efficent of deterritorialization.' Gilles Deleuze and Félix Guattari, *Kafka: Toward a Minor Literature*, trans. Dana Polan (Minneapolis and London: University of Minnesota, 1986), 16.

3   'The second characteristic of minor literatures is that everything in them is political. In "great" literatures, on the contrary, the question of the individual (familial, conjugal, etc.) tends to be connected to other, no less individual questions, and the social milieu serves as environment and background.' Ibid., 16.

4   'The third characteristic is that everything has a collective value. In effect, precisely because talents do not abound in a minor literature, the conditions are not given for an individuated utterance which would be that of some "master" and could be separated from collective utterance.' Ibid., 17.

5   I use the term along the lines of the Deleuzoguattarian concept of 'becoming-revolutionary' which is beyond linear temporalities and, similarly to 'queer', 'Becoming-revolutionary remains indifferent to questions of a future and a past of the revolution; it passes between the two' and is associated with becoming-minoritarian. 'Becoming-minoritarian as the universal figure of consciousness is called autonomy. It is certainly not by using a minor language as a dialect, by regionalizing or ghettoizing, that one becomes revolutionary; rather, by using a number of minority elements, by connecting, conjugating them, one invents a specific, unforeseen, autonomous becoming.' Gilles Deleuze and Félix Guattari, *A Thousand Plateaus: Capitalism and Schizophrenia*, trans. Brian Massumi (Minneapolis and London: University of Minnesota, 1987), 292 and 106 respectively.

6   'Performative language is also that which, after all, both builds and unbuilds concepts in language.' Judith Butler, introduction to *Of Grammatology*, xxii.

7   O'Sullivan, 'Notes Towards a Minor Art Practice'.

8   Interview with Paulistano Jiulian Correia conducted on June 2013, and with Carioca artist Pêdra Costa conducted on October 2014. Traces found in Antonio Gomes da Costa Neto's 'A Linguagem no Candomblé: Um estudo lingüístico sobre as comunidades religiosas afro-brasileiras' as well as articles in the blogosphere, e.g., by Eloisa Aquino, a Brazilian-born zinister. According to Pêdra Costa, who first encountered Pajubá words in Umbanda's terreiro (spiritual place of the Afro-Brazilian religion), these words derived from the religious sphere. According to Eloisa Aquino, it was the need of queers for a more liberal religious practice that pushed them to borrow words from Candomblé practitioners.

9   Laurent Berlant, *Cruel Optimism* (Durham and London: Duke University Press, 2011), 48.
10 Kulick, 'Gay and Lesbian Language', 252.
11 Deleuze and Guattari, *Kafka*, 17.
12 'Indeed, if there is an affirmation of a new community, it is precisely of the always already excluded, a bastard community of the sick and the frail, a hybrid and mutant collectivity always in progress, always open to any and everyone.' O'Sullivan, 'Notes Towards a Minor Art Practice', 8.
13 'At the beginning of *The Castle*, the children speak so quickly that nobody understands what they're saying' Deleuze and Guattari, *Kafka*, 21.
14 O'Sullivan, 'Notes Towards a Minor Art Practice', 2.
15 Kulick, 'Gay and Lesbian Language', 252.
16 Ings, 'Trade Talk', 788.
17 Though there are videos of the TV talk show available on YouTube and other streaming sites, I will avoid sharing the link due to the extremity of the homophobic and transphobic language the extreme cisgenderism and the TV network's involvement in the political sphere to serve the interests of its owner. Similar statements the same person made years earlier in: Δημήτρης Γαλάνης, Πειραιώς Σεραφείμ: «Κατάχρηση της Θεοδότου Ελευθερίας η Πεολειχία», *Το Βήμα*, Σεπτέμβριος 28, 2012, http://www.tovima.gr/society/article/?aid=476946.
18 The overall consensus seems to be that 'sodomy' refers to oral and anal practices between humans, particularly of the same gender, but also any non-procreative practices, and practices with non-human animals. David E. Newton, *Gay and Lesbian Rights: A Reference Handbook*, 2nd Edition, (Santa Barbara: ABC-CLIO, 2009), 85; John M. Scheb, John M. Scheb, II, *Criminal Law and Procedure* (Belmont: Wadsworth Publishing, 2010), 185.
19 Virginia Woolf, *A Room of One's Own* (New York: Harcourt, Brace and Co., 1929).
20 Ahmed, *Willful Subjects*, 154.
21 Rudwick, 'Gay and Zulu, we speak isiNgqumo', 128.
22 Ahmed, *Willful Subjects*, 19.
23 Audre Lorde, *Sister Outsider: Essays and Speeches* (Trumansburg: Crossing Press, 1984), 110-114.
24 Joe E. Jeffreys, 'Joan Jett Blakk for President: Cross-Dressing at the Democratic National Convention', *TDR* (1988-), Vol. 37, No. 3 (Autumn, 1993), 186-195.
25 Ibid.
26 Ibid.

27   Hubert Fichte, *Queer Theory in Education*, ed. William F. Pinar, (Mahwah and London: Lawrence Erlbaum Associates Inc. 1998), 1.

28   'An act of survival. In the silent universe of the Plantation, oral expression, the only form possible for the slaves, was discontinuously organized. As tales, proverbs, sayings, songs appeared—as much in the Creole-speaking world as elsewhere—they bore the stamp of this discontinuity. The texts seem to neglect the essentials of something that Western realism, from the beginning, had been able to cover so well: the situation of landscapes, the lesson of scenery, the reading of customs, the description of the motives of characters. Almost never does one find in them any concrete relating of daily facts and deeds; what one does find, on the other hand, is a symbolic evocation of situations. As if these texts were striving for disguise beneath the symbol, working to say without saying. This is what I have referred to elsewhere as detour, and this is where discontinuity struggles; the same discontinuity the Maroons created through that other detour called marronnage.' Glissant, *Poetics of Relation*, 68.

29   O'Sullivan, 'Notes Towards a Minor Art Practice', 3-5.

30   Street art is not the only such outlet, off-spaces, and virtual spaces have indeed offered spaces of expression and politically-engaged discourse to take place.

31   I say 'basic' as my knowledge of these languages and slangs likely could not formally qualify as code-switching in the sense that bilingual speakers do.

32   I must admit I am unsure about the validity of this, as the use of the heart symbol generally seems to have been much later than 1 Century CE, but the following sources insist on the Brothel Ad theory: Mike Von Joel, 'Urbane Guerrillas: Street Art, Graffiti & Other Vandalism', *State of Art* January-February 2006; Acarlar Köyü, 'The Brothel Advertisement at Ephesus', *Atlas Obscura* https://www.atlasobscura.com/places/brothel-advertisement-at-ephesus (accessed December 3, 2018).

33   Valeria Appel, 'Ghetto Art: Thousand Voices in the City', EDIT3, *Territoires/Territories* (2006), http://www.edit-revue.com/?Article=98 (accessed November 27, 2016). *Bomb It*, DVD, directed by Jon Reiss (Los Angeles, 2008). *Style Wars*, DVD, directed by Tony Silver (New York City: Public Art Films, 1983).

34   Gordon C. C. Douglas, 'The Art of Spatial Resistance: The Global Urban Network of Street Art' (MSc thesis, London School of Economics, 2005).

35   'Coding is the process of ordering matter as it is drawn into a body; by contrast, stratification is the process of creating hierarchal [sic] bodies, while territorialization is the ordering of those bodies in "assemblages", that is to say, an emer-

gent unity joining together heterogeneous bodies in a "consistency".' Zalta, *The Stanford Encyclopedia of Philosophy*.

36 *Lexigram Dictionary*, s.v. 'γκράφιτι' Ετυμολογία: [<αγγλ. graffiti, πληθ. του graffito < ιταλ. graffito < ιταλ. graffio 'χάραγμα' < graffiare 'χαράζω' < λατιν. graphium < αρχ. ελλ. γραφεῖον 'όργανο γραφής']' *Lexigram Dictionary*, s.v. 'graffiti' Lexigram, https://www.lexigram.gr/lex/enni/%CE%B3%CE%BA%CF%81%E1%B-D%B1%CF%86%CE%B9%CF%84%CE%B9 (accessed November 27, 2016).

37 'OLEK's art explores sexuality, feminist ideals and the evolution of communication through colors, conceptual exploration and meticulous detail. OLEK consistently pushes the boundaries between fashion, art, craft and public art, fluidly combining the sculptural and the fanciful. With the old fashion technique of crocheting, she has taken the ephemeral medium of yarn to express everyday occurrences, inspirations and hopes to create a metaphor for the complexity and interconnectedness of our body and psychological processes.' From OLEK's website, http://oleknyc.com/home (accessed November 27, 2016).

38 Tatyana Fazlalizadeh, 'Stop Telling Women To Smile: A Street Art Project Addressing Gender Based Street Harassment' http://www.tlynnfaz.com/Stop-Telling-Women-to-Smile (accessed November 27, 2016).

39 RAW Project 'Space Invaders' https://www.raw.at/materialien (accessed November 27, 2016).

40 This was a project in which I used sideway-chalk (which children use in Germany to colour pavements and squares) to write my CV, a love email, and my will and testament on sidewalks around Berlin. It was meant as a reflection upon the seriousness and privacy which we treat certain documents with. Given the specific kinds of texts chosen, it was also a comment on the difficulty of finding a job in Berlin at the time, no matter how far and wide I disseminated my CV. This led to an existential crisis prompting me to renew my will and explore how it would impact me if I shared it in public. http://annatee.co.uk/strassenmalkreide/ (accessed November 27, 2016).

41 I am referring in particular to the blog 'Aesthetics of Crisis' an ethnographic research project located at the intersection of urban theory, visual culture, and social movement studies. http://aestheticsofcrisis.org/ (accessed November 27, 2016).

42 Tiffany Renée Conklin, 'Street Art, Ideology, and Public Space' (master's thesis, Portland State University, 2012).

43 Kai Jakob, *Street Art in Berlin* (Berlin: Jaron Verlag, 2008).

44 Ibid.

45 'How many people live today in a language that is not their own? Or else, no longer even know their tongue –or do not know it yet- and know a major tongue which they are forced to use poorly?' Deleuze and Guattari, *Kafka*, 19.
46 '(Linguistics) a private language, as invented by a child or between two children, esp twins' The Free Dictionary, s.v. 'idioglossia' http://www.thefreedictionary.com/idioglossia (accessed November 27, 2016).
47 Deleuze and Guattari, *Kafka*, 13-14.
48 O'Sullivan, 'Notes Towards a Minor Art Practice', 4.
49 Maggie MacLure, Rachel Holmes, Liz Jones, and Christina MacRae, 'Silence as Resistance to Analysis: Or, on Not Opening One's Mouth Properly', *Qualitative Inquiry* 16, no. 6 (July 2010): 492–500, 496. doi:10.1177/1077800410364349.
50 Beyond the bears and the cubs, there's otters, and wolves, and rice queens, and polar bears, and twinks, and daddies, and panda bears, and pillow queens.

Mom's the Word or Take Sertraline with Me (if you want to)

1 'Within predominantly gay, but also lesbian literatures of the Euro-American world, the "coming out" story has become an established genre of self-narrative and self-identification (Plummer 1995). A recurring theme in these stories is the association of migration with the fulfillment of the "true" homosexual self outside of the family home of one's childhood: "coming out" means "moving out" of the childhood "home" and relocating oneself elsewhere, in an other "home"(Brown 2000: 50 inter alia).' Anne-Marie Fortier, 'Making Home: Queer Migrations and Motions of Attachment' published by the Department of Sociology, Lancaster University, Lancaster LA1 4YL, UK http://www.lancaster.ac.uk/fass/resources/sociology-online-papers/papers/fortier-making-home.pdf (accessed November 28, 2016).
2 Cvetkovich, *Depression*, 26.
3 'It is easy for scholars in the humanities to feel that arguments about the cultural construction of feelings have been overlooked, but rather than fully indulge that resentment, I have been motivated by a desire to develop forms of scholarship and writing that offer alternatives to critique and new ways to describe feelings—or the intersections of mind and body that encompass not just more cognitive forms of emotion but the embodied senses.' Ibid., 24.
4 bell hooks, *Yearning: Race, Gender, and Cultural Politics* (Boston: South End Press, 1990), 47.

5   'In recent sociology, conceptions of kinship have become dis- joined from the marriage assumption, so that, for example, Carol Stack's now classic study of urban African-American kinship, All Our Kin, shows how kinship functions well through a network of women, some related through biological ties, and some not.' Judith Butler, 'Is Kinship Always Already Heterosexual?' *differences: A Journal of Feminist Cultural Studies* 13.1 (2002): 15.

6   Silvia Federici, 'The Reproduction of Labour-Power in the Global Economy, Marxist Theory and the Unfinished Feminist Revolution', http://endofcapitalism.com/2013/05/29/a-feminist-critique-of-marx-by-silvia-federici/ (accessed December 3, 2018); David Staples, *No Place Like Home: Organizing Home-based Labor in the Era of Structural Adjustment* (London and New York: Routledge, 2006); Dorothy Sue Cobble, *The Sex of Class: Women Transforming American Labor* (Ithaca: Cornell University Press, 2007).

7   Cvetkovich, *Depression*, 165.

8   As a diminutive term from my first language, «σπιτάκι» conveys less of a direct relation to repronormative politics, or economy, and more of a notional, non-fixed space of comfort. It resonates directly with the affective framework I employ here. It is epistemologically situated in a linguistic and cultural context that brings out elements of childhood, fairy-tales, and imaginary, safer spaces. It is not as ambivalent as 'home' is, as it is mainly activated during children's games, where a simple demarcation of a square shape on the ground by dragging one's feet is enough to constitute it and have it act as a safer space where one can rest and regroup from playing tag. It is a space where those chasing you cannot touch you.

9   'Ο «αστείος λόγος» ήταν ο πνευματώδης, και σιγά-σιγά έφτασε να σημαίνει κάτι το ευτράπελο, που προκαλεί το γέλιο. Η διάκριση αυτή χωριού-πόλης έχει περάσει και στα νεότερα ελληνικά, αν σκεφτούμε ότι τα χωρατά, τα αστεία δηλαδή, τα έκαναν οι κάτοικοι της χώρας, της πόλης δηλαδή.' (emphasis in original) Nick Sarantakos, «Η πόλη, το άστυ, ο δήμος», *Sarantakos* (blog), May 5, 2014, https://sarantakos.wordpress.com/2014/05/05/polis/.

10 Jacques Derrida, Thomas Dutoit, David Wood, John P. Leavey, and Ian McLeod, *On the Name* (Stanford: Stanford University Press, 2019), xv, 89, 95, 124.

11 For many people, the opposite is true, and suffer from abusive, oppressive, and violent situations in what they may call 'home'. My focus is on the home some (including some of the aforementioned individuals) create perhaps *precisely* because they have those experiences.

12 An acronym for Portugal, Ireland, Greece, and Spain which have been seen as the failures to the EU economic project with reasons provided for that often including racist caricatures of lazy, corrupt Southerners who rely on the welfare state of Central and Northern Europe and who have no intention of pulling their own weight.

13 Love, *Feeling Backward*, 7.

14 'Can we work differently? Can those who come after work differently, working as willful strangers, by not putting the will of those who come first "first"? Perhaps we need to work back to front. We have to work from behind to challenge the front. We have to work the behind. We can hear the queerness of this hindsight. We can also hear decolonial connotations. Those deemed behind, as lagging behind in the history of becoming modern, can rewrite that history from this view.' Ahmed, *Willful Subjects*, 171.

15 Ahmed, *The Promise of Happiness*, 89.

16 Love, *Feeling Backward*, 146.

17 Muñoz, *Cruising Utopia*, 182.

18 'The very expectation of happiness as an overcoming of bad feeling is how happiness can cause unhappiness.' Ahmed, *The Promise of Happiness*, 175.

19 Love, *Feeling Backward*, 127.

20 'Freedom becomes the freedom to be made happy by different things.' Ahmed, *The Promise of Happiness*, 27.

21 Ibid., 210.

22 Love, *Feeling Backward*, 106.

23 A brief history of the word in the online sources below Jon Levine, 'Yaaass, You Have Black Drag Queens to Thank for the Internet's Favorite Expression', *Mic*, October 7, 2015. https://mic.com/articles/126364/yaaass-you-have-black-drag-queens-to-thank-for-the-internet-s-favorite-expression#.u043eODm2; Jenna Amatulli, 'Here's The Real Origin Of The Word "Yas"', *The Huffington Post*, July 19, 2016. http://www.huffingtonpost.com/entry/heres-the-real-origin-of-the-word-yas_us_578ce747e4b0fa896c3f4306; Madison Moore, 'Gurl! On Code Switching When You're Black And Gay', *Thought Catalogue*, December 3, 2015. http://thoughtcatalog.com/madison-moore/2015/12/gurl-on-code-switching-when-youre-black-and-gay/.

24 Some of those may find their way in hetero relationships as well, but I would argue that these do not constitute normative relationships.

25 Pepper Labeija, *Paris is Burning*, DVD, directed by Jennie Livingston (Off White Productions, US, 1990).

26 The 'houses' were also called 'families' and the reasoning becomes clear in the film through the stories of the protagonists, many of whom have been disowned by their families of origin, due to their queerness some in a young age, and these events become a place for belonging, affirmation, and support. 'Legendary' in ballroom terms refers to a house that has been 'serving', that is, walking or competing on the runway, for twenty years or more) 'Vogue History' on *MyStreetBeats, November 28, 2018*, http://www.mystreetbeats.com/vogue-history (site discontinued).

27 Jose Xtravaganza in Amatulli, 'Here's The Real Origin Of The Word "Yas"'.

28 'Also known as Calo Caló, like Spanglish, makes heavy use of ode-switching. Unlike Spanglish, Caló uses rhyming and in some cases, a type of rhyming slang similar in Spanish to Cockney rhyming slang or African American jive'. *World Heritage Encyclopedia*, s.v. 'Caló (Chicano)' Article Id: WHEBN0000001262. http://self.gutenberg.org/article.aspx?title=cal%C3%B3_(chicano) (accessed November 28, 2018).

29 Anzaldúa, *Borderlands/La Frontera*, 56.

30 Ibid., 55.

31 'Adelphopoiesis, or adelphopoiia from the Greek ἀδελφοποίησις, derived from ἀδελφός (adelphos) "brother" and ποιέω (poieō) "I make", literally "brother-making" is a ceremony practiced historically in some Christian traditions to unite together two people of the same sex (normally men) in church-recognized relationship analogous to siblinghood.' *Wikipedia*, s.v. 'Adelphopoiesis' http://en.wikipedia.org/wiki/Adelphopoiesis (accessed November 28, 2018).

32 O'Sullivan, 'Notes Towards a Minor Art Practice', 2.

33 'The aesthetic practice that I have previously described as disidentification focused on the way in which dominant signs and symbols, often ones that are toxic to minoritarian subjects, can be reimagined through an engaged and animated mode of performance or spectatorship. Muñoz, Cruising Utopia, 169.

34 A 'good life' that is premised on exploitation, consumerism, and a conformist adoption of their ideals.

35 E. Patrick Johnson, 'Mother Knows Best: Black Gay Vernacular and Transgressive Domestic Space', in *Speaking in Queer Tongues*, 251-278.

36 Ibid., 258-259.

37 I am, of course, referring to people who are practising age-play, and not to very young humans.

38 'The original sense seems to have been "wife", specialized by Old English to "wife of a king".' *Etymology Online*, s.v. 'queen', http://www.etymonline.com/index.php?term=queen (accessed December 3, 2018).
39 Deleuze and Guattari, *A Thousand Plateaus*, 23.
40 'Derogatory term for any white or black woman who acts uppity or white' E. Patrick Johnson, 'Mother Knows Best', 252.
41 'auntie /' :nti/noun: older gay man. mother /m /pronoun: me, myself. Often used by older gay men to friends when they're talking about themselves, especially in the phrase your mother: 'pull up a chair and tell your mother all about it' In Polari, someone's mother is likely to be an older, more experienced gay man.' Baker, *Polari*.
42 «μουτζόπουρη, η·μητέρα» and «σεμελοπουρός, ο·πατέρας» Petropoulos, *Kaliarnta*, 92 and 137 respectively.
43 As narrated by George Tsitiridis, in an interview conducted in April 2015 with the author, on the use of Kaliarnta in Salonica in the '90s, '00s, and '10s.
44 Freeman, 'Queer Belongings', 303.
45 'Orphan (n.) –someone who has recently been broken up with.' Nico Lang, '1 Gay Slang Phrases You've Never Heard Before', *Thought Catalogue*, September 21, 2013, http://thoughtcatalog.com/nico-lang/2013/09/51-gay-slang-phrases-youve-never-heard-before/.
46 Kundalia, 'Queer Language'.
47 Freeman, 'Queer Belongings', 303.
48 *Etymology Online*, s.v. 'hospital', http://www.etymonline.com/index.php?term=hospital (accessed December 3, 2018); *Etymology Online*, s.v. 'hospice', http://www.etymonline.com/index.php?term=hospice (accessed December 3, 2018).
49 *Wiktionary, The Free Dictionary*, 'hospes', https://en.wiktionary.org/w/index.php?title=hospes&oldid=41485698 (accessed December 3, 2018).
50 Wiktionary contributors, 'hostis', *Wiktionary, The Free Dictionary*, https://en.wiktionary.org/w/index.php?title=hostis&oldid=41485711 (accessed December 3, 2018).
51 Freeman, 'Queer Belongings', 296.
52 Ibid., 302.
53 'With that recognition, we became a distinct people. Something momentous happened to the Chicano soul- we became aware of our reality and acquired a name and a language (Chicano Spanish) that reflected that reality. Now that we had a name, some of the fragmented pieces began to fall together—who

we were, what we were, how we had evolved. We began to get glimpses of what we might eventually become.' Anzaldúa, *Borderlands/La Frontera*, 44.

54 Halberstam, *The Queer Art of Failure*, 88.
55 Julian and Sandy were two of the regular characters on the *Round the Horne* radio show presented by the BBC between 1965-1968. They were stereotypical camp gay characters and introduced Polari to the general population, being unapologetic in a time when homosexuality was illegal in the UK.
56 Ahmed, *Willful Subjects*, 118.
57 Ahmed adds, 'There can be joy in creating worlds out of the broken pieces of our dwelling spaces: we can not only share our willfulness stories, but pick up some of the pieces too. And we can hear each other in each other; can be moved by each other with each other; we can even just tell each other to let it go, at the moments when holding on demands too much.' Ibid., 169.
58 Sara Ahmed, 'You Are Oppressing Me!' Blog Post on *Feministkilljoys*, February 17, 2016, https://feministkilljoys.com/2016/02/17/you-are-oppressing-me/.
59 *Space is the Place*, DVD, directed by John Coney (USA, 1974).
60 It is important to note the sociotemporal context Sun Ra grew up in, born in 1914 in was Birmingham Alabama, birthplace of Ku Klux Klan, which around that time was in its peak.
61 'The first four songs are the reckoning; realizing what you mean to this society. The middle half of the album, is the celebration; celebrating your dirt, celebrating being a "dirty computer". And then you kind of go through the fear of what that means to stand up for yourself and those who are oftentimes marginalized. And it leads you to the reclamation. Reclaiming what it is to be an American. I too am American. My ancestors built this place. So, it goes through phases. Every song depends on the next song.' Nicole Mastrogiannis, 'Janelle Monáe Reveals Important "Dirty Computer" Messages & Meanings' in iHeartRadio, April 19, 2018 (accessed October 9, 2019). https://www.iheart.com/content/2018-04-20-janelle-mone-reveals-important-dirty-computer-messages-meanings/.
62 Shawn Setaro, 'Reckoning, Celebration, and Reclamation: Janelle Monáe Dissects "Dirty Computer"', *Complex*, October 29, 2018, https://www.complex.com/music/2018/10/janelle-monae-dissects-dirty-computer; Rebecca Bengal, '"You Don't Own or Control Me": Janelle Monáe on her Music, Politics and Undefinable Sexuality', *The Guardian*, February 22, 2018, https://www.theguardian.com/music/2018/feb/22/you-dont-own-or-control-me-janelle-monae-on-her-music-politics-and-undefinable-sexuality.

63 *Wikipedia*, 'Venus Xtravaganza', https://en.wikipedia.org/w/index.php?title=Venus_Xtravaganza&oldid=751068150 (accessed November 23, 2016).
64 Nikki Sullivan, *A Critical Introduction to Queer Theory* (New York: New York University Press, 2003), 95.
65 *Strella*, (Greek: Στρέλλα; international title: A Woman's Way), DVD, directed by Panos H. Koutras (Memento Films, Greece, 2009).
66 Cvetkovich, *Depression*, 205.
67 'Gesture, I argue throughout this book, signals a refusal of a certain kind of finitude. Dance is an especially valuable site for ruminations on queerness and gesture.' Muñoz, *Cruising Utopia*, 65.
68 Ibid., 66.
69 Ibid., 111.
70 Torres, 'In praise of Latin Night at the Queer Club'.
71 Michelle Clunie, Robert Gant, and Thea Gill, *Queer as folk The final season, 5* (New York: Showtime Entertainment), 2006.
72 Zackie Oh! - Μωρή, he died for you, Video, posted April 15, 2017, https://www.youtube.com/watch?v=mQNynlUuh28 This is from a project connected to the Athens Biennale in which he participated. The 6th edition of the Athens Biennale (2018) was dedicated to Zak/Zackie Oh.
73 Muñoz, *Cruising Utopia*, 112.
74 Ibid., 49.
75 [...] 'that *queerness* names the side of those not "fighting for the children" the side outside the consensus by which all politics confirms the absolute value of reproductive futurism.' Lee Edelman, *No Future: Queer Theory and the Death Drive* (Durham: Duke University Press, 2004), 3.
76 At this point I would like to bring it back into connection with different Others and specifically the figure of the migrant. Ahmed writes, 'Anti-immigration discourse thus exercises the figure of the unwilling migrant, or more specifically the migrant who is "unwilling to integrate". To be unwilling to integrate is to be "too willing" to retain an allegiance to another body.' Ahmed, *Willful Subjects*, 128.
77 'To be willful is thus to refuse what we might call "the reproductive duty," as the duty of a part to reproduce the whole or at least to be willing to participate in reproduction.' Ibid., 114.
78 'No wonder that growing up is imagined as leaving playfulness behind you: nonreproductive adult bodies can thus appear as willful children, or perhaps as willfully childlike, as selfish, as spoiled, as refusing the demand to grow up,

perhaps by growing sideways, as Kathryn Bond Stockton (2009) has suggested.' Ibid., 120.
79 Ibid., 91.
80 Ahmed, *Willful Subjects*, 21.

Tô passada!

1 Ramesh Tibile, 'Literary theories of Gayatri Spivak, Homi Bhabha, Ania Loomba, Gauri Viswanathan and Ganesh Devy: an assessment' (PhD dissertation, Shivaji University, 2009), http://hdl.handle.net/10603/4107 (accessed December 2, 2016).
2 Ahmed, *Willful Subjects*, 15.
3 'The Queer Art of Failure is an extended meditation on antidisciplinary forms of knowing specifically tied to queerness; I have made the case for stupidity, failure, and forgetfulness over knowing, mastering, and remembering in terms of contemporary knowledge formations.' Halberstam, *The Queer Art of Failure*, 147.
4 Love, *Feeling Backward*, 160.

Bibliography

Agamben, Giorgio. *The Coming Community*. Translated by Michael Hardt. Minneapolis: University of Minnesota, 1993.
———. *What is an Apparatus? and Other Essays*. Translated by David Kishik and Stefan Pedatella. Stanford: Stanford University Press, 2009.
Ahmed, Sara. 'Happy Objects'. In *The Affect Theory Reader*, edited by Melissa Gregg and Gregory J. Seigworth, 29-51. Durham: Duke University Press, 2010.
———. *The Promise of Happiness*. Durham: Duke University Press, 2010.
———. *Willful Subjects*. Durham: Duke University Press, 2014.
Allsup, Andrew. *Queer Indigenous Rhetorics: Decolonizing the Socio-Symbolic Order of Euro-American Gender and Sexual Imaginaries*. Manhattan, Kan: Kansas State University, 2015.
Anzaldúa, Gloria. *Borderlands / La Frontera: The New Mestiza*. San Francisco: Aunt Lute Books, 2012.
Avendaño, Lukas. 'No Soy Persona Soy Mariposa.' Vimeo video, 21:17. Posted by 'Mario Patiño', November 5, 2015. https://vimeo.com/144735012.
Baim, Tracy, ed. *Out and Proud in Chicago: An Overview of the City's Gay Community*. Chicago: Agate, 2008.
Baker, Paul. *Fantabulosa: A Dictionary of Polari and Gay Slang*. London: Bloomsbury Academic, 2004.
———. *Polari: The Lost Language of Gay Men*. London: Routledge, 2002.
Ballinger, Ariel, Lisa Sacerio, AnjaLi Carrasco, Sarah Elgart, Rachel DeVay Jacobson, Jessica W. Tsai, and Allison K. Zoromski. 'Imagined Spatial Motion and Spatiotemporal Metaphors'. In *Mind Matters: The Wesleyan Journal of Psychology* 2 (2007): 7-18.
Berlant, Laurent. *Cruel Optimism*. Durham: Duke University Press, 2011.

Besnier, Niko. 'The Social Production of Abjection: Desire and Silencing Among Transgender Tongans'. *Social Anthropology: the Journal of the European Association of Social Anthropologists* 12, no. 3 (2004): 301–323.

Boroditsky, Lera. 'Metaphoric Structuring: Understanding Time Through Spatial Metaphors'. *Cognition* 75, (2000): 1-28.

Britton, Celia. *Edouard Glissant and Postcolonial Theory: Strategies of Language and Resistance*. Charlottesville, Va: University Press of Virginia, 1999.

———. *The Sense of Community in French Caribbean Fiction*. Liverpool: Liverpool University Press, 2008.

Brown, Michael P. *Closet Space: Geographies of Metaphor from the Body to the Globe*. London: Routledge, 2000.

Browne, Kath, and Catherine J. Nash, eds. Introduction to *Queer Methods and Methodologies: Intersecting Queer Theories and Social Science Research*. London: Ashgate, 2010.

Butler, Judith. *Bodies That Matter: On The Discursive Limits Of 'Sex'*. New York: Routledge, 1993.

———. *Gender Trouble: Feminism and the Subversion of Identity*. New York: Routledge, 1990.

———. 'Is Kinship Always Already Heterosexual?' *differences: A Journal of Feminist Cultural Studies* 13, no. 1 (2002): 14-44.

Cage, Ken. *Gayle: The Language of Kinks and Queens: a History and Dictionary of Gay Language in South Africa*. Johannesburg: Jacana Media, 2003.

Catacutan, Sonny Atencia. 'Swardspeak: A Queer Perspective'. Presentation in the Multimedia and Popular Culture Class, Los Baños: University of the Philippines Open University, 2013. Accessed December 3, 2018. https://prezi.com/hoog_fqpyosx/swardspeak-a-queer-perspective/.

Chauncey, George. *Gay New York: Gender, Urban Culture, and the Making of the Gay Male World, 1890–1940*. New York: BasicBooks, 1995.

Chesebro, James W. *Gayspeak: Gay Male & Lesbian Communication*. Edited by James W. Chesebro. New York: Pilgrim Press, 1981.

Cobble, Dorothy Sue. *The Sex of Class: Women Transforming American Labor*. Edited by Dorothy Sue Cobble. Ithaca: Cornell University Press, 2007.

Conklin, Tiffany Renée. 'Street Art, Ideology, and Public Space'. Master's thesis, Portland State University, 2012. http://archives.pdx.edu/ds/psu/8294.

Cvetkovich, Ann. *Depression: A Public Feeling*. Durham: Duke University Press, 2012.

Danbolt, Mathias. 'Dismantling the Serious Machine: An Interview with Gavin Butt.' *Trikster*, no. 3, 2009. Accessed November 17, 2016. http://trikster.net/3/butt/1.html.

Davies, Sharyn Graham. *Challenging Gender Norms: Five Genders Among Bugis in Indonesia*. Belmont, Calif: Thomson Higher Education, 2007.

de Bloois, J. 2011. 'Making Ends Meet: Precarity, Art and Political Activism'. *VOLUME* 30 (2011): 4-9.

De Certeau, Michel. *The Practice of Everyday Life*. Translated by Steven Rendall. Berkeley: University of California Press, 1984.

De Quiros Gianan, Emy Ruth. 'The Evolution and Expansion of Gay Language in the Philippines'. Bachelor's thesis, University of Santo Tomas, Philippines, 2008. https://www.academia.edu/36052287/The_Evolution_and_Expansion_of_Gay_Language_in_the_Philippines.

De Villiers, Nicholas. *Opacity and the Closet: Queer Tactics in Foucault, Barthes, and Warhol*. Minneapolis: University Of Minnesota Press, 2012.

Deleuze, Gilles, and Félix Guattari. *A Thousand Plateaus: Capitalism and Schizophrenia*. Translated by Brian Massumi. Minneapolis and London: University of Minnesota, 1987.

———. *Kafka: Toward a Minor Literature*. Translated by Dana Polan. Minneapolis and London: University of Minnesota, 1986.

Derrida, Jacques. 'How to Avoid Speaking: Denials'. In *Derrida and Negative Theology*. Edited by Harold Coward and Toby Foshay. Albany: SUNY Press, 1989.

Derrida, Jacques. *Of Grammatology*. Baltimore: Johns Hopkins University Press, 2016.

Derrida, Jacques, Thomas Dutoit, David Wood, John P. Leavey, and Ian McLeod. *On the Name*. Stanford: Stanford University Press, 2019.

Dolgoy, Reevan. *The Search for Recognition and Social Movement Emergence: Towards an Understanding of the Transformation of the Fa'afafine of Samoa*. Ottawa: National Library of Canada = Bibliothèque nationale du Canada, 2002.

Douglas, Gordon C. C. 'The Art of Spatial Resistance: The Global Urban Network of Street Art'. Master's thesis, London School of Economics, 2005. http://works.bepress.com/gordon-douglas/59/.

Driskill, Qwo-Li. *Queer Indigenous Studies: Critical Interventions in Theory, Politics, and Literature*. Tucson: University of Arizona Press, 2011.

E. Jeffreys, Joe. 'Joan Jett Blakk for President: Cross-Dressing at the Democratic National Convention'. *TDR (1988-)* 37, no. 3 (Autumn, 1993): 186-195. doi:10.2307/1146317.

Eckert, Penelope. 'Three Waves of Variation Study: The Emergence of Meaning in the Study of Sociolinguistic Variation'. *Annual Review of Anthropology* 41 (2012): 87–100.

Edelman, Lee. *No Future: Queer Theory and the Death Drive*. Durham: Duke University Press, 2004.

Endo, Orie (遠藤織枝). 'Nushu'. Paper presented at the Association of Asian Studies Annual Conference, Boston, March 1999. Accessed November 18, 2016. http://nushu.world.coocan.jp/aas99.htm.

Fanon, Frantz. *Black Skin, White Masks*. Translated by Charles Lam Markmann. London: Pluto Press, 1986.

Feu'u, Poiva Junior Ashleigh. 'Ia E Ola Malamalama I Lou Fa'asinomaga: A Comparative Study of the Fa'afafine of Samoa and the Whakawahine of Aotearoa/New Zealand'. Master's thesis, Victoria University of Wellington, 2013. http://hdl.handle.net/10063/3179.

Foucault, Michel. 'Technologies of the Self'. In *Technologies of the Self: A Seminar With Michel Foucault*. Edited by Luther H. Martin, Huck Gutman, and Patrick H. Hutton, 16-49. Massachusetts: Tavistock Publications, 1988.

———. *The History of Sexuality Volume I: An Introduction*. Translated by Robert Hurley. New York: Pantheon Books, 1978.

Fortier, Anne-Marie. 'Making Home: Queer Migrations and Motions of Attachment'. In *Uprootings / Regroundings: Questions Of Home And Migration*, edited by Sara Ahmed, Claudia Castada, Anne-Marie Fortier, and Mimi Sheller, 115-135. Oxford, 2003. https://www.lancaster.ac.uk/fass/resources/sociology-online-papers/papers/fortier-making-home.pdf.

Freeman, Elizabeth. 'Queer Belongings Kinship Theory and Queer Theory'. In *A Companion to Lesbian, Gay, Bisexual, Transgender, and Queer Studies*. Edited by George E. Haggerty and Molly McGarry. MA: Blackwell, 2007.

Gentner, Dedre. 'Spatial Metaphors in Temporal Reasoning'. In *Spatial Schemas and Abstract Thought*, edited by Merideth Gattis, 203-222. Cambridge: The MIT Press, 2001.

Gentner, Dedre, and Mutsumi Imai. 'Is the Future Always Ahead? Evidence for System-Mappings in Understanding Space-Time Metaphors'. In *Proceedings of the Fourteenth Annual Conference of the Cognitive Science Society*, 510-515. Hillsdale, New Jersey: Lawrence Erlbaum, 1992.

Gentner, Dedre, Mutsumi Imai, and Lera Boroditsky. 'As Time Goes by: Evidence for Two Systems in Processing Space → Time Metaphors'. In *Language and Cognitive Processes* 17, no. 5 (2002): 537-565. doi:10.1080/01690960143000317.

Gevisser, Mark, and Edwin Cameron eds. *Defiant Desire, Gay and Lesbian Lives in South Africa*. New York and London: Routledge, 1995.

Gieseking, Jen Jack, William Mangold, Cindi Katz, Setha Low, and Susan Saegert eds. *The People, Place, and Space Reader*. New York and London: Routledge, 2014.

Glissant, Edouard. *Caribbean Discourse: Selected Essays*. Translated by J. Michael Dash. Charlottesville: Univ. Press of Virginia, 1999.

———. *Poetics of Relation*. Translated by Betsy Wing. Ann Arbor: University of Michigan Press, 1997.

Godin, Marie-Noëlle. 'Urban Youth Language in Multicultural Sweden'. *Scandinavian-Canadian Studies / Études Scandinaves Au Canada* 16 (2006): 126-141. Accessed November 18, 2016. http://scancan.net/article.htm?id=godin_1_16.

Graham, Sharyn. 'It's Like One of Those Puzzles: Conceptualising Gender Among Bugis'. *Journal of Gender Studies* 13, no. 2 (2004): 107-116. doi:10.1080/0958923042000217800.

Halberstam, Judith. *The Queer Art of Failure*. Durham and London: Duke University Press, 2011.

Hall, Kira. '"Go Suck Your Husband's Sugarcane!" Hijras and the Use of Sexual Insult.' In *Queerly Phrased: Language, Gender, and Sexuality*, edited by Anna Livia and Kira Hall, 430-460. New York: Oxford University Press, 1997.

———. 'Hijra / Hijrin: Language and Gender Identity'. PhD diss., University of California Berkeley, 1995. http://escholarship.org/uc/item/6m5744jx.

———. 'Intertextual Sexuality: Parodies of Class, Identity, and Desire in Liminal Delhi'. *Journal of Linguistic Anthropology* 15, no. 1 (2005): 125–144.

Hall, Stuart, ed. *Representation: Cultural Representations and Signifying Practices*. London: Sage in association with the Open University, 1997.

Harney, Stefano, and Fred Moten. *The Undercommons: Fugitive Planning & Black Study*. New York: Minor Compositions, 2013.

Hook, Genine. 'Towards a Decolonising Pedagogy: Understanding Australian Indigenous Studies Through Critical Whiteness Theory and Film

Pedagogy'. *The Australian Journal of Indigenous Education* 41, no. 2 (2012): 110-119.

hooks, bell. *Teaching to Transgress: Education As the Practice of Freedom*. New York: Routledge, 1994.

———. *Yearning: Race, Gender, and Cultural Politics*. Boston: South End Press, 1990.

Hutta, Jan Simon. 'Beyond the Politics of Inclusion: Securitization and Agential Formations in Brazilian LGBT Parades'. In *Queer Futures: Reconsidering Ethics, Activism, and the Political*, edited by Elahe Haschemi Yekani, Eveline Kilian, and Beatrice Michaelis, 67-81. London: Routledge, 2016.

Ings, Welby. 'Trade Talk: The Historical Metamorphosis of the Language of the New Zealand Male Prostitute Between 1900–1981'. *Women's History Review* 21, no. 5 (2012): 773-791.

Jakob, Kai. *Street Art in Berlin*. Berlin: Jaron Verlag, 2008.

Katz, Jonathan D. 'Performative Silence and the Politics of Passivity'. In *Making A Scene: Performing Culture into Politics*, edited by Henry Rodgers, and David Burrows, 97-103. Birmingham: Article Press, 2001.

Kaye, Melanie. 'Sign'. In *We Speak in Code: Poems and Other Writings*, 85. Pittsburgh: Motheroot Publications, 1980.

Kelly, Mark G. E. *Foucault's History of Sexuality Volume I, The Will to Knowledge*. Edinburgh: Edinburgh University Press, 2013.

Kempadoo, Kamala. *Sexing the Caribbean: Gender, Race, and Sexual Labor*. New York: Routledge, 2008.

Koutras, Panos, dir. *Strella* (Greek: Στρέλλα; international title: A Woman's Way). Greece: Memento Films, 2009. DVD, 111 min.

Kulick, Don. 'Gay and Lesbian Language'. *Annual Review of Anthropology* 29 (2000): 243–85.

Κωνσταντίνος Π. Καβάφης, *Καβάφης: Ατελή Ποιήματα, 1918-1932*, επιμ. Renata Lavagnini (Αθήνα: Ίκαρος, 1994).

Leap, William L., and Tom Boellstorff, eds. *Speaking in Queer Tongues: Globalization and Gay Language*. Urbana: University of Illinois Press, 2004.

Leung, Christie K. K. 'Women Who Found A Way Creating a Women's Language'. *Off Our Backs* 33, no. 11/12 (2003): 40-43. Accessed November 18, 2016. https://www.jstor.org/stable/20837958.

Lewis, C. S. *The Lion, the Witch and the Wardrobe*. London: Geoffrey Bles, 1950.

Lewis, Vek. *Crossing Sex and Gender in Latin America*. New York: Palgrave Macmillan, 2010.

Livia, Anna. 'Disloyal to Masculinity: Linguistic Gender and Liminal Identity in French'. In *Queerly Phrased: Language, Gender, and Sexuality*, edited by Anna Livia and Kira Hall, 349–68. New York: Oxford University Press, 1997.

Livingston, Jennie. *Paris is Burning*. DVD. Directed by Jennie Livingston. United Kingdom: Second Sight Films Ltd, 2009.

Love, Heather. *Feeling Backward: Loss and the Politics of Queer History*. Cambridge, Mass: Harvard University Press, 2007.

Lorde, Audre. *Sister Outsider: Essays and Speeches*. Trumansburg, NY: Crossing Press, 1984.

Lorenz, Renate. *Queer Art: A Freak Theory*. Bielefeld: Transcript, 2012.

———. *Not Now! Now! Chronopolitics, Art, and Research*. Berlin: Sternberg Press, 2014.

MacLure, Maggie, Rachel Holmes, Liz Jones, and Christina MacRae. 'Silence as Resistance to Analysis: Or, on Not Opening One's Mouth Properly.' *Qualitative Inquiry* 16, no. 6 (July 2010): 492–500. doi:10.1177/1077800410364349.

Mahdavi, Pardis. 'Passionate Uprisings: Young People, Sexuality and Politics In Post-revolutionary Iran'. *Culture, Health & Sexuality* 9, no.5 (September - October 2007): 445-457. doi: 10.1080 / 13691050601 170378.

McBeth, Mark. Review of *Queerly Phrased: Language, Gender, and Sexuality*, by Anna Livia and Kira Hall, eds. *JAC* 20, no. 4 (Fall 2000): 983-988. http://www.jstor.org/stable/20866382.

McLean, Hugh, and Linda Ngcobo. 'abangibhamayo bathi ngimnandi'. In *Defiant Desire: Gay and Lesbian Lives in South Africa*. Edited by Mark Gevisser and Edwin Cameron. New York: Routledge, 1995.

McRuer, Robert. *Crip Theory: Cultural Signs of Queerness and Disability*. New York: New York University Press, 2006.

Meyer, Moe. 'Reclaiming the Discourse on Camp'. In *The Politics And Poetics Of Camp*, edited by Moe Meyer. New York: Routledge, 1994.

Munoz, José Esteban. *Cruising Utopia: The Then and There of Queer Futurity*. New York: New York University Press, 2009.

Murray-Román, Jeannine. *Performance and Personhood in Caribbean Literature: From Alexis to the Digital Age*. Charlottesville and London: University of Virginia Press, 2016.

Newton, David E. *Gay and Lesbian Rights: A Reference Handbook*. 2nd ed. Santa Barbara: ABC-CLIO, 2009.

O'Sullivan, Simon. 'Notes Towards a Minor Art Practice'. *Drain: Journal of Contemporary Art and Culture* 2, no. 2 (2005): 3. Accessed November 26, 2016. http://www.drainmag.com/contentNOVEMBER/RELATED_ESSAYS/Notes_Towards_Minor_Practice.htm.

Omniglot: The Online Encyclopedia of Writing Systems and Languages s.v. 'Nüshu (女书)'. Accessed November 18, 2016. http://www.omniglot.com/writing/nushu.htm.

Petropoulos, Elias. *Kaliarnta*. Athens: Nefeli, 1971.

Pinar, William F., ed. *Queer Theory in Education*. Mahwah and London: Lawrence Erlbaum Associates Inc., 1998.

Probyn, Elspeth. 'Writing Shame'. In *The Affect Theory Reader*. Edited by Melissa Gregg and Gregory J. Seigworth. Durham and London: Duke University Press, 2010.

Reiss, Jon. *Bomb It*. DVD. Directed by Jon Reiss. Los Angeles, 2008.

Revenioti, Paola. *Kaliarnta* DVD. Directed by Paola Revenioti. Athens, 2014.

Rich, Adrienne. 'Cartographies of Silence' in Poems. The World's Poetry Archive, 2012.

Rifkin, Mark. *When Did Indians Become Straight?: Kinship, the History of Sexuality, and Native Sovereignty*. New York: Oxford University Press, 2011.

Rudwick, Stephanie. '"Gay and Zulu, we speak isiNgqumo": Ethnolinguistic Identity Constructions'. *Transformation Critical Perspectives on Southern Africa* 74, no. 1 (2010): 112-134. doi:10.1353/trn.2010.0016.

Safeer Awan, Muhammad, and Muhammad Sheeraz. 'Queer but Language: A Sociolinguistic Study of Farsi'. *International Journal of Humanities and Social Science* 1, no. 10 (2011): 127-135. http://www.ijhssnet.com/journals/Vol_1_No_10_August_2011/17.pdf.

Salzmann, Zdenek, Stanlaw, James, Adachi, Nobuko. *Language, Culture, and Society: An Introduction to Linguistic Anthropology*. Boulder: Westview Press, 2018.

Salzmann, Zdeněk. *Language, Culture, and Society: An Introduction to Linguistic Anthropology*. Boulder, Colo: Westview Press, 1998.

Scheb, John M., and John M. Scheb II. *Criminal Law and Procedure*. 7th ed. Belmont: Wadsworth Publishing, 2010.

Schmidt, Johanna M. 'Redefining Fa'afafine: Western Discourses and the Construction of Transgenderism in Samoa'. *Intersections: Gender, History and Culture in the Asian Context*, no. 6 (August 2001): 1-16. https://www.

waikato.ac.nz/php/research.php?skin=2016&year=2001&mode=show&author=3042971.

———. 'Translating Transgender: Using Western Discourses to Understand Samoan Fa'afāfine'. *Sociology Compass* 11, no. 5 (2017): 1-17. doi:10.1111/soc4.12485.

Seitz, David K. 'Spaces Between Us: Queer Settler Colonialism and Indigenous Decolonization'. *Gender, Place & Culture* 19, no. 5 (2012): 686-687.

Sedgwick, Eve Kosofsky. *Epistemology of the Closet*. Berkeley and Los Angeles: University of California Press, 1990.

———. *Tendencies*. London: Routledge, 1994.

Seidman, Steven. *Beyond the Closet: The Transformation of Gay and Lesbian Life*. New York: Routledge, 2002.

Silver, Tony. *Style Wars*. DVD. Directed by Tony Silver. New York City: Public Art Films, 1983.

Smith, Daniel, and John Protevi. 'Gilles Deleuze'. *The Stanford Encyclopedia of Philosophy* (Winter 2015 Edition). Edited by Edward N. Zalta. Accessed November 17, 2016. http://plato.stanford.edu/archives/win2015/entries/deleuze/.

Sontag, Susan. *Against Interpretation, and Other Essays*. New York: Farrar, Straus & Giroux, 1966.

Staples, David. *No Place Like Home: Organizing Home-based Labor in the Era of Structural Adjustment*. London and New York: Routledge, 2006.

Stephen, Lynn. 'Sexualities and Genders in Zapotec Oaxaca'. *Latin American Perspectives* 29, no. 2 (March 2002): 41-59. doi:10.1177/0094582X0202900203.

Sullivan, Nikki. *A Critical Introduction to Queer Theory*. New York: New York University Press, 2003.

Sun Ra, and John Coney. *Sun Ra: Space Is the Place*. New York: Rhapsody Films, 1998.

Swiss, Thom. '"I'm Melvin, a 4G Hot Spot"'. In *Theories of the Mobile Internet: Materialities and Imaginaries*, edited by Andrew Herman, Jan Hadlaw, and Thom Swiss, 183-192. London and New York: Routledge, 2015.

Thorpe, David. *Do I Sound Gay?* DVD. New York City: Spectrum, 2014.

Tibile, Ramesh. 'Literary Theories of Gayatri Spivak, Homi Bhabha, Ania Loomba, Gauri Viswanathan and Ganesh Devy: an Assessment'. PhD diss., Shivaji University, 2009. http://hdl.handle.net/10603/4107.

Von Bose, Käthe, Ulrike Klöppel, Katrin Köppert, Karin Michalski, and Pat Treusch, eds. *I is for Impasse: Affektive Queerverbindungen in Theorie, Aktivismus, Kunst*. Berlin: b_books Verlag, 2015.

Weber, Shannon. Review of *Language and Gender Research from a Queer Linguistic Perspective: a Critical Evaluation*, by Michaela Koch. *Gender and Language*. 5, no. 1 (2011): 153-157. doi: 10.1558/genl.v5i1.153.

Woolf, Virginia. *A Room of One's Own*. New York: Harcourt, Brace and Company, 1929.

Zoltán, Ildikó Gy. 'The Nature of Slang: Spoken, Creative and Transient'. *The Proceedings of the International Conference "Communication, Context, Interdisciplinarity"*. Section: Language and Discourse 2 (2012): 1010-1015. http://www.diacronia.ro/en/indexing/details/A22587.

Cultural Studies

Elisa Ganivet
Border Wall Aesthetics
Artworks in Border Spaces

2019, 250 p., hardcover, ill.
79,99 € (DE), 978-3-8376-4777-8
E-Book: 79,99 € (DE), ISBN 978-3-8394-4777-2

Jocelyne Porcher, Jean Estebanez (eds.)
Animal Labor
A New Perspective on Human-Animal Relations

2019, 182 p., hardcover
99,99 € (DE), 978-3-8376-4364-0
E-Book: 99,99 € (DE), ISBN 978-3-8394-4364-4

Andreas Sudmann (ed.)
The Democratization of Artificial Intelligence
Net Politics in the Era of Learning Algorithms

2019, 334 p., pb., col. ill.
49,99 € (DE), 978-3-8376-4719-8
E-Book: 49,99 € (DE), ISBN 978-3-8394-4719-2

All print, e-book and open access versions of the titles in our list are available in our online shop www.transcript-verlag.de/en!

Cultural Studies

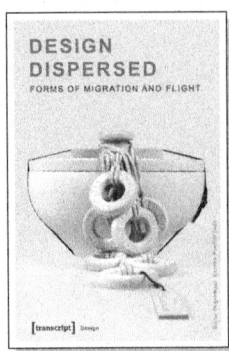

Burcu Dogramaci, Kerstin Pinther (eds.)
Design Dispersed
Forms of Migration and Flight

2019, 274 p., pb., col. ill.
34,99 € (DE), 978-3-8376-4705-1
E-Book: 34,99 € (DE), ISBN 978-3-8394-4705-5

Pál Kelemen, Nicolas Pethes (eds.)
Philology in the Making
Analog/Digital Cultures of Scholarly Writing and Reading

2019, 316 p., pb., ill.
34,99 € (DE), 978-3-8376-4770-9
E-Book: 34,99 € (DE), ISBN 978-3-8394-4770-3

Chris Goldie, Darcy White (eds.)
Northern Light
Landscape, Photography and Evocations of the North

2018, 174 p., hardcover, ill.
79,99 € (DE), 978-3-8376-3975-9
E-Book: 79,99 € (DE), ISBN 978-3-8394-3975-3

**All print, e-book and open access versions of the titles in our list
are available in our online shop www.transcript-verlag.de/en!**